THE COLUMBIA RIVER

LECTOR HOUSE PUBLIC DOMAIN WORKS

This book is a result of an effort made by Lector House towards making a contribution to the preservation and repair of original classic literature. The original text is in the public domain in the United States of America, and possibly other countries depending upon their specific copyright laws.

In an attempt to preserve, improve and recreate the original content, certain conventional norms with regard to typographical mistakes, hyphenations, punctuations and/or other related subject matters, have been corrected upon our consideration. However, few such imperfections might not have been rectified as they were inherited and preserved from the original content to maintain the authenticity and construct, relevant to the work. The work might contain a few prior copyright references as well as page references which have been retained, wherever considered relevant to the part of the construct. We believe that this work holds historical, cultural and/or intellectual importance in the literary works community, therefore despite the oddities, we accounted the work for print as a part of our continuing effort towards preservation of literary work and our contribution towards the development of the society as a whole, driven by our beliefs.

We are grateful to our readers for putting their faith in us and accepting our imperfections with regard to preservation of the historical content. We shall strive hard to meet up to the expectations to improve further to provide an enriching reading experience.

Though, we conduct extensive research in ascertaining the status of copyright before redeveloping a version of the content, in rare cases, a classic work might be incorrectly marked as not-in-copyright. In such cases, if you are the copyright holder, then kindly contact us or write to us, and we shall get back to you with an immediate course of action.

HAPPY READING!

THE COLUMBIA RIVER

WILLIAM DENISON LYMAN

ISBN: 978-93-5614-288-6

Published: 1909

LECTOR HOUSE LLP
E-MAIL: lectorpublishing@gmail.com

St. Peter's Dome, Columbia River, 2300 Feet High

Copyright, Kiser Photograph Co., 1902.

THE COLUMBIA RIVER
ITS HISTORY, ITS MYTHS, ITS SCENERY
ITS COMMERCE

BY

WILLIAM DENISON LYMAN

Professor of History in Whitman College, Walla Walla, Washington

WITH 80 ILLUSTRATIONS AND A MAP

1909

TO MY PARENTS
HORACE LYMAN AND MARY DENISON LYMAN
PIONEERS OF 1849, WHO BORE THEIR PART IN LAYING THE
FOUNDATIONS OF CIVILIZATION UPON THE BANKS
OF THE COLUMBIA, THIS VOLUME IS
DEDICATED BY THE AUTHOR

I see the living tide roll on,
It crowns with rosy towers
The icy capes of Labrador,
The Spaniard's land of flowers;
It streams beyond the splintered ridge
That parts the northern showers.
From eastern rock to sunset wave,
The Continent is ours.

Holmes.

PREFACE

AS one of the American Waterways series, this volume is designed to be a history and description of the Columbia River. The author has sought to convey to his reader a lively sense of the romance, the heroism, and the adventure which belong to this great stream and the parts of the North-west about it, and he has aimed to breathe into his narrative something of the spirit and sentiment—a spirit and sentiment more easily recognised than analysed—which we call "Western." With this end in view, his treatment of the subject has been general rather than detailed, and popular rather than recondite. While he has spared no pains to secure historical accuracy, he has not made it a leading aim to settle controverted points, or to present the minutiæ of historical research and criticism. In short, the book is rather for the general reader than for the specialist. The author hopes so to impress his readers with the majesty of the Columbia as to fill their minds with a longing to see it face to face.

Frequent reference in the body of the book to authorities renders it unnecessary to name them here. Suffice it to say that the author has consulted the standard works of history and description dealing with Oregon—the old Oregon—and its River, and from the voluminous matter there gathered has selected the facts that best combine to make a connected and picturesque narrative. He has treated the subject topically, but there is a general progression throughout, and the endeavour has been to find a natural jointure of chapter to chapter and era to era.

While the book has necessarily been based largely on other books, it may be said that the author has derived his chief inspiration from his own observations along the shores of the River and amid the mountains of Oregon and Washington, where his life has mainly been spent, and from familiar conversations in the cabins of pioneers, or at camp-fires of hunters, or around Indian tepees, or in the pilot-houses of steamboats. In such ways and places one can best catch the spirit of the River and its history.

The author gladly takes this opportunity of making his grateful acknowledgments to Prof. F. G. Young, of Oregon University, for his kindness in reading the manuscript and in making suggestions which his full knowledge and ripe judgment render especially valuable. He wishes also to express his warmest thanks to Mr. Harvey W. Scott, editor of the *Oregonian*, for invaluable counsel. Similar gratitude is due to Prof. Henry Landes of Washington University for important assistance in regard to some of the scientific features of the first chapter.

W. D. L.

Whitman College,

Walla Walla, Wash.,
1909.

CONTENTS

LIST OF ILLUSTRATIONS

LIST OF MAPS

PART I
THE HISTORY

CHAPTER I

THE LAND WHERE THE RIVER FLOWS

Contrasts—The Two Islands—Uplift—Volcanic Action—Flood—Age
of Ice—Story of Wishpoosh and Creation of the Tribes—Outline
of the Mountain Systems—Peculiar Interlocking of the Columbia
and the Kootenai—The Cascade Range—The Inland Empire—
The Valleys West of the Cascade Mountains—The Forests—The
Climate—The Native Races and Some of their Myths—Story of
the Kamiah Monster—The Tomanowas Bridge at the Cascades—
Origin of Three Great Mountains—The Chinook Wind—Myths of
the Unseen Life—Klickitat Story of the Spirit Baby—Beauty of the
Native Names.

WONDERFULLY varied though rivers are, each has a physiognomy of its own. Each preserves its characteristics even in the midst of constant diversity. We recognise it, as we recognise a person in different changes of dress. The Ohio has one face, the Hudson another, and each keeps its essential identity. The traveller would not confuse the Rhine with the Danube, or the Nile with the Volga.

Even more distinctive than most rivers in form and feature is the Columbia, the old Oregon that now hears far other sounds than "his own dashings," the River of the West, the Thegayo, the Rio de los Reyes, the Rio Estrachos, the Rio de Aguilar, the many-named river which unites all parts of the Pacific North-west. It is to its records of romance and heroism, of legend and history, as well as to its alternating scenes of stormy grandeur and tranquil majesty that the reader's attention is now invited. Though among the latest of American rivers to be brought under the control of civilised men, the Columbia was among the earliest to attract the interest of the explorers of all nations, and the struggles of international diplomacy over possession were among the most momentous in history. The distance of the Columbia from the centres of population and the difficulty of reaching it made its development slow, and for this reason its pioneer stage lasted longer than would otherwise have been the case. In this part of its history there was a record of pathos, tragedy, and achievement not surpassed in any of the annals of our country, while, in its later phases, the North-west has had the sweep and energy of growth and power characteristic of genuine American development. Finally, by reason of scenic grandeur, absorbing interest of physical features, the majesty and mystery of its origin in the greatest of American mountains, the swift might of its flow through some of the wildest as well as some of the most beautiful regions of the globe, and at the last by the peculiar grandeur of its entrance into the greatest of the oceans, this "Achilles of Rivers" attracts alike historian, scientist, poet, statesman, and lover of nature.

*   *   *   *   *

"A land of old upheaven from the abyss," a land of deepest deeps and highest heights, of richest verdure here, and barest desolation there, of dense forest on one side, and wide extended prairies on the other; a land, in brief, of contrasts, contrasts in contour, hues, productions, and history;—such is that imperial domain watered by the Columbia River and its affluents. To the artist, the poet, the scientist, and the sportsman, this region presents noble and varied scenes of shore, of mountain, of river, of lake, while to the romancer and historian it offers a wealth of native legend and of record from the heroic ages of American history.

As a fit introduction to the picture of the land as it now appears, there may be presented a brief record of the manner in which it was wrought into its present form. Professor Thomas Condon of Oregon thought that the first land to rise on the Pacific Coast was composed of two islands, one in the region of the Siskiyou Mountains of Northern California and Southern Oregon, and the other in the heart of what are now the Blue Mountains and Saw-tooth Mountains of North-eastern Oregon, South-eastern Washington, and Western Idaho. Other geologists have doubted the existence of the second of these two islands.

Those islands, if both existed, were the nuclei of the Pacific Coast region. The rock consisted of the earlier granite, sandstone, and limestone crust of the earth. For long ages these two islands, washed by the warm seas of that early age, and bearing a life now found in the tropics, were slowly rising and widening their boundaries in all directions.

Next, or perhaps as early, to respond to the pressure of the shrinking crust of the earth and to appear above the sea, was the vast cordon of pinnacled peaks which compose the present Okanogan and Chelan uplift, granite and porphyry, broken by volcanic outflow. These peaks are veined with gold, silver, and copper.

That first age of mountain uplift was ended by the coming on of the age of fire. The granite upheaval of the Blue and the Cascade Mountains was blown apart and cracked asunder by volcanic eruption and seismic force. A vast outflow of basalt and andesite swept westward from the Blue Mountains to meet a similar outflow moving eastward from the Cascades. Thus, throughout the Columbia Basin, the surface is mainly of volcanic rock overlying the shattered fragments of the original earth crust. At many points, however, the primeval granite or sandstone surface was not covered, while at frequent intervals the breaking forth of the fiery floods transformed those original rocks into various forms of gneiss, porphyry, and marble. But the greatest result of the age of volcanic outflow was the elevation of the stupendous isolated snow peaks which now constitute so striking a feature of Columbian landscapes.

With the close of the age of fire, the mountain chains were in place, as they now stand, but the plains and valleys were not yet fashioned. Another series of forces must needs come to elaborate the rude outlines of the land. And so came on the third great age, the age of flood. The upheaval of the mingled granite and volcanic masses of the Cascade and Blue Mountains, while at the same time the Rockies were undergoing the same process, imprisoned a vast sea over the region now known by Westerners as the Inland Empire. In the depths of this sea the sediment from a thousand torrents was deposited to fashion the smooth and level valleys of the Yakima, the Walla Walla, the Spokane, and lesser streams, while a similar process fashioned the valleys of the Willamette and other streams between the Cascades and the Coast Mountains westward.

But while the age of flood was shaping the great valley systems, a fourth age—the age of ice—was working still other changes upon the plastic land. The mountains had been reared by upheaval and volcanic outflow to a stupendous height. Then they became glaciated. The whole Northern Hemisphere, in fact, took on the character of the present Greenland. Enormous glaciers descended the flanks of the mountains, gouging and ploughing out the abysmal cañons which now awe the beholder, and scooping out the deeps where Chelan, Cœur d'Alene, Pend Oreille, Kaniksu, and other great lakes delight the vision of the present day.

Such were the forces that wrought the physical features of the land where the River flows. We do not mean to convey the impression that there was a single age of each, and that they followed each other in regular chronological order. As a matter of fact there were several eras of each, interlocked with each other: upheaval, fire, flood, and frost. But as the resultant of all, the Columbia Basin assumed its present form. The great forces which have thus fashioned this land manifested themselves on a scale of vast energy. Evidences of upheaval, fire, flood, and glacier are exhibited on every side, and these evidences constitute a testimony of geological history of the most interesting nature. Long before this record of the rocks had found a white reader, the native red man had read the open pages, and interpreted them in the light of his ardent fancy.

The Indian conception of the flood, involving also that of the creation of the native tribes, is one of the most fantastic native legends. This is the story of the great beaver, Wishpoosh, of Lake Kichelos. According to this myth the beaver Wishpoosh inhabited that lake on the summit of the Cascade Mountains, the source of the Yakima River.

In the time of the Watetash (animal people) before the advent of men, the king beaver, Wishpoosh, of enormous size and voracious appetite, was in the evil habit of seizing and devouring the lesser creatures and even the vegetation. So destructive did he become that Speelyei, the coyote god of the mid-Columbia region, undertook to check his rapacities.

The struggle only made the monster more insatiate, and in his wrath he tore out the banks of the lake. The gathered floods swept on down the cañon and formed another great lake in the region now known as the Kittitas Valley.

But the struggle between Wishpoosh and Speelyei did not end, and the former in his mad fury went on thrashing around in this greater lake. For a long time the rocky barriers of the Umtanum restrained the flood, but at last they gave way before the onslaughts of the wrathful beaver, and the loosened waters swept on down and filled the great basin now occupied by the fruit and garden ranches of the Cowiche, Natchees, and Atahnum. In like fashion the restraining wall at the gap just below Yakima city was torn out, and a yet greater lake was formed over all the space where we now see the level plains of the Simcoe and Toppenish. The next lake formed in the process covered the yet vaster region at the juncture of the Yakima, Snake and Columbia rivers. For a long time it was dammed in by the Umatilla highlands, but in process of time it, too, was drained by the bursting of the rocky wall before the well-directed attacks of Wishpoosh. The yet greater lake, the greatest of all, now formed between the Umatilla on the east and the Cascade Mountains on the west. But even the towering wall of the Cascades gave way in time and the accumulated floods poured on without further hindrance to the open sea.

Thus was the series of great lakes drained, the level valleys left, and the Great River suffered to flow in its present course. But there is a sequel to the story of the flood. For Wishpoosh, being now in the ocean, laid about him with such fury that he devoured the fish and whales and so threatened all creation that Speelyei perceived that the time had come to end it all. Transforming himself into a floating branch, he drifted to Wishpoosh and was swallowed. Once inside the monster, the wily god resumed his proper size and power; and with his keen-edged knife proceeded to cut the vitals of the belligerent beaver, until at last all life ceased, and the huge carcass was cast up by the tide on Clatsop beach, just south of the mouth of the Great River. And now what to do with the carcass? Speelyei solved the problem by cutting it up and from its different parts fashioning the tribes as each part was adapted. From the head he made the 'Nez Percés, great in council and oratory. From the arms came the Cayuses, powerful with the bow and war-club. The Klickitats were the product of the legs, and they were the runners of the land. The belly was transformed into the gluttonous Chinooks. At the last there was left an indiscriminate mass of hair and gore. This Speelyei hurled up the far distance to the east, and out of it sprung the Snake River Indians.

Such is the native physiography and anthropogenesis of the land of the Oregon.

If now one could rise on the pinions of the Chinook wind (the warm south wind of the Columbia Basin, of which more anon), and from the southern springs of the Owyhee and the Malheur could wing his way to the snowy peaks in British Columbia, from whose fastnesses there issues the foaming torrent of Canoe River, the most northerly of all the tributaries of the Great River, he would obtain, in a noble panorama, a view of the land where the River flows, in its present aspect, as fashioned by the elemental forces of which we have spoken. But not to many is it given thus to be "horsed on the sightless couriers of the air," and we must needs use imagination in lieu of them. Even a map will be the safest guide for most. Inspection of the map will show that the distance to which we have referred covers twelve degrees of latitude, while the distance from the source of the Snake River in the Yellowstone National Park to the Pacific requires a span of fifteen degrees of longitude. The south-eastern part of this vast area occupying Southern Idaho is mainly an arid plain; arid, indeed, in its natural condition, but, when touched by the vivifying waters in union with the ardent sun, it blossoms like a garden of the Lord. Upon these vast plains where the volcanic dust has drifted for ages, now looking so dismal in their monotonous garb of sage-brush, the millions of the future will some time live in peace and plenty, each under his own vine and apple-tree. On the eastern boundary, all the way from Western Wyoming to Eastern British Columbia, stand cordons of stupendous mountains, the western outposts of the great Continental Divide. These constitute one spur after another, from whose profound cañons issues river after river to swell the torrents of the turbid and impetuous Snake on its thousand-mile journey to join the Columbia. Among these tributary streams are the Payette, the Boisé, the Salmon, and the Clearwater. Yet farther north, beyond the system of the Snake, are the Bitter Root, the Missoula, the Pend Oreille, the Spokane, and the Kootenai (we follow here the American spelling, the Canadian being Kootenay), with almost innumerable afflu- ents, draining the huge labyrinths of the Bitter Root Mountains and the Silver Bow.

Thus our northward flight carries us to the international boundary in latitude 49 degrees.

Far beyond that parallel stretches chain after chain of divisions of the great Continental Range, the Selkirks, the Gold Range, Purcell's Range, sky-piercing heights, snow-clad and glaciated. Up and down these interlocking chains the Co- lumbia and the Kootenai, with their great lakes and unexplored tributaries, seem to be playing at hide-and-seek with each other. These rivers form here one of the most singular geographical phenomena of the world, for so strangely are the par- allel chains of mountains tilted that the Kootenai, rising in a small lake on the western flank of the main chain of the Canadian Rockies and flowing south, passes within a mile of the source of the Columbia at Columbia Lake, separated only by a nearly level valley. Connection, in fact, is so easy that a canal once joined the two rivers. From that point of contact the Kootenai flows far south into Idaho, then makes a grand wheel to the north-west, forming Kootenai Lake on the way, then wheeling again in its tortuous course to the west, it joins the greater stream in the midst of the majestic mountain chains which stand guard over the Arrow Lakes. And meanwhile where has the Columbia itself been journeying? After the parting from the Kootenai it flows directly north-west between two stupendous chains of mountains. Reaching its highest northern point in latitude 52 degrees, where it receives the Canoe River, which has come two hundred miles or more from the north, it turns sharply westward, finding a passageway cleft in the mountain wall. Thence making a grand wheel toward the south, it casts its turbid floods into the long expanse of the Arrow Lakes, from which it emerges, clear and bright, soon to join the Kootenai. And how far have they journeyed since they parted? The Columbia about six hundred miles, and the Kootenai hardly less, though having passed within a mile of each other, flowing in opposite directions.

It will be readily seen from this description that the mountains which feed the Columbian system of rivers on the east and north, are of singular grandeur and interest. But now as we bear our way southward again we discover that another mountain system, yet grander and of more curious interest, forms the western boundary of the upper Columbia Basin. This is the Cascade Range. Sublime, majestic, mysterious, this noble chain of mountains, with its tiaras of ice, its girdles of waterfalls, its draperies of forest, its jewels of lakes, must make one search long to find its parallel in any land for all the general features of mountain charm. But over and beyond those more usual delights of the mountains, the Cascade Range has a unique feature, one in which it stands unrivalled among all the mountains of the earth, with the exception possibly of the Andes. This is the feature of the great isolated snow peaks, stationed like sentinels at intervals of from thirty to sixty miles all the way from the British line to California. There is nothing like this elsewhere on the North American continent. The Sierras of California are sublime, but their great peaks are not isolated monarchs like those of the Cascades. The high Sierras are blended together in one mountain wall, in which no single peak dominates any wide extended space. But in the long array of the Cascades, five hundred miles and more from the international boundary to the California line, one glorious peak after another uplifts the banner and sets its regal crown toward sunrise or sunset, king of earth and air to the border where the shadow of the next mountain monarch mingles with its own. Hence these great Cascade peaks have an individuality which gives them a kind of living personality in the life of any one who has lived for any length of time within sight of them.

From the north, moving south, we might gaze at these great peaks, and find no two alike. Baker—how much finer is the native name, Kulshan, the Great White Watcher—first on the north; Shuksan next, the place where the storm-winds gather, in the native tongue; then Glacier Peak, with its girdle of ice, thirteen great glaciers; Stewart next with its dizzy horn of rock set in a field of snow; then the great king-peak of all, Rainier, better named by the natives, Takhoma, the fountain breast of milk-white waters; and after this, Adams, or in the Indian, Klickitat, with St. Helens or Loowit near at hand on the west; then, across the Great River, Hood or Wiyeast, with its pinnacled crest; next southward, Jefferson with its sharp chimney whose top has never yet been touched by human foot; yet beyond, the marvellous group of the Three Sisters, each with its separate personality and yet all together combining in one superb whole; then Mt. Scott, Mt. Thielson, Diamond Peak, Mt. Pitt, and with them we might well include the truncated cone of Mt. Mazama, once the lordliest of the chain, but by some mighty convulsion of nature, shorn of crown and head, and now bearing on its summit instead the most singular body of water, Crater Lake, on all the American continent.

Fifteen is the number of the great peaks named, but there are dozens of lesser heights, snow-crowned and regal. The great Cascade chain is, therefore, the noblest and most significant feature of the topography of the land of the Columbia. Between the Rocky Mountains and the Cascades lies what is locally known as the Inland Empire, mainly a continuous prairie or series of prairies and valleys, wheat land, orchard land, garden land, fertile, beautiful, attractive, broken by an occasional mountain spur, as the irregular mass of the Blue Mountains, but substantially an inhabited land, reaching from Colville, Spokane, and the Okanogan on the north to the Klamath valleys on the south, a region five hundred miles long by two hundred wide, a goodly land, one difficult to excel in all the potentialities of use for human needs.

Such are the distinguishing features of the Columbia Basin on the east side of the Cascade Mountains.

To the west of those mountains is another vast expanse of interior valleys, not so large indeed and not more fertile, but even more beautiful, and by reason of earlier settlement and contiguity to the ocean, better developed.

This series of valleys is enclosed between the Cascade Mountains and the Coast Range, and in a general way parallels the Inland Empire already described. But this statement should be qualified by the explanation that North-western Washington consists of the Puget Sound Basin, which is a distinct geographical system, while South-western Oregon consists of the Umpqua and Rogue River valleys, and these valleys though commercially and politically a part of the Columbia system, are geographically separate, since they debouch directly into the Pacific Ocean. There is left, therefore, for the Columbia region proper west of the Cascade Mountains, the Willamette Valley in Oregon, and the valleys of the Lewis, Kalama, and Cowlitz in Washington, with several smaller valleys on each side. The Willamette Valley is the great distinguishing feature of this part of the Columbia Basin. A more attractive region is hard to find. Mountains snow-clad and majestic, the great peaks of the Cascades already described, guard it on the east, while westward the gentler slopes of the Coast Range separate it from the sea. Between the two ranges lies the valley, two hundred miles long by about a hundred broad, including the foot-hills, a succession of level plains, oak-crowned hills, and fertile bottoms. Not Greece nor Italy nor the Vale of Cashmere can surpass this earthly paradise in all the features that compose the beautiful and grand in nature.

Geologists tell us that this Willamette region was once a counterpart of Puget Sound, only with less depth of water, and that, as the result of centuries of change, the old-time Willamette Sound has become the Willamette Valley. It has now become the most thickly settled farming region of the Columbia Basin, and, as its fitting metropolis, Portland sits at the gateway of the Willamette and Columbia, the "Rose City," handsomest of all Western cities, to welcome the commerce of the world.

The valleys on the Washington side of the Columbia make up together a region of great beauty, fertility, and productiveness, perhaps a hundred miles square, and, though yet but partially developed, contain many beautiful homes.

The larger part of the Columbia Valley west of the Cascade Mountains is, in its natural state, densely timbered. Here are found "the continuous woods where rolls the Oregon and hears no sound but his own dashings." These great fir, spruce, cedar, and pine forests, extending a thousand miles along the Pacific Coast from Central California to the Straits of Fuca (and indeed they continue, though the trees gradually diminish in size, for nearly another thousand miles up the Alaska coast), constitute the world's largest timber supply. The demands upon it have been tremendous during the past twenty years, and the stately growths of centuries have vanished largely from all places in the near vicinity of shipping points. Yet one can still find primeval woods where the coronals of green are borne three hundred feet above the damp and perfumed earth, and where the pillars of the wood sustain so continuous a canopy of foliage that the sunlight is stopped or filters through only in pale and watery rays. Hence all manner of vines and shrubs grow with almost tropic profusion, though with weak and straggling stems.

Throughout the entire Pacific North-west the soil is of extraordinary fertility. It is largely of volcanic dust as fine as flour and seems to contain the constituents of plant life in inexhaustible abundance. Even in the arid belts of Eastern Oregon, where to the eye of the stranger the appearance is of a hopeless waste, those same elements of plant food exist, and with water every manner of tree or vine or flower bursts quickly into perfect life.

The climate of the Columbia Basin is a puzzle to the stranger, but in most of its aspects it quickly becomes an equal delight. As is well known, the Japan ocean current exercises upon the Pacific Coast an effect similar to that of the Gulf Stream on Ireland and England. Hence the states of the Columbia Valley are much warmer in winter than regions of the same latitude on the Atlantic Coast or in the Mississippi Valley. Though the average temperature is higher, yet it is cooler in summer on the Pacific Coast than on the Atlantic. The Pacific climate has much less of extremes. The State of Washington has about the same isothermal line as North Carolina. There is, however, another feature of the Columbia climate not so well known to non-residents, which is worthy of a passing paragraph. This is the division of the country by the Cascade Mountains into a humid western section and a dry eastern one. The mountain wall intercepts the larger part of the vapour rising from the Pacific and flying eastward, and these warm masses of vapour are condensed by the icy barrier and fall in rain on the western side. Hence Western Oregon and Washington are damp and soft, with frequent clouds and fogs. The rainfall, though varying much, is in most places from forty to fifty inches a year. But east of the mountain wall which has "milked the clouds," the air is clear and bright, the sun shines most of the year from cloudless skies, and there seems to be more of tingle and electricity in the atmosphere. The rainfall ranges from ten to thirty inches, and in the drier parts vegetation does not flourish without irrigation.

Any view of primeval Oregon would be incomplete without a glimpse of the native race, that melancholy people, possessed of so many interesting and even noble traits, whose sad lot it has mainly been to struggle against the advent of a civilisation which they could not understand nor resist, and before which they have melted away in pitiful impotency. But they have at least had the highest dignity of defeat, for they have died fighting. They have realised the conception of the Roman Emperor: "*Me stantem mori oportet.*"

The Oregon Indians have essentially the same characteristic traits as other Indians, secretiveness, patience, vindictiveness, stoicism; and, in their best state, fidelity and boundless generosity to friends.

The poor broken fragments of the once populous tribes along the Columbia cannot but affect the present-day observer with pity. Most of the tangible memorials of this fallen race have vanished with them. Not many of the conquerors have been sympathetic or even rational in their treatment of the Indians. Hence memorials of memory and imagination which might have been drawn from them and treasured up have vanished with them into the darkness. Yet many Indian legends have been preserved in one manner and another, and these are sufficient to convince us that the native races are of the same nature as ourselves. Some of the legends which students of Indian lore have gathered, will, perhaps, prove interesting to the reader.

A quaint Nez-Percé myth accounts for the creation as follows: There was during the time of the Watetash a monster living in the country of Kamiah in Central Idaho. This monster had the peculiar property of an irresistible breath, so that when it inhaled, the winds and grass and trees and even different animals would be sucked into its devouring maw. The Coyote god, being grieved for the destruction wrought by this monster, made a coil of rope out of grass and with this went to the summit of Wallowa Mountains to test the suction power of the monster. Appearing like a tiny spear of grass upon the mountain, he blew a challenge to the monster. Descrying the small object in the distance Kamiah began to draw the air inward. But strange to say, Coyote did not move. "Ugh, that is a great medicine," said the monster. Coyote now took his station upon the mountains of the Seven Devils, a good deal closer, and blew his challenge again. Again the Kamiah monster tried to breathe so deeply as to draw the strange challenger into his grasp, but again he failed. "He is a very big medicine," he said once more. And now Coyote mounted the top of the Salmon River Mountains, somewhere near the Buffalo Hump of the present time, and again the monster's breath failed to draw him. The baffled Kamiah was now sure that this was most extraordinary medicine. In reality, Coyote had each time held himself by a grass rope tied to the mountain.

Coyote now called into counsel Kotskots, the fox. Providing him with five knives, Kotskots advised Coyote to force an entrance into the interior of the monster. Entering in, Coyote found people in all stages of emaciation, evidently having had their life gradually sucked out of them. It was also so cold and dark in the interior that they were chilled into almost a condition of insensibility. Looking about him, Coyote began to see great chunks of fat and pitch in the vitals of the monster, and accordingly he rubbed sticks together and started a fire, which being fed with the fat and pitch, soon grew into a cheerful glow. Now, armed with his knives, he ascended the vast interior until he reached the heart. He had already directed Kotskots to rouse up and gather together all the emaciated stowaways and provide that when the monster was cut open they should see how to rush out into the sunlight. Great as was the monster Kamiah, he could not stop the persistent hacking away at his heart which Coyote now entered upon. When the fifth knife was nearly gone, the heart dropped down and Kamiah collapsed into a lifeless mass. The people under the guidance of Kotskots, burst out into the sunshine and scattered themselves abroad. It must be remembered that these were animal people, not human. Coyote called upon them to wait until he should have shown them a last wonder, for, cutting the monster in pieces, he now began to fashion from the pieces a new race of beings to be called men. The portion which he cut from the head he flung northward, and of this was fashioned the Flathead tribe. The feet he cast eastward, making them the Blackfeet. So he continued, making new tribes here and there. But at the last Kotskots interposed an objection. "You have made no people," he said, "for the valley of the Lapwai, which is the most beautiful of all." Realising the force of the suggestion, Coyote mixed the blood of the monster with water and sprinkled it in a rain over the entire valley of the Clearwater. From these drops of blood and water, the Nez Percé tribe was formed. The heart of the monster is still to be seen by all travellers in that country, being a heart-shaped hill in the valley of Kamiah.

Perhaps the most perfect and beautiful of all Indian fire myths of the Columbia, is that connected with the famous "tomanowas bridge" at the Cascades. This myth not only treats of fire, but it also endeavours to account for the peculiar formation of the river and for the great snow peaks in the near vicinity. This myth has various forms, and in order that it may be the better understood, we shall say a word with respect to the peculiar physical features in that part of the Columbia. The River, after having traversed over a thousand miles from its source in the heart of the great Rocky Mountains of Canada, has cleft the Cascade Range asunder with a cañon three thousand feet in depth. While generally swift, that portion between The Dalles and the Cascades is deep and sluggish. There are, moreover, sunken forests on both sides visible at low water, which seem plainly to indicate that at that point the river was dammed up by some great rock slide or volcanic convulsion. Some of the Indians affirm that their grandfathers have told them that there was a time when the river at that point passed under an immense natural bridge, and that there were no obstructions to the passage of boats under the bridge. At the present time there is a cascade of forty feet at that point. This is now overcome by government locks. Among other evidences of some such actual occurrence as the Indians relate, is the fact that the banks at that point are gradually sliding into the river. The prodigious volume of the Columbia, which here rises from fifty to seventy-five feet during the summer flood, is continually eating into the banks. The railroad has slid several inches a year at this point toward the river and requires frequent readjustment. It is obvious at a slight inspection that this weird and sublime point has been the scene of terrific volcanic and probably seismic action. One Indian legend, probably the best known of their stories, is to the effect that the downfall of the bridge and consequent damming of the river was due to a battle between Mt. Hood and Mt. Adams,—or, some say, Mt. St. Helens— in which Mt. Hood hurled a great rock at his antagonist; but, falling short of the mark, the rock demolished the bridge instead. This event has been made use of by Frederick Balch in his story, *The Bridge of the Gods*.

But the finer, though less known legend, which unites both the physical conformation of the Cascades and the three great snow mountains of Hood, Adams, and St. Helens, with the origin of fire, is to this effect. According to the Klickitats, there was once a father and two sons who came from the east down the Columbia to the region in which Dalles City is now located, and there the two sons quarrelled as to who should possess the land. The father, to settle the dispute, shot two arrows, one to the north and one to the west. He told one son to find the arrow to the north and the other the one to the west, and there to settle and bring up their families. The first son, going northward, over what was then a beautiful plain, became the progenitor of the Klickitat tribe, while the other son was the founder of the great Multnomah nation of the Willamette Valley. To separate the two tribes more effectively, Sahale, the Great Spirit, reared the chain of the Cascades, though without any great peaks, and for a long time all things went in harmony. But for convenience' sake, Sahale had created the great tomanowas bridge under which the waters of the Columbia flowed, and on this bridge he had stationed a witch woman called Loowit, who was to take charge of the fire. This was the only fire in the world. As time passed on Loowit observed the deplorable condition of the Indians, destitute of fire and the conveniences which it might bring. She therefore besought Sahale to allow her to bestow fire upon the Indians. Sahale, greatly pleased by the faithfulness and benevolence of Loowit, finally granted her request. The lot of the Indians was wonderfully improved by the acquisition of fire. They began to make better lodges and clothes and had a variety of food and implements, and, in short, were marvellously benefited by the bounteous gift.

But Sahale, in order to show his appreciation of the care with which Loowit had guarded the sacred fire, now determined to offer her any gift she might desire as a reward. Accordingly, in response to his offer, Loowit asked that she be transformed into a young and beautiful girl. This was accordingly affected, and now, as might have been expected, all the Indian chiefs fell deeply in love with the guardian of the tomanowas bridge. Loowit paid little heed to any of them, until finally there came two chiefs, one from the north called Klickitat and one from the south called Wiyeast. Loowit was uncertain which of these two she most desired, and as a result a bitter strife arose between the two. This waxed hotter and hotter, until, with their respective warriors, they entered upon a desperate war. The land was ravaged, all their new comforts were marred, and misery and wretchedness ensued. Sahale repented that he had allowed Loowit to bestow fire upon the Indians, and determined to undo all his work in so far as he could. Accordingly he broke down the tomanowas bridge, which dammed up the river with an impassable reef, and put to death Loowit, Klickitat, and Wiyeast. But, inasmuch as they had been noble and beautiful in life, he determined to give them a fitting commemoration after death. Therefore he reared over them as monuments, the great snow peaks; over Loowit, what we now call Mt. St. Helens; over Wiyeast, the modern Mt. Hood; and, above Klickitat, the great dome which we now call Mt. Adams.

Of the miscellaneous myths which pertain to the forces of nature, one of the best is that accounting for the Chinook wind. All people who have lived long in Oregon or Washington have a conception of that marvellous warm wind which in January and February suddenly sends them almost summer heat amid snow banks and ice-locked streams, and causes all nature to rejoice as with a resurrection of spring time. Scarcely anything can be imagined in nature more picturesque and dramatic than this Chinook wind. The thermometer may be down nearly to zero, a foot of snow may rest like a pall on the earth, or a deadly fog may wrap the earth, when suddenly, as if by the breath of inspiration, the fog parts, the peaks of the mountains may be seen half stripped of snow, and then, roaring and whistling, the warm south wind comes like an army. The snow begins to drip like a pressed sponge, the thermometer goes with a jump to sixty, and within two hours we find ourselves in the climate of Southern California. No wonder the Indians personified this wind. We personify it ourselves.

The Yakima account of the Chinook wind was to the effect that it was caused by five brothers who lived on the Columbia River, not far from the present town of Columbus. Now there is at rare intervals in this country a cold north-east wind, which the Indians on the lower Columbia call the Walla Walla wind because it comes from the north-east. The cold wind was caused by another set of brothers. Both these sets of brothers had grandparents who lived near what is now Umatilla. The two groups of brothers were continually fighting each other, sweeping one way or the other over the country, alternately freezing or thawing it, blowing down trees and causing the dust to fly in clouds, and rendering the country generally very uncomfortable. Finally, the Walla Walla brothers sent a challenge to the Chinook brothers to undertake a wrestling match, the condition being that those who were defeated should forfeit their lives. It was agreed that Speelyei should act as umpire and should inflict the penalty by decapitating the losers. Speelyei secretly advised the grandparents of the Chinook brothers to throw oil on the wrestling ground so that their sons might not fall. In like manner he secretly advised the grandparents of the Walla Walla brothers to throw ice on the ground. Between the ice and the oil it was so slippery that it would be hard for any one to keep upright, but inasmuch as the Walla Walla grandfather got ice on the ground last, the Chinook brothers were all thrown and killed.

The eldest Chinook had an infant baby at home, whose mother brought him up with one sole purpose in view, and that was that he must avenge the death of his father and uncles. By continual practice in pulling up trees he became prodigiously strong, insomuch that he could pull up the largest fir trees and throw them about like weeds. The young man finally reached such a degree of strength that he felt that the time had come for him to perform his great mission. Therefore he went up the Columbia, pulling up trees and tossing them around in different places, and finally passed over into the valley of the Yakima, where he lay down to rest by the creek called the Setas. There he rested for a day and a night, and the marks of his couch are still plainly visible on the mountain side.

Now, turning back again to the Columbia, he sought the hut of his grandparents, and when he had found it, he found also that they were in a most deplorable condition. The Walla Walla brothers had been having it all their own way during these years and had imposed most shamefully upon the old people. When he learned this, the young Chinook told his grandfather to go out into the Columbia to fish for sturgeon, while he in the meantime would lie down in the bottom of the boat and watch for the Walla Walla wind. It was the habit of these tormenting Walla Walla wind brothers to wait until the old man had got his boat filled with fish, and then they, issuing swiftly and silently from the shore, would beset and rob him. This time they started out from the shore as usual, but to their great astonishment, just as they were about to catch him, the boat would shoot on at miraculous speed and leave them far behind. So the old man landed safely and brought his fish to the hut. The young Chinook then took his grandparents to a stream and washed from them the filth which had gathered upon them during all those years of suffering. Strange to say, the filth became transformed into trout, and this is the origin of all the trout along the Columbia.

As soon as the news became known abroad that there was another Chinook champion in the field, the Walla Walla brothers began to demand a new wrestling match. Young Chinook very gladly accepted the challenge, though he had to meet all five. But now Speelyei secretly suggested to the Chinook grandfather that he should wait about throwing the oil on the ground until the ice had all been used up. By means of this change of practice, the Walla Walla brothers fell speedily before the young Chinook. One after another was thrown and beheaded until only the youngest was left. His courage failing, he surrendered without a struggle. Speelyei then pronounced sentence upon him, telling him that he must live, but could henceforth only blow lightly, and never have power to freeze people to death. Speelyei also decreed that in order to keep Chinook within bounds he should blow his hardest at night time, and should blow upon the mountain ridges first in order to prepare people for his coming. Thus there came to be moderation in the winds, but Chinook was always the victor in the end. And thus at the present time, in the perpetual flux and reflux of the oceans of the air, when the north wind sweeps down from the chilly zones of Canada upon the Columbia Basin, his triumph is but transient. For within a few hours, or days at most, while the cattle are threatened with destruction and while ranchers are gazing anxiously about, they will discern a blue-black line upon the southern horizon. In a short time the mountain ridges can be seen bare of snow, and deliverance is at hand. For the next morning, rushing and roaring from the South, comes the blessed Chinook, and the icy grip of the North melts as before a blast from a furnace. The struggle is short and Chinook's victory is sure.

Nearly all our native races had a more or less coherent idea of a future state of rewards and punishments. "The happy hunting ground" of the Indians is often referred to in connection with the Indians of the older part of the United States. Our Indians have ideas in general quite similar. Some believe that there is a hell and a heaven. The Siskiyou Indians in Southern Oregon have a curious idea similar to that of the ancient Egyptians as well as of the Mohammedans. This is to the effect that the regions of the blessed are on the other side of an enormously deep chasm. To pass over this, one must cross on a very narrow and slippery pole. The good can pass, but the bad fall off into empty space, whence they reappear again upon the earth as beasts or birds.

The Klickitat Indians, living along The Dalles of the Columbia have a fine legend of the land of spirits. There lived a young chief and a girl who were devoted to each other and seemed to be the happiest people in the tribe, but suddenly he sickened and died. The girl mourned for him almost to the point of death, and he, having reached the land of the spirits, could find no happiness there for thinking of her. And so it came to pass that a vision began to appear to the girl at night, telling her that she must herself go into the land of the spirits in order to console her lover. Now there is, near that place, one of the most weird and funereal of all the various "memaloose" islands, or death islands, of the Columbia. The writer himself has been upon this island and its spectral and volcanic desolation makes it a fitting location for ghostly tales. It lies just below the "great chute," and even yet has many skeletons upon it. In accordance with the directions of the vision, the girl's father made ready a canoe, placed her in it, and passed out into the Great River by night, to the memaloose island. As the father and his child rowed across the dark and forbidding waters, they began to hear the sounds of singing and dancing and great joy. Upon the shore of the island they were met by four spirit people, who took the girl, but bade the father return, as it was not for him to see into the spirit country. Accordingly the girl was conducted to the great dance-house of the spirits, and there she met her lover, far stronger and more beautiful than when upon earth. That night they spent in unspeakable bliss, but when the light began to break in the east and the song of the robins was heard from the willows on the shore, the singers and the dancers fell asleep.

The girl, too, had gone to sleep, but not soundly like the spirits. When the sun had reached the meridian, she woke, and now, to her horror, she saw that instead of being in the midst of beautiful spirits, she was surrounded by hideous skeletons and loathsome, decaying bodies. Around her waist were the bony arms and skeleton fingers of her lover, and his grinning teeth and gaping eye-sockets seemed to be turned in mockery upon her. Screaming with horror, she leaped up and ran to the edge of the island, where, after hunting a long time, she found a boat, in which she paddled across to the Indian village. Having presented herself to her astonished parents, they became fearful that some great calamity would visit the tribe on account of her return, and accordingly her father took her the next night back to the memaloose island as before. There she met again the happy spirits of the blessed, and there again her lover and she spent another night in ecstatic bliss. In the course of time a child was born to the girl, beautiful beyond description, being half spirit and half human. The spirit bridegroom, being anxious that his mother should see the child, sent a spirit messenger to the village, desiring his mother to come by night to the memaloose island to visit them. She was told, however, that she must not look at the child until ten days had passed. But after the old woman had reached the island, her desire to see the wonderful child was so intense that she took advantage of a moment's inattention on the part of the guard, and, lifting the cloth from the baby board, she stole a look at the sleeping infant. And then, dreadful to relate, the baby died in consequence of this premature human look. Grieved and displeased by this foolish act, the spirit people decreed that the dead should never again return nor hold any communication with the living.

In concluding this chapter we cannot forbear to call the attention of our readers to the rare beauty of many of the native Indian names of localities. These names always have some significance, and ordinarily there is some such poetic or figurative conception involved in the name as plainly reveals the fact that these rude and unfortunate natives have the souls of poets beneath their savage exterior. It is truly lamentable that some of the sonorous and poetic native names have been thrust aside for the commonplace and oft-repeated names of Eastern or European localities or the still less attractive names of discoverers or their unimportant friends.

Think of using the names Salem and Portland for Chemeketa and Multnomah, the native names. Chemeketa means "Here we Rest," or, some say, the "Place of Peace," for it was the council ground of the Willamette Valley Indians. But the

Methodist missionaries thought that it would have a more Biblical sound and conduce to the spiritual welfare of the natives to translate the word into its equivalent, Salem. So they spoiled the wild native beauty of the name for all time. Multnomah means "Down the Waters." But two Yankee sea captains, with a sad deficiency of poetry in them, tossed up a coin to decide whether to employ the name of Boston or Portland, the native town of each, and the latter won the toss.

Oregon has been more fortunate than Washington in its State name, for it has the unique name, stately and sonorous, which old Jonathan Carver first used for the River and which is one of the most distinctive of all the names of States. But whether Oregon is Indian, Spanish, French, or a corruption of something else, or a pure invention of Carver's is one of the mooted points in our history. Idaho, too, has one of the most mellifluous of names, meaning the "Gem of the Mountains."

All three States have many beautiful and appropriate names of rivers, lakes, mountains, and cities. Such are Chelan, "Beautiful Water"; Umatilla, "The Wind-blown Sand"; Walla Walla, "Where the Waters Meet"; Shuksan, "The Place of the Storm Winds"; Spokane, "The People of the Sun"; Kulshan, "The Great White Watcher"; Snoqualmie, "The Falls of the Moon God." Seattle derives its name from the old chief Seattle, or Sealth.

The most bitterly disputed name of all is Tacoma *vs.* Rainier, as the name of the greatest of our mountains. The name of Rainier was derived by Vancouver from that of an officer of the British navy, a man who never knew anything of Oregon and had no part or lot in its discovery or development. Tacoma, or more accurately, *Takhoma* (a peculiar guttural which we cannot fully indicate), was the native Indian name, meaning, according to some, "The Great White Mountain," and according to others meaning "The Fountain-breast of Milk-white Waters."

With these glances at the character of the land, and its native inhabitants, we are now ready to see how they became known to the world.

CHAPTER II

TALES OF THE FIRST WHITE MEN ALONG THE COAST

Nekahni Mountain and Tallapus—Quootshoi and Toulux—Original
Beauty of Clatsop Plains—The Story Told by Celiast and Cultee—
Casting of the "Thing" upon the Beach—The Pop-corn—Burning
of the Ship—Konapee, the Iron-worker—Franchère's Account of
Soto—The Treasure Ship on the Beach at Nekahni Mountain—
The Black Spook and Mysterious Chest—The Inscription Still
Found on the Rock—The Beeswax Ship—Quiaculliby.

WE have told something of the mountains, rivers, and lakes which make up
the framework of our Pacific North-west. We have also tried to see the land
through the eyes of the native red men, and have called back a few of the grotesque, fantastic, sometimes heroic, sometimes pathetic legends which they associated with every phase of their country.

Now the very centre of Indian lore, the Parnassus, the Delphi, the Dodona, of
the lower Columbia River Indians, is the stretch of mingled bluff, plain, lake, sand-
dune, and mountain, marvellously diversified, from the south shore of the Columbia's mouth to the sacred Nekahni Mountain. It is a wonderously picturesque
region. From it came Tallapus, the Hermes Trismegistus of the Oregon Indians. Its
forests were haunted by the Skookums and Cheatcos. From the volcanic pinnacles
of Swallallochast, now known as Saddle Mountain, the thunder bird went forth
on its daily quest of a whale, while at the mountain's foot Quootshoi and Toulux
produced the first men from the monstrous eggs of that same great bird. In short,
that region was rich in legend, as it was, and still is, in scenic beauty.

It is said by the Indians that a hundred years or more ago it was much finer
than now, for the entire breadth of Clatsop Plains was sodded with deep green
grass and bright with flowers almost the whole year through. This bright-hued
plain lay open to the sea, and across its southern end flowed three tide streams,
having the aboriginal names of Nekanikum, Ohanna, and Neahcoxie.

It was a veritable paradise for the Indians. The forests were filled with elk
(moosmoos) and deer (mowitch), while fish of almost every variety thronged the
waters, from that king of all fish now known as the royal chinook of the Columbia
down to such smaller fry as the smelt and the herring, which even now sometimes
so throng the lesser streams that the receding tide leaves them by the thousands on

the muddy flats. On the beach were infinite numbers of clams; and as an evidence of their abundance we can now see shell mounds by the acre, in such quantity, indeed, that some of the modern roads have been paved with shells.

This favoured region was the home of the Clatsops. There, too, according to the legends, the first white men landed. The story of the first appearance of the white men has reached our own times in various forms, but the most coherent account is through the word of Celiast, an Indian woman who died many years ago, but who became the wife of one of the earliest white settlers and the mother of Silas Smith, now dead, but known in his time as one of the best authorities on Indian history. Celiast was the daughter of Kobaiway, a chieftain whose sway extended over the land of the Clatsops in the time of the Astor Company a century ago. Celiast was in fact the best authority for many of the Indian legends. But she is not alone in the knowledge of this appearance of the white men, for a number of other Indians tell the substance of the same tale. Among others an old Indian of Bay Centre, Washington, by the name of Charlie Cultee, related the story to Dr. Franz Boas, whose work in the Smithsonian Institute is known as among the best on the native races. This is the story, a composite of that of Celiast and that of Cultee.

It appears that an old woman living near the ancient Indian village of Ne-Ahkstow, about two miles south of the mouth of the Great River (the Columbia) had lost her son. "She wailed for a whole year, and then she stopped." One day, after her usual custom, she went to the seaside, and walked along the shore towards Clatsop. While on the way she saw something very strange. At first it seemed like a whale, but, when the old woman came close, she saw that it had two trees standing upright in it. She said, "This is no whale; it is a monster." The outside was all covered over with something bright, which they afterwards found was copper. Ropes were tied all over the two trees, and the inside of the Thing was full of iron.

While the old woman gazed in silent wonder, a being that looked like a bear, but had a human face, though with long hair all over it, came out of the Thing that lay there. Then the old woman hastened home in great fear. She thought this bearlike creature must be the spirit of her son, and that the Thing was that about which they had heard in the Ekanum tales.

The people, when they had heard the strange story, hastened with bows and arrows to the spot. There, sure enough, lay the Thing upon the shore, just as the old woman had said. Only instead of one bear there were two standing on the Thing. These two creatures,—whether bears or people the Indians were not sure,—were just at the point of going down the Thing (which they now began to understand was an immense canoe with two trees driven into it) to the beach, with kettles in their hands.

As the bewildered people watched them they started a fire and put corn into the kettles. Very soon it began to pop and fly with great rapidity up and down in the kettles. The pop-corn (the nature of which the Clatsops did not then understand) struck them with more surprise than anything else,—and this is the one part of the story preserved in every version.

Then the corn-popping strangers made signs that they wanted water. The chief sent men to supply them with all their needs, and in the meantime he made a careful examination of the strangers. Finding that their hands were the same as his own, he became satisfied that they were indeed men. One of the Indians ran and climbed up and entered the Thing. Looking into the interior, he found it full of boxes. There were also many strings of buttons half a fathom long. He went out to call in his relatives, but, before he could return, the ship had been set on fire. Or, in the language of Charlie Cultee, "It burnt just like fat." As a result of the burning of the ship, the Clatsops got possession of the iron, copper, and brass.

Now the news of this strange event became noised abroad, and the Indians from all the region thronged to Clatsop to see and feel of these strange men with hands and feet just like ordinary men, yet with long beards and with such peculiar garb as to seem in no sense men. There arose great strife as to who should receive and care for the strange men. Each tribe or village was very anxious to have them, or at least one of them. The Quienaults, the Chehales, and the Willapas, from the beach on the north side, came to press their claims. From up the river came the Cowlitz, the Cascades, and even the Far-off Klickitat. The different tribes almost had a battle for possession, but, according to one account, it was finally settled that one of the strange visitors should stay with the Clatsop chief, and that one should go with the Willapas on the north side of the Great River. According to another, they both stayed at Clatsop.

From this first arrival of white men, the Indians called them all "Tlehonnipts," that is, "Of those who drift ashore." One of the men possessed the magical art of taking pieces of iron and making knives and hatchets. It was indeed to the poor Indians a marvellous gift of Tallapus, their god, that they should have a man among them that could perform that priceless labour, for the possession of iron knives and hatchets meant the indefinite multiplying of canoes, huts, bows and arrows, weapons, and implements of every sort. The iron-maker's name was Konapee. The Indians kept close watch of him for many days and made him work incessantly. But, as the tokens of his skill became numerous, his captors held him in great favour and allowed him more liberty. Being permitted to select a site for a house, he chose a spot on the Columbia which became known to the Indians, even down to the white occupancy of the region, as "Konapee."

Among other possessions, Konapee had a large number of pieces of money, which, from the description, must have been Chinese "cash." From this some have inferred that Konapee must have been a Chinaman, and the wrecked ship a Chinese or Japanese junk. This does not, however, follow. For the Spaniards had become entirely familiar with China, and any Spanish vessel returning from the Philippine Islands or from China would have been likely to have a supply of Chinese money on board.

There is an interesting bit of testimony which seems to belong to this same story of Konapee. It is found in the book by Gabriel Franchère in regard to the founding of Astoria, the book which was the chief authority of Irving in his fascinating narrative entitled *Astoria*. Franchère describes meeting an old man, eighty years old, in 1811, at the Cascades, whose name was Soto, and who said that his father was one of four Spaniards wrecked on Clatsop beach many years before. His father had tried to reach the land of the sunrise by going eastward, but having reached the Cascades was prevented from going farther and had there married an Indian woman, Soto's mother. It is thought likely that the father of Soto was Konapee. The two stories seem to fit quite well. If this be true, it is likely that Konapee's landing was as early as 1725. If all the details of Konapee's life could be known, what a romance might be made of it! There is no reason to suppose that he ever saw other white men or ever got away from the region where the fortune of shipwreck had cast him. Yet he was in possession of one of the greatest geographical secrets of that country, for the hope of the discovery of some great "River of the West," the elusive stream which many believed to be a pure fabrication of Aguilar and other old navigators, had enticed many a "marinere" from many a far "countree."

In any event it is probable that the Columbia River Indians had got a general knowledge of the whites and their arts from Konapee long before the authentic discovery of the river was made. Especially it seems that from him they got a knowledge of iron and implements fashioned from it. Captain Cook mentions that when he visited the coast in 1780 the Indians manifested no surprise at the weapons or implements of iron. In fact even all whites who supposed themselves to be the first to visit this coast found the Indians ready to trade and especially eager to get iron. A new era of trade and business seems to have been inaugurated among these Clatsops and Chinooks dating from about the supposed time of Konapee. But he was by no means the only one of his race to be cast upon the Oregon shore. There is a story of a treasure ship cast upon the beach near Nekahni Mountain. This mountain, the original home of Tallapus, while on its summit the great chief god Nekahni himself dwelt, is one of the noblest pieces of Nature's art all along the shore. Fronting the ocean with a precipitous rampart of rock five hundred feet high and thence rising in a wide sweeping park clad in thick turf, and dotted here and there with beautiful spruce and fir trees, to an elevation of twenty-five hundred feet, the sacred Nekahni presents as fine a combination of the beautiful and sublime as can be seen upon a whole thousand miles of coast. It was a favourite spot with the natives. For lying upon its open and turfy slopes they could gaze upon many miles of sea, and could no doubt light up their signal fires which might be seen over a wide expanse of beach. Very likely there, too, they celebrated the mysterious rites of Nekahni and Tallapus.

One pleasant afternoon in early summer, a large group of natives assembled upon the lower part of Nekahni, almost upon the edge of the precipitous cliff with which it fronts the sea. Gazing into the offing they saw a great object like a huge bird drawing near from the outer sea. It approached the shore, and then from it a small boat with a number of men and a large black box put out to land. Coming to the beach the men took out the box and also a black man whom the Indians supposed to be a spook or evil demon. Going a little way up the beach the men dug a hole into which they lowered the box, and then having struck down the black man they threw him on top of the box and, covering it up, they returned to the ship, which soon disappeared from sight. On account of the black man buried with the box, the superstitious Indians dared not undertake to exhume the contents of the grave. But the story was handed from one generation to another, and it came to constitute the story of the "treasure ship."

In recent times the idea that here some chest, with gold and jewels in the most approved style of buried fortunes, might be found has caused much searching. The ground has been dug over for the sight of the regulation rusty handle which is to lead to the great iron-bound chest with its doubloons of gold and crucifixes of pearls. Parties have come from the Eastern States to join the search. One party even secured the guidance of spirits who professed to locate the treasure. But though the spirit-led enthusiasts turned over every stone and dug up the sand for many feet along the beach, they found never an iron-bound chest, and never a sign of the treasure. There is, however, in plain sight now, on a rock at the foot of Nekahni Mountain, a character cut in the rock bearing a rude resemblance to a cross. Some think it looks more like the letters, I.H.S., the sacred emblem of the Catholic Church. There is also what seems to be quite a distinct arrow pointing in a certain direction. But the treasure remains unfound.

The next legend of the prehistoric white man is that of the "Beeswax Ship." This, too, has a real confirmation in the presence of large quantities of beeswax at a point also near Nekahni Mountain, just north of the mouth of the Nehalem River. Some naturalists claimed at one time that this substance was simply the natural paraffine produced from the products of coal or petroleum. But more recently cakes of the substance stamped with the sacred letters, "I.H.S.," together with tapers, and even one piece with a bee plainly visible within, may be considered incontestable proof that this is indeed beeswax, while the letters, "I.H.S." denote plainly enough the origin of the substance in some Spanish colony. An interesting point in connection with this is the historical fact that on June 16, 1769, the ship *San José* left La Paz, Lower California, for San Diego, and was never heard from again. Some have conjectured that the *San José* was the "Beeswax Ship," driven far north by some storm or mutiny. As to the peculiar fact that a ship should have been entirely loaded with beeswax it has been conjectured that some of the good padres of the Spanish Missions meant to provide a new station with a large amount of wax for the sake of providing tapers for their service, the lighted candles proving then, as they do now, a matter of marvel and wonder to the natives, and, with other features of ceremonial worship, having a great effect to bring them into subjection to the Church.

The Indian legend runs on to the effect that several white men were saved from the wreck of the "Beeswax Ship," and that they lived with them. But having infringed upon the family rights of the natives, they became obnoxious, and were all cut off by an attack from them. One story, however, asserts that there was one man left, a blue-eyed, golden-haired man, that he took a Nehalem woman, and that from him was descended a fair-complexioned progeny, of which a certain chieftain who lived at a beautiful little lake on Clatsop plains, now known as Culliby Lake, was our Quiaculliby.

Such in brief survey, are some of the stories which preserve the record of the space betwixt the Indian age of myth and the period of authentic discovery.

CHAPTER III

HOW ALL NATIONS SOUGHT THE RIVER FROM THE SEA AND HOW THEY FOUND IT

Search for Gold—Economic Effects—Early Extension of Exploration Westward—Cortez—Magellan—Aguilar—Fables of the
Sea—Shakspere and Swift—Maps—Great Wars of the Seventeenth Century and Downfall of Spain—Long Delay—Resump-
tion of Exploration—Spanish Settlement of California—Russia
and Behring—Perez—Heceta—Cook—Fur-trade—Gathering of
Nations—The Yankees—Gray and Kendrick—Meares and Vancouver—The Complete Discovery—Strife between England and
the United States.

THE period of the Renaissance is one, which by reason of splendid achievements in literature, in art, in science, and in discovery, can hardly be dupli-
cated. We are here especially concerned with the discoverers. A mingling of motives impelled those dauntless spirits onward, and among the most potent was
the greed for gold. Much American history is bound up with the mad rush for the
precious metals, and the spread of exploration from the West Indies and Mexico,
the first centres of Spanish power, was one of its results. Only eight years after
the landing of Columbus on San Salvador, the Portuguese Gaspar Cortereal had
conceived the idea of a north-west passage, which in some unexplained manner
became known as the Strait of Anian. In 1543, the Spaniards Cabrillo and Ferrelo
coasted along the shores of California, and the latter was doubtless the first white
man to look upon the coast of Oregon. In 1577, England appeared in the person
of that boldest and most picturesque of the half-discoverers, half-pirates, of that
time, Francis Drake. In that year he set forth on the wonderful voyage in which
he plundered the treasures of the Spanish Main, cut the golden girdle of Manila,
queen of the Spanish Orient, skirted along the coast of California and Oregon,
and at last circumnavigated the globe. Brilliant as were Drake's exploits, they did
not result in the discovery of our Great River. In 1592, just a century after Columbus, Juan de Fuca, whose name is now preserved in the strait leading to Puget
Sound, is said to have made that voyage which is regarded by most historians as
a myth, but which affords so fascinating a bit of narration that it ought to be true.
Two hundred years later John Meares, the English navigator, attached the name
of the stout old Greek pilot to that inlet now familiar to ships of all nations. With
the passage of a few years more, explorations upon the western shore of America

began to assume a more definite form. In 1602 the best equipped squadron thus far sent out left Acapulco under command of Vizcaino, with the aim of carrying out Monterey's great purpose for the northward extension of Spanish power. The fleet being scattered by storm, the *fragata* in command of Martin Aguilar ran up the coast as far as latitude 43 degrees. There they found a cape to which they attached the name still held, Cape Blanco. From that point, following the north-westerly trending of the coast, they soon came abreast of a "rapid and abundant river, with ash trees, willows, and brambles, and other trees of Castile upon its banks." This they endeavoured to enter, but from the strength of the current could not. "And seeing that they had already reached a higher latitude than had been ordered by the viceroy and that the number of the sick was great, they decided to return to Acapulco." Torquemada, the historian, from whom the account is taken, goes on to say:

> It is supposed that this river is one leading to a great city, which was discovered by the Dutch when they were driven thither by storms, and that it is the Strait of Anian, through which the vessels passed in sailing from the North Sea to the South Sea; and that the city called Quivera is in those parts; and that this is the region referred to in the account which His Majesty read, and which induced him to order this expedition.

The interesting question arises, Was the river the Columbia? It is the only large river on the Oregon coast, though the Umpqua, if at flood stage, might have given the impression of size. The latitude is not right, either, though the Spanish narrator does not say how far north of Cape Blanco they went. But whether or not Aguilar really went so far north as the Columbia, his voyage was one of much interest. It gave Spain a warrant to claim the western coast of America; it still further strengthened the idea of the Strait of Anian; it seemed to confirm the romantic conception of a great city or group of cities with civilised inhabitants along that passage way, and it gave the first name to the river, the Rio de Aguilar.

Thenceforth the navigators of all nations accepted as the primary object of their search some great river of the West. Hidden in the fogs of fancy, as it lay shrouded in truth in the mists of the ocean, the supposed Rio de Aguilar yet held the spell of enchantment over many an "ancient mariner" of many a land. Whatsoever nation could actually find the river and establish a definite claim to first discovery, would have, by the generally accepted usage of nations, the right of occupation and ownership.

That was a fruitful time for fables of the sea, and around the Great River many of them gathered. The original of Baron Munchausen seems to have existed in the persons of Captain Lorenzo Ferrer de Maldonado and Admiral Pedro Bartolomé de Fonte. The first of these worthies, whose voyage was said to have been made in 1588, describes in a very circumstantial manner his passage through the Strait of Anian and his exit upon the Asiatic side of the continent. This he averred was marked with a very remarkable rocky eminence which rendered it wonderfully adapted to fortification and defence, the mountain being so steep, in fact, that a missile dropped from the summit would fall directly upon a ship in mid-channel.

It is thought by some students that some unchronicled Spanish navigator may have actually made the inland passage up the Alaskan coast and that some report of it may have become transformed into Maldonado's story. Fonte's story seems to have first appeared in a London publication in 1708, though his voyage was alleged to have been made in 1640. He told a marvellous tale of a great river which led to a magnificent lake on whose banks stood a great city. The river he located in latitude 53 degrees, and he named it the Rio de los Reyes, or River of Kings. This is far north of the Columbia, but the account persisted in popular idea for a long time. The name became associated with those of the Rio de Aguilar and the River of the West.

These and other similar tales, the flotsam and jetsam of ocean myths, gave something of inspiration and suggestion to literature. For even long before the alleged exploits of Fonte, the fertile mind of Shakspere had conceived of Caliban and Ariel and other fancies of the age of Western adventure. And in the next century the prince of political satirists, Jonathan Swift, had located almost exactly at the mouth of the Rio de Aguilar, the land of the Brobdingnagians, while the countries into which the veracious Gulliver was thrown at a later time, Luggnagg and Blubdubrib, were in the Pacific at a somewhat indefinite distance from the land of the Giants.

The land of the Oregon was in short, the land of the great unexplored and of boundless fancy. Some of the old maps illustrating that period are of much interest. Zaltieri's map of 1566 shows a generally accurate conception of the eastern part of America and of the western coast of Mexico and California, but the entire continent above about latitude 60 degrees is occupied with a *mare septentrionale incognito*. Luck's map of 1582 presents a fairly good conception of Florida and Mexico, but is entirely astray on the western coast. The Wytfliet-Ptolemy map of 1597 has a singularly indented coast running nearly east and west in the location of Oregon, while Cape Blanco and a river, the Rio de los Estrachos, in about latitude 51 degrees, seem to be an attempt to denote Aguilar's cape of 1543, and to locate the river by still another name, though in a higher latitude. Maldonado's map of the Strait of Anian of 1609 is manifestly manufactured to suit the occasion, and is interesting only as showing how far mendacity and gullibility could travel hand in hand.

But now the first age of discovery on the coast of Oregon drew to a close. It cannot be said that much of tangible knowledge had been attained. Puzzling questions had been raised. Labyrinths of conjecture, with no definite clues for exit, had been entered. Fascinating romances had been so interwoven with probable fact that no one could untangle them. A general conception of a great river and a great north-west passage had been held up with some distinctness as the goal of navigators. Finally, most important of all, what had been seen was of so enticingly interesting a nature and seemed to promise results so important, that they furnished a motive for continued exploration. It certainly looked as though the nations would continue the search for the Great River of the West. Spain had the inside track of all, though Drake and Cavendish and Hawkins had run down many a richly laden treasure galleon and had laid the booty at the feet of the Virgin Queen, and many an embittered buccaneer of French or English race had hounded the flag of Spain across the breadth of half the seas.

But a great change was impending. There was a new shuffle of the cards in the hands of the Fates and the Furies as the seventeenth century moved on apace. Spain's time had come. Her cup of iniquity was now full. Her whole measure of national policy had been the sword for the pagan and the inquisition for the heretic. The banished Moors of Granada and the murdered "Beggars" of Holland and the wasted Incas and Montezumas of America united to call down the vengeance of Nemesis upon the destroyer of a fair world's peace.

The stupendous struggles engendered by the Reformation, culminating in the Thirty Years' War, went on almost without pause for over a century. That strife, ending at Westphalia in 1648, saw Spain prostrate and the principle of religious toleration triumphant. But almost immediately another struggle arose, the natural successor of the first, the struggle against the absolute monarchy of the Bourbons. As may well be seen, the nations of Europe were so enchained in the strife against Pope and King that they had little thought for new discoveries. Over a hundred and sixty years passed after the voyage of Aguilar before there was another serious movement of discovery on the coast of Oregon.

This new movement of Pacific exploration, destined to continue with no cessation to our own day, was ushered in by Spain. There was even yet much vitality in the fallen mistress of the world. Impelled by both religious zeal and hope of material gain, the immigration of 1769 went forth from La Paz to San Diego and Monterey. That inaugurated the singular and poetic, in some aspects even beautiful, history of Spanish California, an era which has provided so much of romance and poetry for literature in the California of our own times. The march of events had made it plain to the Spanish Government that, if it was to retain a hold on the Pacific Coast, it must bestir itself. Russia, England, and France, released in a measure from the pressure of European struggles, were fitting out expeditions to resume the arrested efforts of the sixteenth century. It seemed plain also that colonial America was going to be an active rival on the seas. And well may it have so seemed, for, in the sign of the Yankee sailor, the conquest was to be made.

But just at that important juncture a most favouring condition arose for Spain. The government of England precipitated the struggle of the American Revolution. France soon joined to strike her island rival a deadly blow by assisting in the liberation of the colonies. For the time, Spain had nearly a clear field for Pacific discovery, so far as England and France were concerned. As for Russia, the danger was more imminent. Russia had, indeed, begun to look in the direction of Pacific expansion a long time prior to the Spanish immigration to California. That vast monarchy, transformed by the genius of Peter the Great, had stretched its arms from the Baltic to the Aleutian Archipelago, and had looked from the frozen seas of Siberia to the open Pacific as a fairer field for expansion. Many years elapsed, however, before Peter's great designs could be fulfilled. Not till 1741 did Vitus Behring thread the thousand islands of Sitka and gaze upon the glaciated crest of Mt. St. Elias. And it was not till thirty years later that it became understood that the Bay of Avatcha was connected by the open sea with China. In 1771 the first cargo of furs was shipped directly from Avatcha to Canton. Then first the vastness of the Pacific Ocean was comprehended. Then first it was understood that the same waters which lashed the frozen ramparts of Kamchatka encircled the coral islands of the South Sea and roared against the stormy barriers of Cape Horn.

The Russians had not found the Great River, though it appears that Behring in 1771 had gone as far south as latitude 46 degrees, just the parallel of the mouth of the Columbia. But he was so far off the coast as not to see it.

Three Spanish voyages followed in rapid succession: that of Perez in 1774, of Heceta in 1775, and of Bodega in 1779. The only notable things in connection with the voyage of Perez were his discovery of Queen Charlotte's Island, with the sea-otter furs traded by the natives, the first sight of that superb group of mountains which we now call the Olympic, but which the Spaniards named the Sierra de Santa Rosalia, and finally the fine harbour of Nootka on Vancouver Island, named by Perez Port San Lorenzo, for years the centre of the fur-trade and the general rendezvous of ships of all nations. But no river was found.

With another year a still completer expedition was fitted out, Bruno Heceta being commander and Francisco de la Bodega y Quadra, second in command. This voyage was the most important and interesting thus far in the history of the Columbia River exploration. For Heceta actually found the Great River, so long sought and so constantly eluding discovery. On June 10, 1775, Heceta passed Cape Mendocino, and entered a small bay just northward. There he entered into friendly relations with the natives and took solemn possession of the country in the name of His Catholic Majesty of Spain. Sailing thence northward, he again touched land just south of the Straits of Fuca, but there he met disaster at the ill-omened point subsequently named Destruction Island. For there his boat landing for exploration was set upon by the savage inhabitants, and the entire boat-load murdered. Moving southward again, on August 15th, in latitude 46 degrees 10 minutes, Heceta found himself abreast of some great river. Deciding that this must be indeed the mysterious Strait of Fuca, or the long concealed river of the other ancient navigators, he made two efforts to enter, but the powerful current and uncertain depths deterred him, and he at last gave up the effort and bore away for Monterey. Three additional names were bestowed upon the River at this time. Thinking the entrance a bay, Heceta named it, in honour of the day, Ensenada de Asuncion. Later it was more commonly known as Ensenada de Heceta, while the Spanish charts designated the river as Rio de San Roque. The name of Cabo de Frondoso (Leafy Cape) was bestowed upon the low promontory on the south, now known as Point Adams, while upon the picturesque headland on the north which we now designate as Cape Hancock, the devout Spaniards conferred the name of Cabo de San Roque, August 16th being the day sacred to that saint.

The original account given by Heceta is so interesting that we insert it here:

> On the 17th day of August I sailed along the coast to the 46th degree, and observed that from the latitude 47 degrees 4 minutes to that of 46 degrees 10 minutes, it runs in the angle of 18 degrees of the second quadrant, and from that latitude to 46 degrees

4 minutes, in the angle of 12 degrees of the same quadrant; the soundings, the shore, the wooded character of the country, and the little islands, being the same as on the preceding days.

On the evening of this day I discovered a large bay, to which I gave the name Assumption Bay, and a plan of which will be found in this journal. Its latitude and longitude are determined according to the most exact means afforded by theory and practice. The latitudes of the two most prominent capes of this bay are calculated from the observations of this day.

Having arrived opposite this bay at six in the evening, and placed the ship nearly midway between the two capes, I sounded and found bottom in four brazas [nearly four fathoms]. The currents and eddies were so strong that, notwithstanding a press of sail, it was difficult to get out clear of the northern cape, towards which the current ran, though its direction was eastward in consequence of the tide being at flood. These currents and eddies caused me to believe that the place is the mouth of some great river, or of some passage to another sea. Had I not been certain of the latitude of this bay, from my observations of the same day, I might easily have believed it to be the passage discovered by Juan de Fuca, in 1592, which is placed on the charts between the 47th and the 48th degrees; where I am certain no such strait exists; because I anchored on the 14th day of July midway between these latitudes, and carefully examined everything around. Notwithstanding the great difference between this bay and the passage mentioned by De Fuca, I have little difficulty in conceiving they may be the same, having observed equal or greater differences in the latitudes of other capes and ports on this coast, as I will show at the proper time; and in all cases latitudes thus assigned are higher than the real ones.

I did not enter and anchor in this port, which in my plan I suppose to be formed by an island, notwithstanding my strong desire to do so; because, having consulted with the second captain, Don Juan Perez, and the pilot Don Christoval Revilla, they insisted I ought not to attempt it, as, if we let go the anchor, we should not have men enough to get it up, and to attend to the other operations which would be thereby necessary. Considering this, and also, that in order to reach the anchorage, I should be obliged to lower my long boat (the only boat I had) and to man it with at least fourteen of the crew, as I could not manage with fewer, and also as it was then late in the day, I resolved to put out; and at the distance of three leagues I lay to. In the course of that night, I experienced heavy currents to the south-west, which made it impossible to enter the bay on the following morning, as I was far to leeward. These currents, however, convinced me that a great quantity of water rushed from this bay on the ebb of the tide.

The two capes which I name in my plan, Cape San Roque and Cape Frondoso, lie in the angle of 10 degrees of the third quadrant. They are both faced with red earth and are of little elevation.

On the 18th I observed Cape Frondoso, with another cape, to which I gave the name of Cape Falcon, situated in the latitude of 45 degrees 43 minutes, and they lay at an angle of 22 degrees of the third quadrant, and from the last mentioned cape I traced the coast running in the angle of 5 degrees of the second quadrant. This land is mountainous, but not very high, nor so well wooded as that lying between the latitudes of 48 degrees 30 minutes, and 46 degrees. On sounding I found great differences: at a distance of seven leagues I got bottom at 84 brazas; and nearer the coast I sometimes found no bottom; from which I am inclined to believe there are reefs or shoals on these coasts, which is also shown by the colour of the water. In some places the coast presents a beach, in others, it is rocky.

A flat-topped mountain, which I named the Table, will enable any navigator to know the position of Cape Falcon without observing it; as it is in the latitude of 45 degrees 28 minutes, and may be seen at a great distance, being somewhat elevated.

It may be added that the Cape Falcon of Heceta was the bold elevation fronting the sea, known now as Tillamook Head, while the Table Mountain was doubtless what we now call Nekahni Mountain, both points especially the scenes of Indian myth.

Such was the actual discovery of the Columbia River, and as such the Spaniards justly laid claim to Oregon. Their treaty with the United States in 1819 was the formal conveyance of their claims to us. Nevertheless Heceta only half discovered the River. It seems very strange that with the all-important object of two centuries' search before him, he should so readily have succumbed to the fear of the powerful outstanding current. But the Spaniards were not in general the patient and persistent students of the shores that the English and Americans were. Their charts were in general worthless. Nevertheless Spain came nearest "making good" of any of the European powers. In 1779 Bodega and Arteaga sailed far north and sighted a vast snow peak "higher than Orizaba," which was doubtless St. Elias. In the same year Martinez and De Haro established themselves at Nootka. Subsequent voyages of Bodega, Valdez, and Galiano, and their first circumnavigation of Vancouver Island (named by them Quadra's Island, but, by mutual courtesy and good-will of the British and Spanish rivals, designated Vancouver's and Quadra's Island), gave them a clear title to the Pacific Coast of North America from latitude 60 degrees to Mexico.

But "that is another story." What of the Great River? In the very year of the declaration of American independence, the most elaborate expedition yet fitted out for western discovery, set forth from England in command of that Columbus of the eighteenth century, Captain James Cook. After nearly two years of important movements in the Southern Hemisphere and among the Pacific Islands, Cook turned to that goal of all nations, the coast of Oregon. But the same singular fatality which had baffled many of the explorers thus far, attended this most skilful navigator and best equipped squadron thus far seen on Pacific waters. For Cook passed and repassed the near vicinity of both the Straits of Fuca and the Columbia River, but without finding either. Killed by the treacherous natives of Hawaii in 1778, Cook left a great name, a more intelligent conception of world geography than was known before, and greatly strengthened claims by Great Britain to the ownership of pivotal points of the Pacific. Of all the great English navigators, Cook is perhaps best entitled to join the grand chorus that sings the *Songs of Seven Seas*. But he did not see the Great River of the West. What had become of it? After the fleeting vision which it accorded to Heceta, it seemed to have gone into hiding.

But a new set of motives came into play immediately after Cook's voyage. The two ships, the *Resolution* and *Discovery*, took with them to China a quantity of furs from Nootka. A few years earlier, as previously stated, the Russian fur-trade from Avatcha to China had been inaugurated. A great demand for peltries sprang up at once. A new régime dawned in Chinese and East India trade. Gold, silver, and jewels had not thus far rewarded the search of explorers. They were reserved for our later days of need. But the fur-trade was as good as gold. The North Pacific Coast, already interesting, assumed a new importance in the eyes of Europeans. The "struggle for possession" was on. The ships of all nations converged upon the fabled Strait and River of Oregon. English, Dutch, French, Portuguese, Spanish, Americans, began in the decade of the eighties to crowd to the land where the sea-otter, beaver, seal, and many other of the most profitable furs could be obtained for a trifle. The dangers of trading and the chances of the sea were great, but the profits of success were yet greater.

The fur-trade began to take the place of the gold hunt as a matter of international strife. The manner in which our own country, weak and discordant as its different members were when just emerging from the Revolutionary War, entered the lists, and by the marvellous allotment of Fortune or the design of Providence, slipped in between the greater nations and secured the prize of Oregon, is one of the epics of history, one which ought to have some native Tasso or Calderon to celebrate its triumph.

Following quickly upon the conclusion of the American War, came a series of British, French, and Russian voyages, which gradually centred more particularly about Vancouver Island and Nootka Sound. The British exceeded the others in numbers and enterprise. Among them we find names now preserved at many conspicuous points on the northern coast: as Portlock, Hanna, Dixon, Duncan, and Barclay. The most notable of the French was La Pérouse, who was best equipped for scientific research of any one. A number of Russian names appear at that period, most of which may yet be found upon the maps of Alaska, as Schelikoff, Ismyloff, Betschareff, Resanoff, Krustenstern, and Baranoff.

But none of them set eyes on the River, and it seemed more mythical than ever. As a result, however, of their various expeditions, incomplete though they were, each nation followed the usual practice of claiming everything in sight, either in sight of the eye or the imagination, and demanded the whole coast by priority of discovery.

Never did a geographical entity seem so to play the *ignis fatuus* with the world as did the River. Thirteen years elapsed from the discovery of the Rio San Roque by Heceta before any one of the dozens who had meanwhile passed up and down the coast, looked in again between the Cabo de Frondoso and the Cabo de San Roque. Then there came on one negative and two positive discoveries, and the elusive stream was really found never to be lost again.

The negative discovery was that of Captain John Meares in 1788. Since England afterwards endeavoured to make the voyages of Meares an important link in her chain of proof to the ownership of Oregon, it is worthy of some special attention. It happened on this wise. Meares came first to the coast of Oregon in 1786, in command of the *Nootka* to trade for furs for the East India Company. With the *Nootka* was the *Sea-Otter*, in command of Captain Walter Tipping. Both seem to have been brave and capable seamen. But disaster followed on their track. For having sailed far up the coast, they followed the Aleutian Archipelago eastward to Prince William's Sound. Separated on the journey, the *Nootka* reached a safe haven, but her consort never arrived, nor was she ever heard of more. The *Nootka*, after an Arctic winter of distress and after losing a large part of the crew through the ravages of scurvy, abandoned the trade and returned to China. Discouraged by the outcome, the East India Company abandoned the American trade and confined themselves henceforth to India.

But Meares, finding that the Portuguese had special privileges in the fur-trade and in the harbour of Nootka, entered into an arrangement with some Portuguese traders whereby he went nominally as supercargo, but really as captain of the *Felice*, under the Portuguese flag. With her sailed the *Iphigenia* with William Douglas occupying a place similar to that of Meares. In estimating the subsequent pretensions of Great Britain, the student of history may well remember that these two mariners, though Englishmen, were sailing under the flag of Portugal.

Reaching again the coast of Oregon, Meares looked in, June 29, 1788, at the broad entrance of an extensive strait which he believed to be the mythical Strait of Juan de Fuca of two centuries earlier, but which he did not pause to explore. He had resolved to solve the riddle of the Rio San Roque or the Ensenada de Asuncion or de Heceta, and turned his prow southward. On July 5th, in latitude 46 degrees 10 minutes, he perceived a deep bay which he considered at once to be the object of his search. Essaying to enter, he found the water shoaling with dangerous rapidity and a prodigious easterly swell breaking on the shore. From the masthead it seemed that the breakers extended clear across the entrance. With rather curious timidity for a bold Briton right on the eve of a discovery for which all nations had been looking, Meares lost courage and hauled out, attaching the name Deception Bay to the inlet and Cape Disappointment to the northern promontory, the last a name still officially used.

Meares left as his final conclusion in the matter, the following memorandum:

"We can now assert that there is no such river as that of St. Roc exists, as laid down in the Spanish charts." In view of this statement of the case it would certainly seem that he could not be accepted as a witness for English discovery, even if the Portuguese flag had not been flying at his masthead.

After bestowing the name of Lookout upon the great headland christened Cape Falcon by Heceta and known to us as Tillamook Head, Meares squared away for Nootka, and there he spent a very profitable season in the fur-trade.

But into the harbour of Nootka that same year of 1788, there sailed the ship of destiny, the *Columbia Rediviva*, in command of John Kendrick. With the *Columbia* came the *Lady Washington*, commanded by Robert Gray. These were the advance guard of Yankee ships which the energies of our liberated forefathers were sending forth as an earnest of the coming conquest of Oregon by the universal Yankee nation.

Gray and Kendrick were engaged in the fur-trade, and their energy and intelligence made it speedily profitable. It took a long time and a long arm, sure enough, in that day, to complete the great circuit of the outfitting, the bartering, the transferring, the return trip, and the final sale;—three years in all. The ship would be fitted out in Boston or New York with trinkets, axes, hatchets, and tobacco, and proceed by the Horn to the coast of Oregon,—six months or sometimes eight. Then up and down the coast, as far as known, they would trade with natives for the precious furs, making a profit of a thousand per cent. on the investment. Gray on one occasion got for an axe a quantity of furs worth $8000. The fur-barter would take another six or eight months. Then with hold packed with bales of furs, the ship would square away for Macao or Canton, six or eight months more. In China, the cargo of furs would go out and a cargo of nankeens, teas, and silks go in, with a great margin of profit at both ends. Then away again to Boston, there to sell the proceeds of that three years' "round-up" of the seas, for probably ten times the entire cost of outfitting and subsistence. The glory, fascination, and gain of the ocean were in it, and also its dangers. Of this sufficient witness is found in vanished ships, murdered crews, storm, scurvy, famine, and war. But it was a great age. Gray and Kendrick were as good specimens of their keen, facile, far-sighted countrymen, as Meares and Vancouver were of the self-opinionated, determined, yet withal manly and thorough Britons.

Among other pressing matters, such as looking out for good fur-trade in order to recoup the Boston merchants who had put their good money into the venture, and looking out for the health of their crew, steering clear of the uncharted reefs and avoiding the treacherous natives, Gray and Kendrick remembered that they were also good Americans. They must see that the new Stars and Stripes had their due upon the new coast.

The first voyage of the two Yankee skippers was ended and they set forth for another round in 1791, but with ships exchanged, Gray commanding the *Columbia* on this second voyage. The year 1792 was now come, and it was a great year in the annals of Oregon, three hundred years from Columbus, two hundred from Juan de Fuca. The struggle between England and Spain over conflicting rights at Nootka, which at one time threatened war, had been settled with a measure of amicability. As a commissioner to represent Great Britain, Captain George Vancouver was sent out, while Bodega y Quadra was empowered to act in like capacity for Spain. Spaniards and Britons alike realised that, whatever the Nootka treaty may have been, possession was nine points of the law, and both redoubled their efforts to push discovery, and especially to make the first complete exploration of the Straits of Fuca and the supposed Great River. There were great names among the Spaniards in that year, some of which still commemorate some of the most interesting geographical points, as Quimper, Malaspina, Fidalgo, Caamano, Elisa, Bustamente, Valdez, and Galiano. A list of British names now applied to many points, as Vancouver, Puget, Georgia, Baker, Hood, Rainier, St. Helens, Whidby, Vashon, Townsend, and others, attests the name-bestowing care of the British commander.

In going to Nootka as British commissioner, Vancouver was under instructions to make the most careful examination of the coast, especially of the rivers or any interoceanic channels, and thereby clear up the many conundrums of the ocean on that shore. With the best ship, the war sloop *Discovery*, accompanied by the armed tender *Chatham*, in command of Lieutenant W. R. Broughton, and with the best crew and best general equipment yet seen on the coast, it would have been expected that the doughty Briton would have found all the important places yet unfound. That the Americans beat him in finding the River and that the Spaniards beat him in the race through the Straits and around Vancouver Island, may be regarded as due partly to a little British obstinacy at a critical time, but mainly due to the appointment of the Fates.

On April 27, 1792, Vancouver passed a "conspicuous point of land composed of a cluster of hummocks, moderately high and projecting into the sea." This cape was in latitude 46 degrees 19 minutes, and Vancouver decided that here were doubtless the Cape Disappointment and Deception Bay of Meares. In spite of the significant fact that the sea here changed its colour, the British commander was so prepossessed with the idea that Meares must have decided correctly the nature of the entrance (for how was it possible for an English sailor to be wrong and a Spaniard right?) that he decided that the opening was not worthy of more attention and passed on up the coast. So the English lost their second great chance of being first to enter the River.

Two days later the lookout reported a sail, and as the ships drew together, the newcomer was seen to be flying the Stars and Stripes. It was the *Columbia Rediviva*, Captain Robert Gray, of Boston. In response to Vancouver's rather patronising queries, the Yankee skipper gave a summary of his log for some months past. Among other things he stated that he had passed what seemed to be a powerful river in latitude 46 degrees 10 minutes, which for nine days he had tried in vain to enter, being repelled by the strength of the current. He now proposed returning to that point and renewing his effort. Vancouver declined to reconsider his previous decision that there could be no large river, and passed on to make his very elaborate exploration of the Straits of Fuca and their connected waters, and to discover to his great chagrin, that the Spaniards had forestalled him in point of time.

The vessels parted. Gray sailed south and on May 10, 1792, paused abreast of the same reflex of water where before for nine days he had tried vainly to enter. The morning of the 11th dawned clear and favourable, light wind, gentle sea, a broad, clear channel, plainly of sufficient depth. The time was now come. The man and the occasion met. Gray seems from the first to have been ready to take some chances for the sake of some great success. He always hugged the shore closely enough to be on intimate terms with it. And he was ready boldly to seize and use favouring circumstances. So, as laconically stated in his log-book, he ran in with all sail set, and at ten o'clock found himself in a large river of fresh water, at a point about twenty miles from the ocean.

The geographical Sphinx was answered. Gray was its Œdipus, though unlike the ancient Theban myth there was no need that either the Sphinx of the Oregon coast or its discoverer perish. The River recognised and welcomed its master.

The next day the *Columbia* moved fifteen miles up the stream. Finding that he was out of the channel, Gray stopped further progress and turned again seaward. Natives, apparently friendly disposed, thronged in canoes round the ship, and a large quantity of furs was secured.

The River already bore many names, but Gray added another, and it was the one that has remained, the name of his good ship *Columbia*. Upon the southern cape he bestowed the name of Adams, and upon the northern, the name Hancock. These also remain.

The great exploit was completed. The long sought River of the West was found, and by an American. The path of destiny for the new Republic of the West was made secure. Without Oregon we probably would not have acquired California, and without a Pacific Coast, the United States would inevitably have been but a second-class power, the prey to European intrigue. The vast importance of the issue then becomes clear. Gray's happy voyage, that Yankee foresight and confidence in his seamanship and intuitive suiting of times and conditions to results which marks the vital turning points of history, differentiate Gray's discovery from all others upon our north-west coast.

As we view the matter now, a century and more later, we can see that our national destiny, and especially the vast part that we now seem at the point of taking in world interests through the commerce of the Pacific, hung in the balance to a certain extent upon the stubborn adherence by Vancouver, the Briton, to the preconceived opinion that there was no important river at the point designated by his Spanish predecessor, and the contrasted readiness of the American Gray to embrace boldly the chances of some great discovery. It is true that the "Oregon Question" was not to be settled for several decades. Much diplomacy and contention, almost to the verge of war, were yet to come, but Gray's fortunate dash, "with all sail set, in between the breakers to a large river of fresh water," gave our nation a lead in the ultimate adjustment of the case, which we never lost.

We have said that there was one negative discovery—that of Meares—and two positive ones. Gray's was one of the two, and that of Broughton, in command of the *Chatham* accompanying Vancouver, was the other.

On the 20th of May, the *Columbia Rediviva*—a most auspicious name—bade adieu to the scene of her glory, and with the Stars and Stripes floating in triumph at her mizzen-mast, turned northward. Again the American captain encountered Vancouver and narrated to him his discovery of the Columbia. With deep chagrin at his own failure in the two most important objects of discovery in his voyage, the British commander directed Broughton to return to latitude 46 degrees 10 minutes, enter the river, and proceed as far up as time allowed.

Accordingly, on October 21st, the companion ships parted at the mouth of the River, the *Discovery* proceeding to Monterey, while the *Chatham* crossed the bar, described by Broughton as very bad, and endeavoured to ascend the bay that stretched out beautiful and broad before them. But finding the channel intricate and soundings variable, the lieutenant deemed it advisable to leave the ship at a point which must have been about twenty miles from the ocean, and to proceed thence in the cutter.

There is one thing observable in Vancouver's account of this expedition of Broughton, and that is extreme solicitude to establish these two propositions:— first, that the lower part of the Columbia is a bay and that its true mouth is at a point above that reached by Gray; and second, that the River is much smaller than it really is. It is hard to reconcile the language used in Broughton's report as given by Vancouver with the supposition of candour and honesty. For while it is true that the lower part of the River is of bay-like expanse from four to nine miles in width, yet it is entirely fresh and has all river characteristics. One of the points especially made by Gray was that he filled his casks with fresh water. Moreover, the bar is entirely at the ocean limit. So completely does the River debouch into the Ocean, in fact, that in the great flood of 1894 the clams were killed on the ocean beaches for a distance of several miles on either side of the outer headlands through the freshening of the sea.

As to the size of the River, Broughton gives its width repeatedly as half a mile or a quarter of a mile, whereas it is at almost no point below the Cascades less than a mile in width, and a mile and a half is more usual. Broughton expresses the conviction that it can never be used for navigation by vessels of any size. In view of the vast commerce now constantly passing in and out, the absurdity of that idea is and has been for years sufficiently exhibited. The animus of the British explorers is obvious. By showing that the mouth of the River was really an inlet of the sea, they hoped to lay a claim to British occupancy as against Gray's discovery, and by belittling the size of the River they hoped to save their own credit with the British Admiralty for having lost so great a chance for first occupation.

Broughton ascended the River to a point near the modern town of Washougal. He bestowed British names after the general fashion, as Mt. Hood, Cape George, Vancouver Point, Puget's Island, Young's Bay, Menzies' Island, and Whidby's River. With true British assurance, he felt that he had "every reason to believe that the subjects of no other civilised nation or state had ever entered this river before; in this opinion he was confirmed by Mr. Gray's sketch, in which it does not appear that Mr. Gray either saw or was ever within five leagues of its entrance." Therefore he "took possession of the river, and the country in its vicinity, in His Britannic Majesty's name."

In view of all the circumstances of Gray's discovery, and his impartation of it to the British, this language of Vancouver has a coolness, as John Fiske remarks, which would be very refreshing on a hot day.

On November 10th, the *Chatham* crossed the bar outward bound for Monterey to join the *Discovery*.

Such, in rapid view, were the essential facts in the long and curiously complicated finding of our River. We see that various nations bore each a part. We see the foundation of the subsequent contention between Great Britain and the United States.

CHAPTER IV

THE FIRST STEPS ACROSS THE WILDERNESS IN SEARCH OF THE RIVER

Jefferson and Ledyard—Verendrye—Montcachabe, the Indian—The Indians—The Canadians—Results of the Louisiana Purchase—Fitting out the Lewis and Clark Expedition—The Winter with the Mandans—Crossing of the Great Divide—Meeting of Sacajawea and Cameahwait—Descent from the Mountains to the Clearwater and Kimooenim—Canoe Journey Down the Snake and Columbia—First Sight of Mt. Hood—Clark in the Rôle of a Magician—The Timm or Great Falls—The Sunken Forests—First Appearances of the Tide—The Winter of 1805-06 at Fort Clatsop—The Beginning of the Return Trip—Faithfulness of the Indians—Reception of Lewis and Clark in the States—The Hunt Expedition—The *Voyageurs* and Trappers—Slow Progress to the Snake River—Disasters and Distress along the "Accursed Mad River"—Starvation—New Year's Day of 1812—A Respite from Suffering in the Umatilla—First Sight of the Columbia and the Mid-winter Descent to Astoria—Melancholy Lot of Crooks and Day—Results of the Hunt Expedition.

THE Pacific North-west was discovered both by land and by sea. To Thomas Jefferson, the great apostle of Democracy, is due the gathering of American interests in the far West, and the opening of the road by which American sovereignty was to reach the Pacific. His great mind outran that of the ordinary statesman of his time, and, with what seems at first sight the strangest inconsistency in our political history, he was the State-rights theorist and at the same time the creator of nationality beyond any other one of our early statesmen. Away back in 1786, Jefferson met John Ledyard, one of Cook's associates in his great voyage to the Pacific Ocean, and grasped from the eager and energetic Yankee sailor, the idea of American destiny on the Pacific Coast. The fertile mind of Jefferson may justly be considered as the fountain of American exploration up the Missouri, across the crest of the Shining Mountains, as they then called the Rockies, and down the Columbia to the Pacific. Although Jefferson never himself took any steps beyond the Alleghanies, he was the inspiration of all the Americans who did take those steps.

Since we are speaking of first steps across the wilderness we should not forget that those of other nationalities than ours first crossed the American continent.

The honour of the pioneer expedition to the crest of the Rocky Mountains belongs to the Frenchman, Verendrye. In 1773 he set forth from Montreal for the Rocky Mountains, and made many important explorations. His party is said to have reached the vicinity of the site of Helena, but never saw the sunset side of the Great Divide.

We are told by the interesting French writer, La Page, that the first man to proceed across the continent to the shores of the Pacific was a Yazoo Indian, Montcachabe or Montcacht Ape by name. According to the story, his two-year journey across the great wilderness through every species of peril and hardship, savage beasts and forbidding mountains and deserts, hostile Indians often barring his progress for many days, was one of the most remarkable explorations ever made by man. This Yazoo Indian with the long name was a veritable Columbus in the nature of his achievements. But results for the world could hardly follow his enterprise.

The first traveller to lead a party of civilised men through the Shining, or the Stony Mountains, finally known as Rocky Mountains, to the Pacific Ocean, was Alexander Mackenzie, a canny Scotchman, leading a party of Scotch and French Canadian explorers. In 1793 he reached the Pacific Coast at the point of 52 degrees 24 minutes 48 seconds north latitude. His inscription upon a rock with letters of vermilion and grease, were read many years afterwards: "Alexander Mackenzie, from Canada by land, July 22, 1793."

But the explorations of Canadians were too far north to come within the scope of the Pacific North-west of our day. We must therefore take up the American expeditions which proceeded from the master mind of Jefferson. The first of these was the expedition of Lewis and Clark. This expedition did more to broaden the American mind and to fix our national destiny than any similar event in our whole history.

As soon as Jefferson was inaugurated president, he had urged upon Congress the fitting out of an expedition "to explore the Missouri River and such principal streams of it as, by its course of communication with the waters of the Pacific Ocean, whether the Columbia, Oregon, Colorado, or any other river, may offer the most direct and practical water communication across the continent, for the purposes of commerce."

But before anything had actually been accomplished in the way of exploration, that vast and important event, the Louisiana Purchase, had been effected. The significance of this event was but little understood at the time, even by statesmen, but Jefferson realised that a great thing had been accomplished towards the development of the nation. His enthusiasm and hopefulness spread to Congress and to the leaders of opinion throughout the land. A like enthusiasm soon possessed the mass of population, and emigration westward began. Already the older West was teeming with that race of pioneers which has made up the life and the grandeur of the nineteenth century. The American hive began to swarm. "Out West" began to mean something more than Ohio and Kentucky. The distant sources of the Missouri and the heights of the Shining Mountains, with all the fantastic tales that had been told of them, were drawing our grandfathers farther and farther from the old colonial America of the eastern coast, and were beginning to modify the whole course of American history. The atmosphere of boundless expectation gathered over farm and town in the older States and the proposed expedition of Lewis and Clark fascinated the people as much as the voyage of Columbus fascinated the Spain of his day.

And what manner of men were in charge of this expedition, thus filled with both interest and peril? Meriwether Lewis was the leader of the party. He was a captain in the U. S. Army who was well known to Jefferson and who had been selected by him as possessed of the endurance, boldness, and energy which made him the fittest man within Jefferson's knowledge for the duties of commander. His whole life, from his boyhood days in Virginia, had been one of bold adventure. It is related that at the tender age of eight, he was already illustrious for successful midnight forays upon the coon and possum. He had not received a scientific education, but immediately upon receiving the appointment of commander of the expedition, he entered with great energy upon the acquisition of knowledge along geographical lines which would best fit him for preserving an accurate record of his journey. William Clark, the lieutenant of the expedition, was also a United States officer, a man of very good judgment, boldness, and skill in organising his work, and readiness in meeting every kind of emergency. The party was made up of fourteen United States regular soldiers, nine Kentucky volunteers, two French voyageurs, a hunter, an interpreter and a negro servant. The soldiers were offered the munificent bounty of retirement upon full pay, with a grant of land. By Jefferson's directions, the party were encouraged to keep complete records of all they saw and did. They carried out the instruction so fully that seven journals besides those of Lewis and Clark themselves, were carefully kept, and in them a record was made of every important, as well as unimportant, discovery, even down to the ingredients of their meals and their doses of medicine. It is safe to say that no expedition was ever more fully or accurately reported. Although not a single one of the party possessed literary attainments, there is nevertheless a singular charm about the combined record which has been recognised to this day by repeated editions of the work. It was well understood that the success of the expedition depended largely upon making friends with the Indians, and the explorers were therefore completely fitted out with beads, mirrors, knives, and all manner of trinkets.

The summer of 1804 was spent in an easy and uneventful journey of five months up the Missouri to the country of the Mandan Indians, in what is now Dakota. There they determined to winter. The winter was devoted to making the acquaintance of Indians and to collecting botanical and zoölogical specimens, of which they sent President Jefferson a large amount by a portion of the party which now left them and descended the River. And, while speaking of their relations to Indians, it is very interesting to note the attitude Jefferson instructed them to take in respect to the native tribes. He insisted upon a policy of peace and good-will toward all the tribes upon the route. It is observable that Jefferson refers in a most considerate and friendly manner to the Indians, and instructs the explorers to arrange, if possible, to have some of the more important chiefs induced to come back with the explorers to the city of Washington. He also points out the desirability of urging any bright young Indians to receive such arts as might be useful to them when in contact with the white men. Jefferson even goes so far as to advise the explorers to take along vaccine matter that the Indians might be instructed in the advantages of vaccination. A number of medallion medals were made that were intended to be given as presents to Indian chiefs, the inscription of which was "Peace and Friendship," with the design of clasped hands. These medals, it may be remarked, seem to have been prized by the Indians as among their greatest treasures. Several of them have been found in Indian graves; one even in a grave of the Nez Percé Indians in Idaho.

While among the Mandans, the expedition was joined by the most attractive personage in it, that is to say, Sacajawea. This young Indian woman, the only woman in the expedition, seems to have furnished the picturesque element in the composition of the party, and she has in later days become the subject of great interest on the part of students of Pacific Coast history.

On April 7th, everything was in readiness for resuming their journey up the River. The explorers embarked again in a squadron of six canoes and two pirogues.

On the twelfth day of August, an advance party of the explorers crossed the Great Divide of the Rocky Mountains, the birthplace of mighty rivers. Descending the western slope, they found themselves in the country of the Shoshone Indians. Captain Lewis was leading this advance expedition, and, as he neared the highest point of the pass, he realised the significance of the transition from the waters of the Missouri to those of the Columbia. A quotation from his narrative at this most interesting point of the journey gives the reader a better conception than any description could, of the feelings of the explorers:

> The road was still plain, and as it led directly toward the mountains, the stream gradually became smaller, till after their advancing two miles further, it had so greatly diminished in width that one of the men in a fit of enthusiasm, with one foot on each side of the rivulet, thanked God that he had lived to bestride the Missouri. As they proceeded, their hope of seeing the waters of the Columbia rose to almost painful anxiety; when at the distance of four miles from the last abrupt turn of the stream, they reached a small gap formed by the high mountains which recede on either side, leaving room for the Indian road. From the foot of one of the lowest of these mountains, which arises with a gentle ascent of about half a mile, issued the remotest water of the Missouri. They had now reached the hidden sources of that river, which had never before been seen by civilised man; and as they quenched their thirst at the chaste and icy fountain, —as they sat down by the brink of that little rivulet, which yielded its distant and modest tribute to the parent ocean, —they felt themselves rewarded for all their labours and difficulties. They left reluctantly this interesting spot, and pursuing the Indian road through the interval of the hills, arrived at the top of a ridge from which they

saw high mountains, partially covered with snow, still to the west of them. The ridge on which they stood formed the dividing line between the waters of the Atlantic and the Pacific Oceans. They found the descent much steeper than on the eastern side, and at the distance of three-quarters of a mile, reached a handsome, bold creek of cold, clear water running to the westward. They stopped to taste for the first time the waters of the Columbia.

Mt. Adams from the South.

Photo. by W. D. Lyman.

Capt. Robert Gray.

The Columbia Rediviva.

The party was now upon the western slope of the Great Divide, in the vicinity of the present Fort Lemhi in Eastern Idaho. They supposed that they were almost to the Pacific, not realising that a thousand miles of difficult and dangerous travel and more than two months of time still separated them from their wished-for goal. The journey, in fact, from the springs of the Missouri to the navigable waters of the Columbia, proved to be the most critical of the whole series.

Soon after passing the crest of the mountains, the party encountered a band of sixty Indians of the Shoshone tribe, coming to meet them at full speed, upon fine horses, and armed for battle. Captain Lewis, who always showed great discretion with Indians, took the Stars and Stripes in his hand, and advanced alone to meet the party. As soon as the Indians perceived that he was a white man, they showed signs of great rejoicing, and the three leaders of the war-party, dismounting, embraced the American captain with great exuberance, shouting words which he afterwards discovered meant, "We are rejoiced! We are rejoiced!" The valiant captain, however, was much more pleased with the hearty good-will of their intentions than in the manner of its expression, inasmuch as they had transferred a good portion of the war paint from their own faces to his. Lewis now brought up his companions and entered upon a long and friendly conference with the chief of the party, whose name was Cameahwait. Captain Lewis, as the representative of the great American nation, set forth to the eager listeners about him, a glowing report as to the benevolence of the Great Father at Washington, and his desire that his brothers of the West should come into friendly relations with him and trade their furs for the beads and blankets and knives which the Indians so highly prize. He also explained to them that they would receive from his government guns and ammunition which would enable them to cope with the dreaded Sioux or the pitiless Blackfeet. Captain Lewis also greatly aroused the curiosity of these Indians by indicating to them that he had with him a woman of their tribe, and also a man who was perfectly black and yet not painted. He now made a proposition to Cameahwait to go back with him and his companions to the forks of the Missouri where they had left the main party with their goods and boats. Cameahwait very gladly agreed to do this and also to provide them with horses for the journey westward to the navigable waters of the Columbia.

After a journey of several days upon the back trail, the party found themselves again at the forks of the Missouri, but, somewhat to their surprise and consternation, the main party was not there. The Indians at first were very much excited, and, believing that they had been deceived and that the white men were enticing them to destruction, they were at the point of wreaking vengeance upon them. But with great tact and boldness, Lewis gave the chief his gun and ammunition, telling him that if it proved that he had been a deceiver, they might instantly kill him. Reassured, the Indians proceeded onward and in a short time they could descry the boats, making their way slowly up the impetuous stream toward a bold promontory where the Indians were stationed. In the bow of the foremost boat was seated Sacajawea, clad in her bright red blanket, and gazing eagerly at the group of Indians, thinking it possible that they might be of her own tribe. As the boat approached the band, the keen-sighted little Indian woman soon perceived that these people were indeed of her own Shoshone tribe. Quickly disembarking, she made her way to them, when suddenly her eyes fell upon the chief, Cameah-wait. Then to the astonishment of the white men who were with her, she broke forth suddenly into a torrent of tears which were soon changed into joyful smiles as the chief, with almost as much emotion as herself, rushed forward to embrace her. She then explained to Captain Lewis that Cameahwait was her own brother, whom she had not seen since, as a little girl, she had been seized by the Mandans and carried into captivity.

Of course there was now the kindliest feeling between the party of explorers and the Indians. They found everything that they needed, horses, provisions, and guides, placed at their disposal. They were at that time, as would be seen by an inspection of the map, at the head waters of Salmon River. They hoped that they might find a route down that powerful stream to navigable water. But the Indians assured them that the river was white with foam for many miles and disappeared in a chain of terrific snowy mountains. It became necessary, therefore, to find a more northerly route, and on the last day of August, with twenty-nine horses, having bidden a hearty good-bye to the hospitable Shoshones, they turned north-westward and soon became entangled in the savage ridges and defiles, already spotted with snow, of the Bitter Root Mountains.

They were at this time among some of the upper branches of the second largest tributary of the Columbia, named by them Clark's Fork, though at the present time more commonly known by the more rhythmic title of Pend Oreille. After several days of the most difficult, and indeed dangerous, journeying of their entire trip, they abandoned the northern route, turned southward, and soon reached the wild and beautiful stream which they called the Kooskooskie, commonly known to modern times as the Clearwater, one of the finest of all the fine rivers of Idaho, the "Gem of the Mountains."

But they were not yet by any means clear of danger. The country still frowned on them with the same forbidding crags, and the same blinding snow storms as before. They were approaching the starvation point. The craggy precipices were marked with almost daily accidents to men and beasts. Their only food was the flesh of their precious horses. Under these harassing circumstances, it was decided that the wisest thing was for Captain Clark to take six of his best men and press rapidly forward in search of game and a more favourable country. After a hard journey of twenty miles, he found himself upon the crest of a towering cliff, from which stretched in front a vast open plain. This was the great plain, now covered with wheat-fields and orchards, lying east and north of the present city of Lewiston, Idaho. Having made their way down the declivities of the Bitter Root Mountains to the prairie, where they found a climate that seemed almost tropical after the bitter cold of the high mountains, the advance guard camped and waited for the main party to come up.

Rejoicing at their release from the distressing conditions of their passage of the Bitter Root Mountains, they passed onward to a beautiful mountain-enclosed valley, which must have been in the near vicinity of what is known as the Kamiah Valley of the present time. Here they found themselves with a large body of Indians who became known subsequently as the Nez Percés. These Indians appeared to be the most honest, intelligent, and attractive they had yet met,—eager to assist them, kind and helpful, although shrewd and business-like in their trading.

The Nez Percés imparted to them the joyful news that the Great River was not far distant. Seeing the Clearwater to be a fine, navigable stream, the explorers determined to abandon the weary land journey and once more commit their fortunes to the waters. They left their horses with the Nez Percés, asking that they should meet them at that point in the following spring when they expected to be on their return trip. The scrupulous fidelity with which the Nez Percés carried out their trust is some evidence of the oft-made assertion that the treachery characteristic of the Indians was learned afterwards from the whites.

With five large and well-filled canoes, and with a good supply of eatables and all the other necessaries of life, the explorers now cast themselves upon the clear, swift current of the Kooskooskie, and on the 10th of October reached that striking and interesting place where the beautiful modern town of Lewiston is located, at the junction of the Clearwater and the Snake. The turbid, angry, sullen Snake, so striking a contrast with the lesser stream, received from the explorers the name of Kimooenim, its Indian name. Subsequently they christened it Lewis's Fork, but the still less attractive name of Snake is the one by which it is universally known.

The journey of a hundred and twenty miles from the junction of the Clearwater and the Snake to the junction of the latter stream with the mighty Columbia, seems to have been a calm and uneventful journey, though the explorers record every manner of event, whether important or unimportant. Knowledge of their approach seems to have reached the Indian world, and when on October 16th they reached the point where the modern city of Pasco is located, they were met by a regular procession of two hundred Indians. The two great rivers were then at their lowest point in the year, and they found by measurement that the Columbia was 960 yards in width and the Snake, 575 yards. In the glimmering haze of the pleasant October day they noted how the vast, bare prairie stretched southward until it was broken by the rounded summits of the Blue Mountains. To their astonishment, they found that the Sohulks, who lived at the junction of the rivers, so differed from other Indians that the men were content with one wife and that they would actually assist her in the drudgery of the family life. After several days spent in rest and getting fish, which seemed to throng the river in almost countless numbers, they resumed their journey upon the magnificent flood of the Columbia. Soon after passing what we now call the Umatilla Highland, they caught their first glimpse, clear-cut against the horizon of the south-west, of the bold cone of Mt. Hood, glistening with its eternal snows. Landing upon the broad prairie near where Umatilla is now located, Captain Clark shot a crane and a duck. He then perceived a group of Indians who were almost paralysed with terror and yet able to make their way with considerable expedition to a little group of tepees. Having entered one of these, Captain Clark discovered thirty-two Indians, men, women, and children, all of whom seemed to be in the greatest terror, wailing and wringing their hands. Endeavouring by kind looks and gestures to soothe their perturbation, Captain Clark held up a burning glass to catch a stray sunbeam with which to light his pipe. Whereupon the consternation of the Indians was redoubled, to be soothed only by the arrival of the two Indian guides who were accompanying the party. The terrified Indians explained to the guides that they knew that Captain Clark must have some bad medicine about him, for he had dropped out of the sky with a dead crane and a duck, accompanied by a terrible noise.

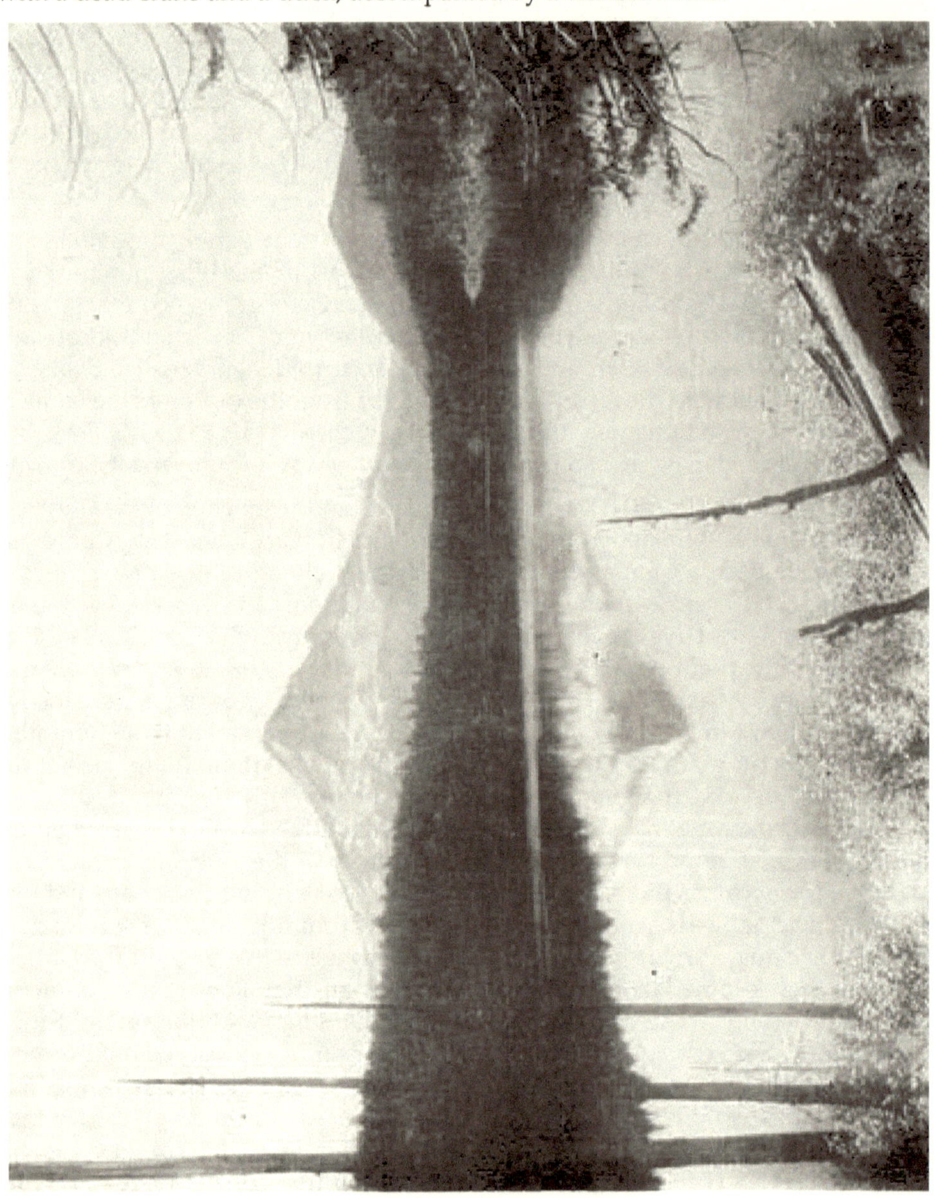

Mt. Hood from Lost Lake.

Photo. by E. H. Moorehouse.

The Indians being now convinced that he was a mortal man, and, moreover, having heard the sound of the violin which the negro servant carried with him, became so enamoured with the strangers that they stayed up with them all night, and in the morning collected by hundreds to bid them good-bye.

The Indians had now given them to understand that in a short time they would reach the place which they knew as "Timm." This seems to have been an Indian word for falls. It still appears in the name Tumwater Falls applied to the falls at Celilo on the Columbia. A weird, savage place this proved to be; crags of basalt, thrust through the soil, like clenched hands, seemed almost to grasp the rushing river. Making several portages, the voyagers reached that extraordinary place now called The Dalles, or the "big chute," where all the waters of the Columbia are squeezed into a crack only a hundred and fifty feet in width. The River, in fact, is "turned on edge." The explorers, finding the shore so rough that it was difficult to carry their boats over, steered boldly through that witch's caldron. Though they must have been carried with frightful rapidity through the boiling stream, they reached the end of the cataract without accident. At this point they began to be aware of the fact that they were reaching the sphere of the white traders from the ocean, for they began to see blankets, axes, brass kettles, and other articles of civilised manufacture. The Indians, too, were more saucy, suspicious, and treacherous than those of the upper country.

Being launched upon the calm, deep flood of the River below The Dalles, they observed the phenomenon of the submerged forest, which at a low state of water is still conspicuous. They correctly inferred that this indicated a damming up of the River at some recent time. They thought indeed that it could not have been more than twenty years previous. We know, however, that submerged trees or piles, as indicated by remains of old Roman wharves in Britain, may remain intact for hundreds of years. This place on the Columbia is, however, one of the most interesting of its many interesting phenomena. It is evident that within very recent times, geologically speaking, there was a prodigious rock-slide from the mountains which closed the River, producing the cataract of the Cascades and raising the River above, some forty feet.

Here the explorers had their last portage. On the second day of November they reached the foot of the Cascades and perceived the movement of the tide, which made it plain to them that the ocean was near at hand. Yet, in reality, it was much farther than they thought, for the majestic lower River extends one hundred and sixty miles from the foot of the last cataract to the Pacific. It is interesting to notice comments made by the explorers upon the green and fertile islands at the lower end of the Cascades, and that spired and turreted volcanic cliff which they called Beacon Rock, but which we know now as Castle Rock.

The rest of the journey of Lewis and Clark was a calm floating down the tranquil flood of the lower Columbia in the midst of the fog and clouds which at that season of the year generally embrace all objects. On November 7th the mist suddenly broke away before them, the bold mountainous shores vanished in front, and, through the parted headlands, they looked forth into the expanse of the ocean.

Eliot Glacier, Mt. Hood.

Photo. by E. H. Moorehouse.

Their journey was now ended. They had demonstrated the possibility of crossing the continent and of linking together the waters of the Missouri and the Columbia.

The winter of 1805-06 was spent in log buildings at a point named by the explorers, Fort Clatsop, situated on the Lewis and Clark River at the south side of the Columbia a few miles from the present site of Astoria. The location of this fort has been identified in modern times, as has also the location of the salt cairn, upon what is now known as the Seaside Beach, commemorated by an inscription.

One of the interesting little human touches in the narrative of Captain Lewis describes the casting of a whale upon Clatsop Beach and the journey of the party to see the great marine curiosity, as well as to secure some of its fat and blubber. The Indian woman, Sacajawea, was to be left behind to keep camp while they were all at the beach, but she put up the earnest plea that inasmuch as she had never seen any such curiosity as the "big fish," and as she had journeyed all those weary miles from the country of the Mandans, it seemed hard that she should be denied the privilege of satisfying her eyes with a view of the whale. Lewis remarks that the request of the poor woman seemed so reasonable that they at once fixed up camp in such manner that it could be left, and took her with them, to her intense satisfaction.

After four months spent in the fogs and mists of the coast, and without seeing any of the ships which the Indians said were accustomed to come in considerable numbers during the spring and summer, the party turned their faces homeward on the 23d of March, 1806. The commander posted upon the fort a notice which read as follows:

> The object of this last is that through the medium of some civilised person who may see the same, it may be made known to the world that the party consisting of the persons whose names are hereunto annexed and who were sent out by the Government of the United States to explore the interior of the continent of North America, did penetrate the same by way of the Missouri and Columbia Rivers, to the discharge of the latter into the Pacific Ocean, at which they arrived on the 14th day of November, 1805, and departed on their return to the United States by the same route by which they had come.

They also gave to the chiefs of the Clatsops and Chinooks certificates, to which they attached great importance and which were afterwards exhibited to other explorers, setting forth the just and hospitable treatment which these Indians had accorded the party.

The return from Fort Clatsop to the Missouri was in the main a pleasant and successful journey without extraordinary event, except the fact that upon their return they discovered the Willamette River, which, strange to say, had eluded their observation on their journey down the River in November. The journal contains the somewhat quaint statement that the chief cultivable region which they discovered in Oregon was Wapatoo Island, now known as Sauvie's Island, at the mouth of the Willamette. They express the conviction that that fertile tract of country and the region adjoining might sometime support a population of fifty thousand people. They seem to regard this as an extraordinary prophecy of prosperity. Inasmuch as there are already over four times that number of people in the city of Portland, it would seem that Lewis and Clark were hardly "boomers" in the modern sense of the word.

One interesting thing in connection with the Lewis and Clark expedition receives special emphasis from them in the account of their return journey, and that is, the faithfulness, honesty, and devotion of the Indians when entrusted with any charge, as the care of horses or canoes. This character of the Indians was so marked that one can hardly avoid the conclusion that the subsequent troubles with the Indians were due very largely to abuse by the whites.

No better summary can be given of the scope of this historic journey than that by Captain Lewis himself in his journal. He says:

> The road by which we went out by way of the Missouri to its head is three thousand ninety-six miles; thence by land by way of Lewis River over to Clark's River and down that to the entrance of Traveller's Rest Creek, where all the roads from different routes meet; thence across the rugged part of the Rocky Mountains to the navigable waters of the Columbia, three hundred and ninety-eight miles, thence down the river six hundred and forty miles to the Pacific Ocean, making a total distance of four thousand one hundred and thirty-four miles. On our return in 1806 we reduced the distance from the Mississippi to the Pacific Ocean to three thousand five hundred and fifty-five miles.

The safe return of the explorers to their homes created a sensation throughout the United States and the world. Leaders and men were suitably rewarded. Though the expedition was not marked by many remarkable adventures or dramatic events, and though the narration given by the explorers is of a plain and simple kind with no attempt at literary ornamentation, yet occurring, as the expedition did, at such a peculiar juncture in our history, and having such an effect to bridge the chasm between the old time and the new, this Lewis and Clark expedition has continued to receive, and justly, more attention than any other journey in our history. President Jefferson, paying a tribute to Captain Lewis in 1813, expressed himself thus:

> Never did a similar event excite more joy throughout the United States; the humblest of its citizens have taken a lively interest in the issue of this journey and looked with impatience for the information it would furnish. Nothing short of the official journals of this extraordinary and interesting journey will exhibit the importance of the service, the courage, devotion, zeal, and perseverance, under circumstances calculated to discourage, which animated this little band of heroes, throughout the long dangerous, and tedious travel.

The expedition of Lewis and Clark may justly be considered as constituting the first steps across the wilderness. The breadth of the American continent was now known. The general relations of its rivers and mountain systems and prairies were understood. Something of its prodigality of resources became set forth to the world. A dim consciousness of the connection of this vast Pacific domain with the progress of American destiny appeared to our grandfathers. And although the wilderness traversed by this complete expedition did not come into possession of the United States for many years, yet it might well be said that our subsequent acquirement of it was due to the Lewis and Clark expedition.

Of the many remarkable explorations which followed, with all of their adventure and tragedy, we cannot here speak. For several years all the expeditions to the far West were the outgrowth of the fur-trade. Most remarkable of these early journeys was that of the Hunt party which was the land division of the great Astor movement to establish the Pacific Fur Company. That company was established by John Jacob Astor of New York for the purpose of making a bold and far-reaching attempt to control the fur-trade of the Pacific Coast in the interests of the United States. While the sea division was upon its journey around Cape Horn, the land division was in process of organisation at St. Louis. Wilson Price Hunt, the commander of this division, was the second partner in the Astor company. He had been merchandising for some years at St. Louis, and had become impressed with the financial profits of the fur-trade as well as with the vast possibilities of American development on the continent. Hunt was a fine type of the pioneer promoter of that age. Brave, humane, cheerful, and resolute, he appears to us as the very flower of the adventurous Argonauts who were searching for the seal and beaver fleeces of the far West.

With Hunt were associated four other partners of the expedition, Crooks, McKenzie, Miller, and McCellan. Accompanying the party were two English naturalists, Bradbury and Nuttall, who did the first scientific study of the Rocky Mountain region. There were forty Canadian *voyageurs* whose duties consisted of rowing, transporting, cooking, and general drudgery. The remaining twelve of the party consisted of a group of American hunters and trappers, the leader of whom was a Virginian named John Day. The company was in all respects fitted out most bountifully.

There were at that time two great classes of trappers. The first and most numerous were the Canadian *voyageurs*. These were mainly of French descent, many of them being half-breeds. Almost amphibious by nature and training, gay and amiable in disposition, with true French vivacity and ingenuity, gliding over every harsh experience with laugh and song, possessed of quick sympathies and humane instincts which enabled them to readily find the best side of the Indians,— these French *voyageurs* constituted a most interesting as well as indispensable class in the trapper's business.

The free trappers were an entirely different class of men. They were usually American by birth, Virginia and Kentucky being the homes of most of them. Patient and indefatigable in their work of trapping, yet, when on their annual trip to the towns, given to wild dissipation and savage revellings, indifferent to sympathy or company, harsh and cruel to the Indians, bold and overbearing, with blood always in their eyes, thunder in their voices, and guns in their hands, yet underneath all of their harsh exterior having noble hearts, could they but be reached, these now vanished trappers have gone to a place in history alongside of the old Spartans and the followers of Pizarro and Cortez in Spanish conquest.

Of the many adventures of the Hunt party on the journey up the Missouri, we cannot speak. For some reason, although taking a more direct route than did Lewis and Clark, and having, to all appearance, a better equipped party, they did not make so good time. Guided by Indians, they crossed chain after chain of mountains, supposing each to be the summit, only to find another yet to succeed. At last on the 15th of September, they stood upon a lofty eminence over which they could gaze both eastward and westward. Scanning attentively the western horizon, the guide pointed out three shining peaks, whose bases, he told them, were touched by a tributary of the Columbia River. These peaks are now known as the Three Tetons.

And now the party set forth upon the long descent of the western slope, passing mountain after mountain and stream after stream, some of the way in boats which the *voyageurs* made from the green timber of the forests, and much of the way being obliged to carry their effects around cataracts and rapids, and thus losing much time. Nevertheless, they found one long stretch of over a hundred miles upon the upper Snake which they navigated with comparative ease. But having reached what is now known as the Seven Devils country in South-western Idaho, they found themselves in a chain of rapids and precipitous bluffs where neither boats nor horses, apparently nothing but wings, could be of service. This was in fact the beginning of over a hundred miles of the most ragged and inaccessible region upon the whole course of the Snake River, a region which even to this day contains neither road nor steamboat route, and by which the great State of Idaho is separated into two divisions, neither directly accessible to the other by any ordinary modes of travel.

After a forty-mile tramp up and down the river, Hunt decided that the only way to escape the difficulties with which they were surrounded, was to divide the party into four divisions, hoping that one of them might find game and a way out of the forbidding volcanic wastes in which they were beleaguered. Two of the parties soon returned. One, being in charge of McKenzie, continued upon its course northward and reached the mouth of the Columbia, without ever again seeing the main party.

During the weeks that followed, the main party, lost amid the great mountains which lie eastward from the present vicinity of Baker City and Wallowa Lake, suffered all the torments of famine and cold. In places the river ran through volcanic sluiceways, roaring and raging; in some cases, although within hearing, yet entirely inaccessible, so that although within sound of its angry raving, the travellers were often obliged to lie down with tongues parched and swollen for lack of water. The party applied to this long volcanic "chute" the name of the Devil's Scuttle-hole, and to the river they applied the name *La Rivière Maudite Enragée*, or "Accursed Mad River."

The lives of the party were evidently at stake. In the emergency Hunt determined to divide his force into two divisions, one on the north and one on the south side of the river. From the 9th of November until the first part of December they urged on this dismal and heart-sickening march. They passed a few wretched Indian camps where they managed to secure dogs for food, and once they got a few horses. The frightened and half-starved Indians could give them no clear information as to the location of the Great River, but they signified that they supposed it to be yet a long way off. The party was evidently approaching something, for gigantic snowy mountains now loomed dimly through the winter mists. Finding it impossible to make headway against blinding snowstorms and up the icy crags, they turned their course down to the river itself and made a cheerless camp. In the morning they were startled by seeing upon the opposite side of the river, a group of men more wretched and desolate than themselves. It soon appeared that this was the other party, which had entirely failed in finding either food or guidance from the Indians. Finding it necessary that some provision should be made for these dying men, Hunt constructed a rude canoe from the limbs of trees and the skin of one of the horses. In this crazy craft one of the daring Canadian *voyageurs* made his way with some of the horse meat, which, poor as it was, was sufficient to save life for the time.

With their little remaining strength, they pressed on down the river until they reached another small village of the wretched Snake Indians. Urging these Indians to provide for them a guide, and at last securing one by the most bounteous offers of rewards, Hunt succeeded in gathering all of his party together, with the exception of six sick men whom they were obliged to leave to the tender mercies of the Indians.

For another fortnight, the cold and hungry party floundered painfully through the snow across the rugged mountains which lie between what we now know as the Powder River Valley and the Grande Ronde. Reaching a lofty mountain height on the last day of December, they looked far down into a fair and snowless prairie, bathed in sunshine and appearing to the winter-worn travellers like a gleam of summer. Moreover, they soon discerned a group of Indian lodges which they judged were well supplied with dogs and horses. Thither hastening eagerly, they soon found themselves in a beautiful valley, which from their description must have been the Grande Ronde Valley. Beautiful at all times, it must have seemed trebly so to these ragged and famished wanderers.

The next morning the new year of 1812 shone in upon them bright and cheerful, as if to make amends for the stern severity of the outgoing year. And now the Canadians insisted upon having their New Year's holiday. Not even death and famine could rob the light-hearted *voyageurs* of their festivals. So with dance and song and with dog meat, roasted, boiled, fried, and fricasseed, they met the newly-crowned year with their Gallic happiness and abandon.

The Indians assured them that they could reach the Great River within three days. But they found it twice that, and their way led across another lofty chain of snowy mountains, before the canopy of clouds which hung above them parted. There, looking far down from their snowy eyre, they beheld the boundless and sunny plains of the Great River. Swiftly descending the slopes of the mountains, they emerged upon that finest land of all Eastern Oregon, the plains of the Umatilla. Here they found the tribe of the Tushepaw Indians with thirty-four lodges and two hundred horses. More significant than these to Hunt were axes, kettles, and other implements of white construction, indicating that these Indians had already come into communication with the traders upon the lower River. In answer to his eager questions, the Tushepaws informed him that the Great River was but two days distant and that a small party of white men had just descended it. Being now certain that this was the advance guard which had left him at the Devil's Scuttle-hole, Hunt felt sure that they were safe and was therefore relieved of one great anxiety.

After a few days' rest upon the pleasant prairies and in the comparatively genial climate of the Umatilla, the party set forth upon horses obtained from the Tushepaws, and after a pleasant ride of two days across the rolling prairie, they beheld flowing at their feet, a majestic stream, deep and blue, a mile in width, sweeping toward the sunset, evidently the Columbia. At the great falls of the River, known to the Indians as the Timm or the Tumwater, just above what we now call Dalles City, Hunt exchanged his horses for canoes. This last stage of two hundred and twenty miles by boat down the River, was calm and peaceful and a refreshing rest after the distress and disaster of their winter journey through the mountains. Not till the 15th of February, however, did they reach the newly christened town of Astoria. Rounding the bluffs of Tongue Point, they beheld with full hearts the Stars and Stripes floating over the only civilised abode west of St. Louis. Westward they saw the parted headlands between which the River pours its floods into the ocean. As the boats drew near the shore, the whole population, trappers, sailors, and Indians, came down to meet them. Foremost in the crowd they saw the members of the party which had gone on ahead through the Snake River Mountains. Having had no hope that Hunt and his men could survive the famine and the cold, these members of the advance guard were the more rejoiced to see them. The Canadians, with their French vivacity, rushed into each other's arms, sobbing and hugging like so many schoolgirls. Even the nonchalant Americans and the stiff-jawed Scotchmen smiled and gave themselves up to the gladness of the hour. The next two or three days were mainly devoted to eating and telling stories.

As we have seen, they had lost several of their number from starvation and drowning along the banks of the Snake River. They had also left six sick men with the Indians in the heart of the mountains. They had little hope of ever seeing these again, but the next summer the party on their way up the Columbia River, saw two wretched looking beings, naked and haggard, wandering on the river bank near the mouth of the Umatilla. Stopping to investigate, they discovered that these were Day and Crooks, the leaders of the party which they had left behind. Their forlorn plight was relieved with food and clothes, and, having been taken into the boat, they related their dismal tale. It appeared that they had been provided sufficiently by the Indians to sustain their lives through the winter. In the spring they had left the Canadians among the Indians, and had set forth in the hope of reaching the Great River. But having reached The Dalles, they had been robbed of rifles and ammunition, stripped of their clothing, and driven forth into the wilderness. They were almost at the point of a final surrender to ill-fortune when they beheld the rescuing boat. So, with joyful hearts, they turned their boat's prow to Astoria, which they reached in safety. But poor Day never regained his health. His mind was shattered by the hardships of his journey, and he soon pined away and died. The barren and rugged shores of the John Day River in Eastern Oregon take on an added interest in view of the sad story of the brave hunter who discovered them, and who wandered in destitution for so many days beside them. Strange to say, the four Canadians who remained among the Indians were afterwards found alive, though utterly destitute of all things. Hence it appears that the loss of life in this difficult journey was not great.

The journeys here narrated may be considered as covering what we have designated as the first steps across the wilderness. Within a few years, many parties of trappers, explorers, and adventurers, with some scientists, and a little later, parties of missionaries, made their way over the great plains, through the defiles of the mountains, and down the barren shores of the Snake River to the Columbia and the sea. Each party had its special experiences, and made its special contribution to geographical or commercial advancement. But to the parties led by Lewis and Clark and by Hunt, we must accord the greatest meed of praise for having broken the first pathways across the continent and for having linked the two oceans by the footsteps of civilised men.

CHAPTER V

THE FUR-TRADERS, THEIR BATEAUX, AND THEIR STATIONS

Importance of the Fur-trade as Connected with all Other Parts of the History—Fur-hunters Compared with Gold-hunters—Sea-otter—Ledyard's Exploration—The European Inaugurators of the Trade—Beginnings of the American Trade—The Great British Companies and their Struggles with the French—Mackenzie's Journey across the Continent—Thompson's Descent of the Columbia—Union of the Two Great Canadian Companies—The American Fur Companies—Henry's Fort—The Winship Enterprise on the River—John Jacob Astor and the Pacific Fur Company—Rivalry with the North-westers—Arrangements for Expeditions by Land and Sea, and the Personnel of these—Voyage of the *Tonquin* and her Disastrous Approach of the River—Founding of Astoria—Appearance of Thompson and the North-westers—Interior Expedition and Founding of Fort Okonogan—McDougall, the Smallpox Chief and Bridegroom of the Indian Princess—Evil Tidings in Regard to the *Tonquin*—Other Disasters—War of 1812 and Sale of Astoria to the North-westers—Restoration of Astoria to the Americans—Monopolisation of the River by the Hudson's Bay Company—Their Expeditions—Hard Lot of Madame Dorion and her Children—Adventures of Alexander Ross—The Forts and General Plan of Work—Fort Vancouver and its Remarkable Advantages—Dr. McLoughlin, or the "White Eagle"—Profits of the Fur-trade—The Canoes and Bateaux and the *Voyageurs*—The Routes of the Brigades—Later Americans.

AS the reader will doubtless already have discovered, we are presenting the history of the River topically rather than chronologically. The various great stages of progress, discovery by sea, discovery by land, fur-trade, Indian wars, missionary undertakings, international contests, beginnings of steamboat navigation, and settlement, overlap each other, and each topic compels us in a measure to anticipate its successors. This is especially true of the topic treated of in this chapter.

The fur-trade was an important factor in the eras of discovery both by land and by sea, in the Indian wars and in the era of settlement, while the strife of nations for the possession of the land of Oregon is almost a history of the fur companies and their international policies. Remembering this synthetic nature of these features of our history, we shall endeavour, with as little repetition as possible, to present a coherent picture of that great era of the fur-traders.

Without doubt one of the earliest uses to which man has put the lower animals is that of clothing his body in their captured skins. The acquisition of furs has been a special feature of the colder climes. It is obviously also a feature of discovery and conquest, for it is the wilderness only which yields any considerable number of fur-producing animals. Thus navigation, commerce, discovery, invention, economics, finally international wars and policies, have been rooted to a large degree in this primal business. The fur-hunters have held the hunters of gold and precious stones and spicery a close race in the rank of world movers. Indeed it may well be questioned whether results of greater moment to humanity have not proceeded from the quest for furs than from that for gold.

The Spaniards expended their energies in the gold and silver hunt in Mexico and Peru and annihilated the races of those lands in their pitiless rapacity. The other great exploring nations of the sixteenth century, especially the French, while not indifferent to the possibility of encountering the precious metals, found more certain and permanent results in the less feverish and dazzling pursuit of the wild animals of the wilderness. Neither the hunters for gold nor those for peltries were the state-builders and home-builders without whom our American Union would not exist. But they were the avant-couriers of both. Our land of Oregon has had the peculiar fortune of being opened by both for both.

China furnished the most active and convenient market for furs to those who secured their supplies on the Pacific Coast of North America. The Russians were the first Europeans to enter the Chinese market, and they began their voyages as early as 1741.

The sea-otter seems to have had its chief habitat on the Pacific shore from Oregon to Alaska, and, as the ships of all nations began to crowd upon the location of the fabled Strait of Anian, the trade with the natives for these precious furs became constantly augmented, until the curious and interesting creatures, so fatally attractive, were added to the long list of "lower creatures" whom the greed of the "higher creatures" has exterminated. A book by Coxe published in London in 1787 first made known to the English-speaking people the rich profits of the Russians from the transportation of the sea-otter skins to China. He instanced a case of a profit of $50,000 from a single cargo. It had, however, been known in 1785 from the report of the voyage of Captain Cook that the North-west Coast of America contained a new source of wealth from the accumulation of these furs by the Indians and their eager desire to trade them for trinkets and implements of civilised manufacture.

The first American to comprehend the greatness of the fur-trade on the North-west Coast of the Pacific, both as a means of profit to himself and as a patriotic impulse to direct his own nation into the channels of westward expansion, was John Ledyard. Thomas Jefferson and John Paul Jones became deeply interested in Ledyard's extravagant hopes of future wealth and glory, but all his efforts came to naught, and in 1788 this brilliant adventurer, just on the eve of setting out to explore the interior of Africa, suddenly put an end to his own life at Cairo, Egypt. Ledyard should always be remembered by his countrymen, for, though his glowing visions were unfulfilled, he was an important link in the great chain which bound Oregon to our own country.

During these same years, several Englishmen, already noted in the chapter on discovery, Portlock, Dixon, Hanna, Barclay, and Meares, were actively engaged in the fur-trade, while the voyages of La Pérouse and Marchand carried the flag of France on the same quest, and Spain's once illustrious emblem of world dominion was borne by Quadra, Valdes, Galiano, Fidalgo, Quimper, Caamano, and several others. While these explorers all were impelled in part by national pride and diplomacy, the hope of sharing the spoils of the sea-otter droves was the chief lure to the tempestuous seas of the North Pacific.

In Bullfinch's *Oregon and El Dorado* is a very interesting narration of the inception of the American part in the fur-trade of Oregon. In a building known as the Coolidge Building in Boston a company were gathered together in 1787 discussing the reports, then first made public, of Cook's voyages. Mr. Joseph Barrell, a rich merchant of Boston, was much impressed with Cook's account of the chances of barter with the Indians for furs and the disposal of them in China for yet more profitable cargoes of teas, silks, and other characteristic commodities of that land. As a result of this conference, a company was formed in Boston to prosecute such enterprise, the members of the company, Messrs. Barrell, Brown, Bulfinch, Darby, Hatch, and Pintard, being among the foremost of the business men in Boston in that good year of the creation of the American Constitution.

The enterprising Yankees rapidly drew to the front, so that during the years from 1790 to 1818, the records show one hundred and eight American vessels regularly engaged in the business, while only twenty-two English, with a few Portuguese and French are found. It should, of course be remembered that the tremendous strife of the Napoleonic Wars was engrossing the attention of European nations during that time. So well known did the Boston navigators become in that period that the common name of Americans used by the Oregon Indians was "Bostons." Robert Gray, the discoverer of the Columbia River, was fitted out by Bulfinch and others of the first Boston Company. During the period under consideration the profits of the traffic were usually very great, though variable, sometimes actual losses being incurred, while disaster from wreck, storm, scurvy, and murderous Indians was frequent. During the two years, 1786 and 1787, if Dixon is to be followed, there were sold in Canton five thousand eight hundred sea-otter hides for $160,700. Swan figures that with the four years ending with 1802, forty-eight thousand five hundred skins were sold. Sturgis states that he knew a capital of $50,000 to yield a gross income of $284,000. He relates that he had collected as high as six thousand fine skins in a single voyage and once secured five hundred and sixty of the best quality in one day. The Indians, however, learned to become very expert traders, and as they discovered the eagerness with which the whites sought their furs, they raised the price. They became, moreover, very capricious and unreliable, so that the phenomenal profits could no longer be obtained.

The stage of the history of the fur-trade of which we have thus far spoken may be called its first era of a free-for-all rush to the new seas, with no vast moneyed interests in any position of leadership. But commercial conditions were already in existence which were bound to reverse the situation.

Great operators, gigantic companies, foreshadowings of the great trusts of the present, with monopolistic aims, were seeking the ear of the British Government, while enterprises, larger, though not so monopolistic, were rapidly forming in the United States. The great monopolies of Europe had indeed existed long prior to the period of the Oregon fur-traders. As far back as the beginning of the sixteenth century, De Monts, Pontgrave, Champlain, and other great French explorers had secured monopolies on the fur-trade from Louis XIII. and his minister, Richelieu. Later La Salle, Hennepin, D'Iberville, and others had the same advantages. The St. Lawrence, the Great Lakes, and the upper Mississippi were the great "preserve" of these great concessionaires. The English and their American Colonists set themselves in battle array against the monopolistic Bourbon methods of handling the vast domain which the genius and enterprise of De Monts and Champlain had won for France, with the result that upon the heights of Abraham the Fleur-de-Lis was lowered before the Cross of St. George, and North America became English instead of Gallic, and one of the world's milestones was set for good. Then by one of those beautiful ironies of history which baffle all prescience, victorious Britain violated the principles of her own conquest and adopted the methods of Bourbon tyranny and monopoly, with the result that another milestone was set on the highway of liberty and the new continent became American instead of European.

But out of the struggles of that century, French, English, and American, out of the final distribution of territory, by which England retained Canada and with it a large French and Indian population, mingled with English and Scotch,—out of these curious comminglings, economic, commercial, political, religious, and ethnic, grew the great English fur companies, whose history was largely wrought out on the shores of the Columbia, and from whose juxtaposition with the American State-builder the romance and epic grandeur of the history of the River largely comes.

Many enterprises were started by the French and English in the seventeenth century, but the Hudson's Bay Company became the Goliath of them all. The first charter of this gigantic organisation was granted in 1670 by Charles II. to Prince Rupert and seventeen others, with a capital stock of ten thousand five hundred pounds. From this small beginning, the profits were so great that, notwithstanding the loss of two hundred thousand pounds from the French wars during the latter part of the century, the Company declared dividends of from twenty-five to fifty per cent.

The field of operations was gradually extended from the south-eastern regions contiguous to Hudson's Bay until it embraced the vast and dreary expanses of snowy prairie traversed by the Saskatchewan, the Athabasca, the Peace, and finally the Mackenzie. Many of the greatest expeditions by land under British auspices which resulted in great geographical discoveries were primarily designed for the expansion of the fur-trade.

Just at the critical moment, both for the great Canadian Fur Company, as well as for discovery and acquisition in the region of the Columbia, a most important and remarkable champion entered the lists. This was the North-west Fur Company of Montreal. It was one of the legitimate consequences of the treaty of Paris in 1763, ceding Canada to Great Britain. The French in Canada became British subjects by that treaty, and many of them had extensive interests as well as experience in the fur business. Furthermore a number of Scotchmen of great enterprise and intelligence betook themselves to Canada, eager to partake of the boundless opportunities offered by the new shuffle of the cards. These Scotchmen and Frenchmen became natural partners in the foundation of enterprises independent of the Hudson's Bay monopoly. In 1783 a group of the boldest and most energetic of these active spirits, of whom the leaders were McGillivray, McTavish, Benjamin and Joseph Frobisher, Rechebleve, Thain, and Frazer, united in the formation of the North-west Fur Company. Bitter rivalry soon arose between the new company and the old monopoly. Following the usual history of special privilege, the old company, which had now been in existence one hundred and thirteen years, had learned to depend more on privilege than on enterprise, and had become somewhat degenerate. The North-westers "rustled" for new business in new regions. In 1789 Alexander Mackenzie, as one of the North-westers, made his way, with incredible hardship, down the river which bears his name to the Frozen Ocean. A few years later he made the first journey to the shore of the Pacific, commemorating his course by painting on a rock on the shore of the Cascade Inlet, north-east of Vancouver Island, these words: "Alexander Mackenzie, from Canada, by land, the twenty-second of July, one thousand seven hundred and ninety-three."

As a result of the new undertakings set on foot by the North-westers and the reawakened Hudson's Bay Company, both companies entered the Columbia Valley. The struggle for possession of Oregon between the English and American fur companies and their government was on. In the summer of 1810 David Thompson of the North-west company crossed the continental divide by the Athabasca Pass in latitude 52° 25'. The North-westers had heard of the Astor enterprise in New York and realised that they must be up and doing if they would control the land of the Oregon. Although the character of soil, climate, and productions of the Columbia Valley was but imperfectly known, enough had been derived from Lewis and Clark, and from ocean discoveries to make it plain that the Columbia furnished the most convenient access to the interior from the sea, and that its numerous tributaries furnished a network of boatable waters unequalled on the Western slope, while there was every reason to suppose that its forests abounded in fur-bearing animals and that its climate would admit of much longer seasons of work than was possible in the biting winters of the Athabasca. It became vital to the continental magnitude of the designs of the Canadian companies that they control Oregon.

For greater topical clearness we will anticipate a little at this point and state that after several years of intense rivalry it became plain to the British Parliament that it was suicidal to allow a policy of division in the face of a common enemy. Hence in 1821, by act of Parliament, the two companies were reorganised and united under a charter which was to last twenty-one years (and as a matter of fact was renewed at the end of that time), and under the provisions of which the North-westers were to have equal shares in both stock and offices, though the name of the Hudson's Bay Company, was retained. It will be remembered therefore, that up to the year 1821, the two great Canadian companies were distinct, and that during that time the North-west Company was much the more active and aggressive in the Columbia Valley, but that after that date the entire force of the Canadian Companies was combined under the name of the old monopoly. But however bitter the first enmity of the Canadian rivals, they agreed on the general proposition that the Americans must be checkmated, and during the score of years prior to their coalition they were seizing the pivotal points of the Oregon country. During the next two decades they created a vast network of forts and stations, and reduced the country contiguous to the River and its tributaries to a system so elaborate and interesting as to be worthy of extended study. We can sketch only its more general features. And the more perfectly to understand them, we must arrest here the story of the great Canadian monopoly and bring up the movement of the American fur companies.

It may be noted, first of all, that by reason of the quicker colonisation and settlement and consequent establishment of agriculture and other arts pertaining to home life, the region of the United States east of the Mississippi never became the natural habitat of the trapper and fur-trader to anything like the degree of Canada and the western part of our own land. Nevertheless extensive fur interests grew up on the Mississippi during the French régime, and in 1763-4 August and Pierre Choteau located a trading post on the present site of St. Louis, and the fascinating history of that great capital began.

Most of the American trading companies confined their operations to the east side of the Rocky Mountains. But the Missouri Fur Company of St. Louis, composed of a miscellaneous group of Americans and Hispano-Gallo-Americans, under the presidency of Manuel Lisa, a bold and enterprising Spaniard, took a step over the crest of the mountains and established the first trading post upon the waters of the Columbia. This was in 1809. Andrew Henry, one of the partners of the aforesaid company, crossed the mountains in that year and a year later built a fort on a branch of Snake River. This seems to have been on what subsequently became known as Henry's River. It was in one of the wildest and grandest regions of all that wild grand section of Snake River. Henry's River drains the north side of the Three Tetons, while the south branch, known afterwards as Lewis and finally as Snake River, drains the south of that group of mountains. *Henry must be remembered as the first American and the first white man recorded in history who built any structure upon any tributary of our River, and the year was 1810.* Both Henry and his Company had hopes of accomplishing great things in the way of the fur-trade in that very favourable region. But the next year the Indians were so threatening that the fort was forsaken and the party returned to the Missouri. When the Hunt party in the fall of 1811 sought refuge at this point they found only a group of abandoned huts, with no provisions or equipment of which they could make any use.

But though Henry's fort was but a transient matter, his American countrymen were beginning to press through the open gateways of both mountain and sea. In the early part of 1809 the Winship brothers of Boston, together with several other keen-sighted Yankees, formed a project for a definite post on the Columbia River, proposing to reach their destination by ship. Accordingly they fitted out an old vessel known as the *Albatross*, with Nathan Winship as captain, William Gale as captain's assistant, and William Smith as first mate. Captain Gale kept a journal of the entire enterprise, and it is one of the most interesting and valuable of the many ship's records of the North-western Coast.

Setting sail with a crew of twenty-two men and an excellent supply of stores and ammunition, and abundance of tools and hardware for erecting needful buildings, the *Albatross* left Boston in the summer of 1809. After a slow and tedious, but very healthful and comfortable voyage, stopping at the Hawaiian Islands on the route, the *Albatross* reached the mouth of the Columbia River on May 26, 1810. Many American and other ships had entered the mouth of the River prior to that date, but so far as known none had ascended any considerable distance. Apparently Gray and Broughton were the only shipmasters who had ascended above the wide expanse now known as Gray's Bay, while the Lewis and Clark expedition contained the only white men who had seen the river above tide-water. The Winship enterprise may be regarded with great interest, therefore, as the first real attempt to plant a permanent establishment on the banks of the River.

Winship and his companions spent some days in careful examination of the river banks and as a result of their search they decided on a strip of valley land formed by a narrowing of the River on the north and an indentation of the mountain on the south. This pleasant strip of fertile land is located on the south bank of the lordly stream, and its lower end is about forty-five miles from the ocean. Being partially covered with a beautiful grove of oak trees, the first to be seen on the ascent of the River, the place received the name of Oak Point. It may be noted that this name was subsequently transferred to a promontory nearly opposite on the north bank, and this circumstance has led many to locate erroneously the site of the first buildings designed for permanent use on the banks of the Columbia. And such these were, for the Lewis and Clark structures at what they called Fort Clatsop, erected four and a half years earlier, were meant only for a winter's use. But the Winship party had glowing visions of a great emporium of the fur-trade, another Montreal or St. Louis, to inaugurate a new era for their country and themselves. They designed paying the Indians for their lands and in every way treating them justly. They seem in short to have had a very high conception of the dignity and worth of their enterprise. They were worthy of the highest success, and the student of to-day cannot but grieve that their high hopes were dashed with disaster.

Tying the *Albatross* to the bank on June 4th, they entered at once with great energy on the task of felling trees, rearing a large log house, clearing a garden spot, in which they at once began the planting of seeds, and getting ready to trade with the natives. But within four days the River began to rise rapidly, and the busy fort-builders perceived to their dismay that they had located on land subject to inundation. All the work thus far done went for naught, and they pulled their fort to pieces and floated the logs down stream a quarter of a mile to a higher place. There they resumed their buildings with redoubled energy. But within a week a much more dangerous situation again, and this time permanently, arrested their grand project. This time it was the very men toward whom they had entertained such just and benevolent designs, the Indians, who thwarted the plans. For, as Captain Gale narrates in a most entertaining manner, a large body of Chinooks and Che-heeles, armed with bows and arrows, and some muskets, made their appearance, announcing that they were on their way to war against the Culaworth tribe who had killed one of their chiefs a year before. But the next day the Indians massing themselves about the whites, gave such plain indications that the previous declaration was a pretence that the party hastily got into a position of defence. Their cannon on board the *Albatross* had already been loaded in anticipation of emergencies, and so plain was it that they could make a deadly defence that the threatened attack did not come. A long "pow-wow" ensued instead, and the Chinooks insisted that the builders must select a site lower down the river. After due consideration the party decided that any determined opposition by the Indians would so impair their enterprise, even though they might be able to defend themselves, that it would be best to seek a new location. Accordingly they reloaded their effects, dropped down the River, and finally decided to make a voyage down the California coast and return the next year. Return they did, but by that time the next year the Pacific Fur Company had already located at Astoria the first permanent American settlement, and the Winship enterprise faded away. That the design of the Winships was not at all chimerical is apparent from the fact that within twenty years the Hudson's Bay Company had made of Vancouver, sixty miles farther up the River, the very kind of a trading entrepôt of which the Winships had dreamed. Their dream was reasonable, but the time and place were unpropitious.

A quotation from Captain Gale's journal will give a conception of his feelings:

> June 12th.—The ship dropped further down the River, and it was now determined to abandon all attempts to force a settlement. We have taken off the goats and hogs which were left on shore for the use of the settlement, and thus we have to abandon the business, after having, with great difficulty and labour, got about forty-five miles above Cape Disappointment; and with great trouble began to clear the land and build a house a second time, after cutting timber enough to finish nearly one-half, and having two of our hands disabled in the work. It is, indeed, cutting to be obliged to knuckle to those whom you have not the least fear of, but whom, from motives of prudence, you are obliged to treat with forbearance. What can be more disagreeable than to sit at the table with a number of these rascally chiefs, who while they supply their greedy mouths with your food with one hand, their bloods boil within them to cut your throat with the other, without the least provocation.

On the way out of the River Captain Winship learned that the Chinooks designed capturing his vessel, and would doubtless have done so, had not his vigilance prevented.

While the crew of the *Albatross* were engaged in these adventures the largest American Fur Company yet formed was getting ready to effect a lodgment on the shores of the Columbia. This was the Pacific Fur Company. John Jacob Astor was the founder of this enterprise. Though unfortunate in almost every feature of its history and its final outcome, this company had a magnificent conception, a royal grandeur of opportunity, and it possessed also the felicity, shared by no one of its predecessors, of the genius of a great literary star to illuminate its records. To Washington Irving it owes much of its fame. Yet the commercial genius of Astor could not prevent errors of judgment by the management any more than the literary genius of Irving was able to conceal their errors, or the genius of American liberty able to order events so as to prevent victory for a time by the "Britishers." As we view the history in the large it may be that we shall conclude that the British triumph at first was the best introduction to American triumph in the end.

John Jacob Astor may, perhaps, be justly regarded as the first of the great promoters or financial magnates who have made the United States the world's El Dorado. Coming from Germany to this land of opportunity after the close of the Revolutionary War, he soon manifested that keen intuition in money matters, as well as intense devotion to accumulation, which has led to the colossal fortunes of his own descendants and of the other multimillionaires of this age. Having made quite a fortune by transporting furs to London, Mr. Astor turned to larger fields. With his broad and keen geographical and commercial insight, he could readily grasp the same fact which the North-westers of Montreal were also considering, that the Columbia River might well become the key to an international fur-trade, as well as a strategic point for American expansion westward. He made overtures to the North-westers for a partnership, but they declined. Then he determined to be the chief manager, and to associate individual Americans and Canadians with himself. With the promptitude of the skilful general, he proceeded to form his company and make his plan of campaign in time to anticipate the apparent designs of the active Canadians. They saw, as well as Astor did, the magnitude of the stake and at once made ready to play their part. For, as already noted, David Thompson crossed the Rockies by the Athabasca Pass in 1810, spent the winter at Lake Windermere on the Columbia River, and in the summer of 1811 reached Astoria, only to find the Astor Company already established there. It should be especially noted that the Thompson party was the first to descend the River from near its source to the ocean, although of course Lewis and Clark had anticipated them on the portion below the junction of the Snake with the main River.

Mr. Astor's plans provided for an expedition by sea and one by land. The first was to convey stores and equipment for founding and defending the proposed capital of the empire of the fur-traders. Of the expedition by land under Hunt we have already given a full account in the preceding chapter, since its events rather allied it to the era of exploration than that of the traders. The organisation of Mr. Astor's company provided that there should be a capital stock of a hundred shares, of which he should hold half and his associates half. Mr. Astor was to furnish the money, though not to exceed four hundred thousand dollars, and was to bear all losses for five years. The term of the association was fixed at twenty years, though with the privilege of dissolving it in five years if it proved unprofitable. The general plan and the details of the expedition had been decided upon by the master mind of the founder with statesmanlike ability. It comes, therefore, as a surprise to the reader that Mr. Astor should have made a capital mistake at the very beginning of his undertaking. This mistake was in the selection of his associates and the captains of some of his ships. Of the partners, five were Americans and five were Canadians. Two only of the Americans remained with the company long enough to have any determining influence on its policies. Take the fact that the majority of the active partners and almost all the clerks, trappers, and other employees of the company were Canadians, and put it beside the other fact that war was imminent with Great Britain and did actually break out within two years, and the dangerous nature of the situation can be seen. Of the ship-captains, the first one, Captain Jonathan Thorn of the *Tonquin*, was a man of such overbearing and obstinate nature that disaster seemed to be fairly invited by placing him in such vitally responsible a position. The captain of the second ship, the *Beaver*, was Cornelius Sowles, and he seems to have been as timid and irresolute as Captain Thorn was bold and implacable. Both lacked judgment. It was probably natural that Mr. Astor, having had his main prior experience as a fur-dealer in connection with the Canadians centring at Montreal, should have looked in that direction for associates. But inasmuch as war between England and the United States seemed a practical certainty, it was a great error, in founding a vast enterprise in remote regions whose ownership was not yet definitely recognised, to share with citizens of Great Britain the determination of the important issues of the enterprise. It would have saved Mr. Astor great loss and chagrin if he had observed the maxim: "Put none but Americans on guard." As to the captains of the two vessels, that was an error that any one might have made. Yet for a man of Astor's exceptional ability and shrewdness to err so conspicuously in judging the character of the men appointed to such important places seems indeed strange.

To these facts in regard to the personnel of the partners, the captains, and the force, must be added two others; *i. e.*, war and shipwreck. The combination of all these conditions made the history of the Astoria enterprise what it was. Yet, with all of its adversity, this was one of the best conceived, and, in most of its details, the best equipped and executed of all the great enterprises which have appeared in the commercial history of our country. As an element in the development of the land of the Oregon, it must be accorded the first place after the period of discovery.

The *Tonquin* left New York on September 6, 1810. She carried a fine equipment of all things needed for founding the proposed emporium. She was manned by a crew of twenty-one and conveyed members of the fur-trading force to the number of thirty-three. Stopping at the Sandwich Islands, an added force of twenty-four natives was taken aboard. At various times on the journey the rigid ideas of naval discipline and the imperious temper of Captain Thorn came near producing mutiny among the partners and clerks. When the *Tonquin* hove to off the mouth of the Columbia on March 22, 1811, the eager voyagers saw little to attract. The wind was blowing in heavy squalls, and the sea ran high. Nevertheless the hard-hearted Captain issued orders to the first mate, Fox, with a boat's crew of four men, to go into the foaming waves and sound the channel. The boat was insufficiently provided, and it seemed scarcely short of murder to despatch a crew under such circumstances. But the tyrannical captain would listen to no remonstrances, and the poor little boat went tossing over the billows on her forlorn hope. Such indeed it proved to be, for neither boat nor any one of the crew was ever heard of again. This was a wholly unnecessary sacrifice of life, for the *Tonquin* was in no danger, and time could just as well have been taken for more propitious weather.

Astoria in 1845.

From an Old Print.

The next day, the wind and sea having abated, the *Tonquin* drew near the dreaded bar, but, no entrance that satisfied the captain appearing, the ship again stood off to spend the night in deep water. On the next day, the 24th, the wind fell and a serene sky seemed to invite another attempt. The pinnace in command of Mr. Aikin, with two white men and two Kanakas, was sent out to find the channel. Following the pinnace the ship moved in so rapidly under a freshening breeze that she passed the pinnace, the unfortunate men on board finding it impossible to effect an entrance and being borne by the refluent current into the mad surge where ocean tide and outflowing river met in foamy strife. So the pinnace disappeared. But meanwhile the crew had all their energies engaged to save the *Tonquin*. For the wind failed at the critical moment and the ship struck the sands with violence. Night came on. Had the men been classically trained (as in fact Franchère was) they might have remembered Virgil, *Ponto nox incubat atra.* But they had no time for classical or other quotations. Hastily dropping the anchors they lay to in the midst of the tumult of waters, in that worst of situations, on an unknown coast in the dark and in storm. But as Franchère expresses it, Providence came to their succour, and the tide flooding and the wind rising, they weighed the anchors, and in spite of the obscurity of the night, they gained a safe harbour in a little cove inside of Cape Disappointment, apparently just about abreast of the present town of Ilwaco.

Astoria. Looking up and across the Columbia River.

Photo. by Woodfield.

Thus the *Tonquin* was saved, and with the light of morning it could be seen that she was fairly within the bar. Natives soon made their appearance, desirous of trading beaver-skins. But the crew were in no mood for commerce while any hope existed for finding the lost sailors. Taking a course toward the shore by what must have been nearly the present route from Ilwaco to Long Beach, the captain and a party with him, began a search and soon found Weeks, one of the crew of the pinnace. He was stark naked and suffering intensely from the cold. As soon as sufficiently revived he narrated the loss of the pinnace in the breakers, the death of three of the crew, and the casting of himself and one of the Kanakas upon the beach. The point where they were cast would seem to have been near the present location of the life-saving station.

The two survivors of the ill-fated pinnace having been revived, the party returned to the *Tonquin*, which was now riding safely at anchor in the bay on the north side of the river, named Baker's Bay by Broughton nineteen years before. Joy for their own escape from such imminent perils was mingled with melancholy at the loss of their eight companions of the two boats, and with the melancholy there was a sense of bitterness toward the captain, who was to blame, at least for the loss of the small boat.

But now the new land was all before them where to choose, and since Captain Thorn was in great haste to depart and begin his trading cruise along the coast, the partners on the *Tonquin*, Messrs. McKay, McDougal, David Stuart, and Robert Stuart, decided somewhat hurriedly to locate at the point which had received from Lieutenant Broughton the name of Point George. Franchère gives a pleasant picture of the beauty of the trees and sky, and the surprise of the party to find that, though it was only the 12th of April when they set to work upon the great trees which covered the site of their chosen capital, yet spring was already far advanced. They did not then understand the effect of the Japan current upon the Pacific Coast climate.

An incident of special interest soon after landing was the appearance on June 15th of two strange Indians, a man and a woman, bearing a letter addressed to *Mr. John Stuart, Fort Estekatadene, New Caledonia*. These two Indians wore long robes of dressed deerskins with leggings and moccasins more like the Indians of the Rocky Mountains. They could not understand the speech of the Astoria Indians nor of any of the mixture of dialects which the white men tried on them, until one of the Canadian clerks addressed them in the Knisteneaux language with which they seemed to be partially familiar. After several days of stay at the fort the two wandering Indians succeeded in making it clear to the traders that they had been sent out by a clerk named Finnan McDonald of the North-west Fur Company from a fort which that company had just established on the Spokane River. They said that they had lost their way and in consequence had descended the *Tacousah-Tessah* (and this Franchère understood to be the Indian name for the Columbia, though the general impression among the Indians is that Tacousah-Tessah, or Tacoutche-Tesse, signified Frazer River). From the revelation gradually drawn from these two Indians (and the surprising discovery was made that they were both women) the very important conclusion was drawn that the North-west Fur Company was already prepared to contest with the Astor Company the possession of the River. The peculiar feature of the situation was that the most of the Astorians, though American by the existing business tie, were Canadian and British by blood and sympathy, and hence were very likely to fraternise with the Montreal traders.

However the Astorians decided to send an expedition into the interior to verify the story given by the two Indian women, but, just as they were ready to go, a large canoe with the British flag floating from her stern appeared, from which, when it had reached the landing, there leaped ashore an active, well-dressed man who introduced himself as David Thompson, of the North-west Company. This was the same man, the reader will remember, who had crossed the Rocky Mountains the year before, had wintered near the head of the River, and had then descended it, seeking a location for the Columbia River emporium of the Canadian company. But he was too late. It was quite strange by what narrow margins on several occasions the British failed to forestall the Yankees.

One of the Lagoons of the Upper Columbia River, near Golden, B. C.

Photo. by C. F. Yates, Golden.

Saddle Mountain, or Swallalochost, near Astoria, Famous in Indian Myth.

Photo. by Woodfield.

On July 23d the delayed expedition of the Astorians set forth far to the interior, and as a result of their investigations, David Stuart, in charge of the party, began the erection of a trading house at the mouth of the Okanogan, five hundred and forty miles above Astoria. It was on September 2, 1811, that this post was begun, and hence Fort Okanogan may be regarded as the first American establishment in the present State of Washington. It was antedated a few months by the post of the North-west Company at the entrance of the Little Spokane into the Spokane, near the present site of the City of Spokane.

During the fall of 1811 the Indians around Astoria became very threatening. Direful rumours, too, in regard to the destruction of the *Tonquin* began to disquiet the Astorians. In the emergency the wary McDougall, then acting as the head of the Company, bethought himself of a very effective expedient. He had learned that dreadful loss of life among the Indians had resulted a few years before from smallpox and that the Indians were mortally afraid of it. Calling into his room several of the principal chiefs, he asked if they remembered the smallpox. Their serious faces were sufficient proof that they did. McDougall then held up a small vial and continued with awful solemnity: "Listen to me. I am the great smallpox chief. In this little bottle I keep the smallpox. If I uncork the bottle and let it out I will kill every man, woman, and child of the Indians. Now go in peace, but if you make war upon us I will open the bottle, and you will die." The chiefs filed out in terror, and peace was preserved.

McDougall still further cemented the bond of union with the natives by becoming united in wedlock with the daughter of Comcomly, the one-eyed chieftain of the Chinooks. After numerous and thorough ablutions had somewhat mitigated the oiliness and general fishiness of the Chinook princess, she was clad in the most brilliant style of the native beauty, a grand holiday was declared at Astoria, and white men and Indians joined in the wedding feast and made the welkin ring with their demonstrations. Thus did the daughter of Comcomly become the first lady of the land, and thus did peace brood over the broad waters of the lower River.

During the winter of 1811-12 the two instalments of the Hunt party made their appearance, after their distressful journey from St. Louis as already narrated in Chapter IV. In May, 1812, the company's ship *Beaver* arrived from New York, loaded with stores and trading equipment, and bringing a considerable addition to the force of men. In the following month sixty men were despatched up-river, and by them a trading post was located at Spokane and another on the Snake River somewhere near the present site of Lewiston, while one section of the party went across the mountains and down the Missouri to convey dispatches to Mr. Astor.

At this stage of the history of the Astoria enterprise, every aspect was encouraging. The trade in furs on the Spokane, the Okanogan, the Snake, the Cœur d'Alene was excellent, a successful cruise along the coast by the *Beaver* seemed sure, and the Indians about the mouth of the River were friendly and well disposed. Mr. Astor's great undertaking seemed sure to be crowned with success. In the midst of all the signs of hope came tidings of dismay. It became known with certainty that the *Tonquin* had been destroyed. This appalling disaster was related directly to the Astoria Company by the only survivor. This was an Indian of the Chehalis tribe whose name is given by Irving as Lamazee, by Ross as Lamazu, and by Bancroft as Lamanse. He had escaped from the Indians who had held him after the destruction of the *Tonquin* and had finally found his way to Astoria, there to tell his tale, one of the most sanguinary in the long roll of struggles with the Indians. The next great disaster was the wrecking of the *Lark*, the third of the Company's ships from New York. During the same period Mr. Hunt, the partner next in rank to Mr. Astor and the one above all who could have acted wisely and patriotically in the forthcoming crisis, had gone in the *Beaver* on a trading cruise among the Russians of Sitka, and by a most remarkable series of detentions he had been kept away from Astoria for over a year.

To cap the climax of misfortunes, the War of 1812 burst upon the knowledge of the fur-traders and seemed to force upon such of the partners as were of British nationality the question of their paramount duty. As a result of the crisis, McDougal and McKenzie, although against the wishes of the other partners present, sold out to the agent of the North-westers, who had repaired at once to Astoria upon knowledge of the declaration of war. Thus the great Astoria enterprise was abandoned, and the Stars and Stripes went down and the Union Jack went up. Soon after the transfer, the British man-of-war *Raccoon*, Captain Black, arrived at Astoria, expecting to have seized the place as a rich prize of war. Imagine the disgust of the expectant British mariners to discover that the post had already been sold to British subjects, that their long journey was useless, and that their hopes of prize money had vanished.

With the close of the War of 1812 a series of negotiations between the ministers of the two countries took place in regard to the possession of the River, by which it was finally decided that Astoria should be restored to the United States. Accordingly, on the 6th of October, 1818, the British Commissioners, Captain F. Hickey, of His Majesty's Ship *Blossom*, and J. Keith, representing the North-west Fur Company, signed an act of delivery restoring Fort George (Astoria) to the United States. Mr. J. B. Prevost, Commissioner for the United States, signed the act of acceptance. Astoria was once again American property.

While the River was now nominally in possession of the United States, it was practically under the control of the British fur companies. The Pacific Fur Company ceased to operate, and the North-westers entered upon active work both by sea and land in exploring the vast and profitable domain which the misfortunes of their American rivals, supplemented in a most timely manner by the treachery of McDougall and McKenzie, had put within their power. The canny Scotchmen, McDougall, McTavish, McKenzie, McDonald, and the various other Macs who now guided the plans of the North-westers, signalled their entrance into power by despatching companies to the various pivotal points of the great Columbia Basin, the Walla Walla, Yakima, Okanogan, Spokane, and Snake rivers. Two incidents may be related to illustrate the character of people and the conditions of that wilderness period.

Steamer "Beaver", the First Steamer on the Pacific, 1836.

Portland, Oregon, in 1851.

From an Old Print.

A party of ninety men in ten canoes left Astoria for up-river points on April 4, 1814. While passing the mouth of the Yakima, about three hundred and fifty miles up the River, the men were surprised to see three canoes putting out from shore and to hear a child's voice calling out, "*Arretez donc! arretez donc!*" Stopping to investigate, the party found in one of the boats the Indian wife of Pierre Dorion, with her children. Dorion, with five other Canadians, had gone the previous summer with a party under command of John Reed of the Astor Company. While trapping and hunting, deep in the mountains of Snake River, the party had been massacred by Indians. The woman and her two boys had alone escaped the massacre. It was the dead of winter and the snows lay deep on the Blue Mountains. But the wife of Dorion found shelter in a remote fastness of the mountains, putting up a bark hut for a shelter and subsisting on the carcasses of some of her horses. In the spring, the pitiful little company of mother and children descended to Walla Walla and found there more kindly disposed natives, who cared for them and turned them over to the protection of the whites. A more thrilling story of suffering and heroism than this of Madame Dorion and her children has never come up from the chronicles of the wild West.

Equally illustrative of the life of the fur-traders is the account given by Alexander Ross of one of his many adventures in the Columbia country. In 1814 Ross went from Okanogan to Yakima to secure horses. With him were four other whites and three Indian women. The Yakima Valley was then as now a paradise of the Indians. There the tribes gathered by the thousands in the spring to dig camas, to race horses, and to gamble, as well as to form alliances and make plans for war. When the little company of traders reached the encampment, they discovered to their astonishment that it was a veritable city. Six thousand men, women, and children, with ten thousand horses, and uncounted dogs and many shackled bears and wolves, were strewn across the plain. It was a dangerous situation for the traders, for it became plain to them that the Indians were unfriendly. But assuming an air of careless bravado, Ross proceeded to display his store of trinkets for the purpose of starting a traffic in horses. Assuming a very hilarious manner the Indians would seize and drive away the animals as fast as the white men got them. Then the Indians began to deprive them of clothes and food. Finally they made ready to seize their three women as slaves. Ross managed to have the women escape temporarily, but then the savages were worse than ever. Matters reached a crisis when an obstreperous chief named Yaktana snatched a knife from the hands of one of the Canadians. A desperate struggle was just at the point of breaking out, which would inevitably have resulted in the death of all the white men, when a sudden intuition flashed through the quick mind of Ross, and rushing between the combatants he handed his own knife, a much more elegant one, to Yaktana, saying in a friendly tone, "This is a chief's knife. Take it and give back the other." There was an instant revulsion. Yaktana was so much flattered that he turned at once into a stanch supporter of the shrewd trader. Food was brought. The horses were restored. Equipment was provided. The three women were regained, and the company made their way without further trouble to Okanogan.

We have already mentioned the important fact that in 1821 the two great Canadian Companies, the North-western and the Hudson's Bay, decided to unite. With the union, the great era of fur-trade in the Columbia Basin fairly began, to continue about twenty-five years, yielding then to the American immigrant. That twenty-five years of the dominance of the great Fur Company contained nearly all the poetry and romance as well as the profit and statesmanship of the business. The entire region of the River, as well as that of the Puget Sound country, was mapped out in a most systematic manner with one chief central fort, Vancouver on the Columbia. A more magnificent location for the purpose cannot be conceived. It is now the site of a flourishing city and of the United States Fort Headquarters for the North-west, generally conceded to be the finest fort location in the United States. Fort Vancouver was established in 1825 upon a superb bench of land gently sloping back from the River for two miles. Great trees fringed the site, Mt. Hood lifted its pinnacled majesty sixty miles to the eastward, the sinuous mazes of the Willamette Valley stretched out far southward, while the lordly River was in full view a dozen miles up and down. Every natural advantage and delight which wild nature could offer was here in fullness. Ships could readily ascend the hundred miles from the ocean to unload their merchandise and take on their cargoes of precious furs, the furs collected at the outlay of so much toil and suffering over the area of hundreds of miles. Every species of game and fish abounded in the waters and along the banks of the River. Deer and elk tossed their antlers between the stately firs of the upland, and pheasant and grouse whirred among the branches. Geese, cranes, ducks, and swans, in countless numbers, darkened the lagoons amid the many islands enclosed by the mouths of the Willamette and the adjacent waters of the larger stream. Fish of many varieties, the royal Chinook salmon, king of food fish, being at the head in beauty and edibility, though surpassed in size by the gigantic sturgeon, which sometimes weighed a thousand pounds, abounded in the River. No epicure of the world's capitals could command such viands as nature brought to the doors of the denizens of Fort Vancouver.

The fort itself was laid out on a scale of amplitude suitable to the spaciousness of the site. It was enclosed with a picket wall twenty feet high, with massive buttresses of timber inside. This enclosure was a parallelogram seven hundred and fifty by five hundred feet. Inside were about forty buildings, the governor's residence of generous dimensions being in the centre. Two chapels provided for the spiritual needs of the company, while schoolhouse, stores, "bachelors' halls," and shops of various kinds attested the variety of the needs. Along the bank of the River, outside the enclosure, lay quite a village of cottages for the married employees, together with hospital, boathouses, granaries, warehouses, threshing mills, and dairy buildings.

Taken altogether Fort Vancouver was the model fort of the western slope. Moreover, the fertile soil and genial, humid climate soon encouraged the factors of the Company to experiment with gardens and orchards, and, within a few years after founding, fifteen hundred acres of land were in the finest state of productivity, while three thousand head of cattle, twenty-five hundred sheep, three hundred brood mares, and over a hundred milch cows, added their bounteous contributions to the already plentiful resources of the fort.

With this rich larder, with the spacious buildings, with the annual arrivals and departures of ships by sea and fleets of bateaux by river, with hunting trips and Indian policies, with the intercoast traffic with the Russians on the north and the Spaniards on the south,—there was as much to engage and delight the minds of these people as if they had lived in the heart of civilisation.

Any account of Fort Vancouver would be incomplete without some reference to Dr. John McLoughlin, chief factor of the Company in the Columbia district from 1824 to the time of his retirement from the Company in 1846 and settlement at Oregon City, Oregon, as an American citizen. Rarely has any one in the stormy history of the Columbia Basin received such unvarying and unqualified praise as has this truly great man. Physically, mentally, and morally, Dr. McLoughlin was altogether exceptional among the mixed population that gathered about the emporium of the traders. Six feet four inches in height, his noble and expressive face crowned with a great cascade of snowy hair, firm yet kindly, prompt and businesslike yet sympathetic and helpful, "Old Whitehead" or "White Eagle," as the Indians called him, was a true-born king of men.

We have said that Fort Vancouver was the great central fort. The others commanding the pivotal points upon the River and its tributaries were Fort Hall and Fort Boisé on the Snake, Spokane House on the Spokane near the present metropolis of the Inland Empire, Fort Colville on the river of the same name near its junction with the Columbia, Fort Okanogan at the junction of the stream of that name with the great River, Fort Owen in the Cœur d'Alene region, Fort Simcoe in the Yakima country, Fort Walla Walla, first known as Fort Nez Percé, on the Columbia at the mouth of the Walla Walla, and Fort George on the former site of Astoria. These forts were all laid out in the same general fashion as Fort Vancouver, though no one was so large, elaborate, or comfortable. Besides the forts there were a number of small trading posts. The chief furs procured in the interior were beaver, and those on the coast were sea-otter. Many others, as the mink, sharp-toothed otter, fox, lynx, raccoon, were found in abundance.

The profits of the business were immense. Alexander Ross relates that he secured one morning before breakfast one hundred and ten beaver skins for a single yard of white cloth. Ross spent one hundred and eighty-eight days alone in the Yakima country. During that time he collected one thousand five hundred and fifty beavers, besides other peltries, worth in the Canton market two thousand two hundred and fifty pounds, which cost him in his objects of trade only thirty-five pounds. That was while Ross was connected with the Astor Company.

In completing this necessarily hurried chapter on the fascinating era of the fur-traders, we cannot omit a brief reference to the movements of the regular brigades of boats up and down the River, for these comprised a great part of both the business and the romance of the age. The course of these brigades was from the southern shores of Hudson Bay, through Manitoba, to the crest of the Rockies at the head of the Columbia. Water was utilised to the greatest possible extent, while at the portages and across the mountains horse-power and man-power were employed. Once afloat upon the Columbia, the brigades braved most of the rapids, paying occasional toll of men and goods to the envious deities of the waters, yet with marvellous skill and general fortune making their way down the thousand or more miles from Boat Encampment to Fort Vancouver. The descent was easy compared with the ascent. The first journey of the east-bound brigade of the North-westers from Astoria to Montreal was in 1814, and it required the time from April 4th to May 11th to reach the mouth of Canoe River, the point at which they entered upon the mountain climb to the head of the Athabasca.

The boatmen were French-Canadians, a hardy, mercurial, light-hearted race, half French, with the natural grace and politeness of their race, and having the pleasant patois which has made them the theme of much popular present-day literature. They were half Indian, either in tastes and manners or in blood, with the atmosphere of forests and streams clinging to every word and gesture. They were perhaps the best boatmen in the world. Upon those matchless lakes into which the Columbia and its tributaries expand at intervals the fur-laden boats would glide at ease, while the wild songs of the *coureurs des bois* would echo from shore to shore in lazy sibilations, apparently betokening no thought of serious or earnest business. But once the rapids were reached, the gay and rollicking knight of the paddle became all attention. With keen eyes fixed on every swirl or rock, he guided the light craft with a ready skill which would be inconceivable to one less daring and experienced. The brigades would run almost all the rapids from Death Rapids to the sea, making portages at Kettle Falls, Tumwater or Celilo Falls, and the Cascades, though at some stages of the water they could run down even them. They always had to carry around those points in ascending the River. In spite of all the skill of the *voyageurs* the Columbia and the Snake, the Pend Oreille and the Kootenai have exacted a heavy toll of life from those who have laid their compelling hands upon the white manes of chute and cataract. Many, even of the *voyageurs*, are the human skeletons that have whitened the volcanic beds of the great streams.

The boats used by the fur brigades were either log canoes obtained of the Indians or bateaux. The former were hollowed from the magnificent cedars which grew on the banks of the River, sometimes fifty or sixty feet long, with prow carved in fantastic, even beautiful fashion. They would hold from six to twenty persons with from half a ton to two or three tons of load, yet were so light that two men could carry one of the medium size while four could handle one of any size around a portage. But the *voyageurs* never took quite so much to the canoes as did the Indians, whose skill in handling them in high waves is described by Ross and Franchère as something astonishing. And even the Indians of the present show much the same ability, though the splendid cedar canoes are no longer made, and only here and there can one of the picturesque survivors be seen.

The bateaux were boats of peculiar shape, being built very high and broad so that in an unloaded condition they seemed to rest on the water almost like a paper shell. Both ends were high and pointed as prows. They were propelled with oars and steered with paddles. One of the usual size was about thirty feet long and five feet wide. Being of light-draft, double-enders, capable of holding large loads and yet easily conveyed around portages, more steady and roomy than canoes, these bateaux were the typical Columbia River medium of commerce during the era of the fur-traders. They, too, have mainly vanished from the scenes of their former glory. Canoes, bateaux, cries and yells of Indians, songs of *voyageurs*, have gone into the engulfing limbo of the bygone, along with the keen-eyed Scotch factor and the sharp-featured Yankee skipper. Yet the swans and geese and ducks still darken the more placid expanses of the River and the salmon still start the widening circles in almost undiminished numbers, while the glaciated heights of Hood and Adams and St. Helens (we would rather say Wiyeast, Klickitat, and Loowit) still stand guard over the unchanging waters.

This part of our topic has mainly centred upon the British possession of the River. A full history of the fur era on the River would demand a chapter on the later attempts of three remarkable men to reestablish American interests in the disputed territory. These men were Jedediah Smith, Capt. E. L. Bonneville, and Nathaniel J. Wyeth. But though these men belong properly to this era, their efforts in the fur-trade were relatively unimportant in comparison with the influence of their lives in the direction of permanent American occupation. It seemed the appointment of destiny that the American should play second fiddle to his British rival in the fur-trade. But as tenfold, a thousandfold compensation, the American farmers, home-builders, and tradesmen were to acquire final possession of one of the goodliest lands on which the Stars and Stripes has ever floated. The bateaux and canoes must needs give way to the steamboat and the launch, the *coureur des bois* to the lumberman and the miner and farmer, and the picturesque emporium of the British fur-trader on the River to the modern American city. We shall, therefore, more fittingly chronicle the later American fur-traders as a part of the march of their countrymen to permanent ownership of Oregon.

CHAPTER VI

THE COMING OF THE MISSIONARIES
TO THE TRIBES OF THE RIVER

Journey of the Nez Percé Chiefs to Find the White Man's Book of
  Life—Interest Excited among Christian People by this Event—
  Methodist Church Leads in Preparing for a Missionary Party—
  Jason Lee and his Mission near Chemeketa—The Reinforcement
  by the *Lausanne*—Importance of Jason Lee as a Force in Oregon
  History—The Missions of the American Board at Walla Walla,
  Lapwai, and Tshimakain—Preliminary Journey of Whitman and
  Parker in 1835—The Wedding Journey from Missouri to the Co-
  lumbia in 1836—Dr. Whitman and his Associates and their Traits
  of Character—On the Summit of South Pass—Whitman's Wag-
  gon—Arrival at Vancouver and Conference with McLoughlin—
  Locations of the Missionaries—Reinforcement in 1838—Friendship of the Nez Percés—First Printing Press—Whitman's Ride in
  1842-43—The Catholic Missions—Fathers Blanchet, Demers, and
  De Smet—Influence of the Missions.

IN 1832 a strange thing happened. Four Indians appeared in St. Louis seeking
the "White Man's Book of Life." At that time General William Clark was superintendent of Indian affairs, located at St. Louis. He was familiar with the Western
Indians and had greatly sympathised with them.

Learning of these strange Indians and their stranger quest, General Clark
sought them, and entered into communication with them. It is usually stated that
these Indians were Flatheads from the Pend Oreille region, but Miss Kate Macbeth,
a missionary for many years to the Nez Percés, became convinced that three were
Nez Percés and the fourth a Flathead. How they had learned that the white man
had a "Book of Life" is not known. Captain Bonneville's journal states that Pierre
Pambrun had given many of the Oregon Indians instruction in the rudiments of
the Catholic worship. Some have conjectured that Jedediah Smith, a noted American trapper, and, most remarkable of all, a devout Christian, may have imparted
religious thoughts to them. Miss Macbeth believed that the motive of the mission
was to find Lewis and Clark, the explorers, whose visit in 1804-05 had produced a
profound impression on the Nez Percés. The first published account of these four
Indians appeared in the *New York Christian Advocate* for March 1, 1833. This was
in the form of a letter from G. P. Disoway, in which he enclosed a letter to himself

from his agent, William Walker, an interpreter for the Wyandotte Indians. Walker was at St. Louis at the time, and met these four Indians in General Clark's office. He was much impressed with their appearance, and learned that General Clark had given them as full an account as possible of the nature and history of man, of the advent of the Saviour, and of His work for men. Walker states that two of the four men died in St. Louis, and as to whether the others reached their native land he did not know.

In the *Illinois Patriot* of October, 1833, the same topic was taken up, together with the statement that Walker's report had excited so much interest that a committee of the Illinois Synod had been appointed to investigate and report on what seemed the duty of the churches in the premises. The committee accordingly went to St. Louis and confirmed the account by conference with General Clark. They also made it an object to learn all available facts in regard to the general conditions among the Indians west of the Rocky Mountains.

One of the most valuable records in respect to these Indians is from George Catlin, the noted painter and student of Indian life. Catlin was on the steamer going up the Missouri toward Fort Benton with these two remaining Indians on their homeward journey. His account of them in the *Smithsonian Report* for 1885 is thus:

> These two men, when I painted them, were in beautiful Sioux dresses which had been presented to them in a talk with the Sioux, who treated them very kindly, while passing through the Sioux country. These two men were part of a delegation that came across the mountains to St. Louis, a few years since, to inquire for the truth of representation which they said some white man had made among them, that our religion was better than theirs, and that they would all be lost if they did not embrace it. Two old and venerable men of this party died in St. Louis, and I travelled two thousand miles, companion with these two fellows, toward their own country, and became much pleased with their manners and dispositions. When I first heard the objects of their extraordinary mission across the mountains, I could scarcely believe it; but, on conversing with General Clark on a future occasion, I was fully convinced of the fact.

It appears from still another account of the matter that the two surviving Indians were disappointed in that they did not actually get possession of the "Book." A speech of one of the chiefs as he left General Clark has been published in a number of books, and is well worthy of preservation. It should be stated, however, that this speech has no authentic source, nor does it appear anywhere how it was obtained. It is commonly stated that it was "taken down" at the time by one of the clerks in General Clark's office. The historian Mowry is authority for the statement that one of the Indians gave the substance of the speech to the missionary, Spalding, at a later time. It has, also, a somewhat conventionalised sound. Yet with whatever discredit may be cast upon it, it possesses so many elements of interest that it may well be given here. This is the reported speech.

I come to you over the trail of many moons from the setting sun. You were the friend of my fathers, who have all gone the long way. I came with an eye partly open for my people, who sit in darkness. I go back with both eyes closed. How can I go back blind, to my blind people? I made my way to you with strong arms through many enemies and strange lands that I might carry back much to them. I go back with both arms broken and empty. Two fathers came with us. They were the braves of many winters and wars. We leave them asleep here by your great water and wigwams. They were tired in many moons and their moccasins wore out.

My people sent me to get the White Man's Book of Heaven. You took me to where you allow your women to dance, as we do not ours, and the book was not there. You took me to where they worship the great Spirit with candles, and the book was not there. You showed me images of the good spirits and the pictures of the good land beyond, but the book was not among them to tell us the way. I am going back the long and sad trail to my people in the dark land. You make my feet heavy with gifts and my moccasins will grow old in carrying them, yet the book is not among them. When I tell my poor blind people after one more snow, in the big council, that I did not bring the book, no word will be spoken by our old men or by our young braves. One by one they will rise up and go out in silence. My people will die in darkness, and they will go on a long path to other hunting grounds. No white man will go with them, and no White Man's Book to make the way plain. I have no more words.

Taken altogether, it may be said that this event, as preserved in these various ways, constitutes one of the most pleasing and significant, though pathetic, incidents in Indian history. It was, moreover, pregnant with results. It might almost be said that it was the key to American possession of Oregon. For upon the acquisition of the story by the Christian people of the United States, there rose an immediate demand that something be done to carry the Gospel to the Indians of the Oregon country. This story was interpreted as a Macedonian cry. The period was one of strong religious feeling, as well as missionary zeal. The warm-hearted followers of the Cross felt at once that here was a providential opening to honour that Cross and to advance its kingdom upon the western border of civilisation.

The Methodist Church was first to take up the work of sending forth missionaries to the Oregon Indians. To Wilbur Fiske of Wesleyan University seems due the credit of the first move. He enlisted the interest of Jason Lee, a former student at Wesleyan University, but then engaged in missionary work in the province of Quebec. Lee was a tall, athletic young man, full of zeal and consecration, not polished or graceful in manner, but powerful in spirit. He grasped at once the great possibilities in the proposition of Dr. Fiske, and, going to Boston, became appointed by the New England Conference as superintendent of a mission to Oregon.

Daniel Lee, Cyrus Shepard, and P. L. Edwards were named his associates.

In 1834, this mission band learned that Nathaniel Wyeth, famous as a fur-trader, was expecting to cross the continent, sending his goods by the brig *May Dacre* to the Columbia River. Such an opportunity was too favourable to be lost, and the Methodist Board at once opened negotiations with Captain Wyeth, with the result that this first missionary company to Oregon went with him and arrived safely at Vancouver on the Columbia, the headquarters of the Hudson's Bay Company. The *May Dacre* reached her destination soon after, and thus Mr. Lee and his comrades found themselves at the threshold of their labours. The first intention had been to locate among the Nez Percés and Flatheads, the ones from whom the Macedonian cry had gone up. But Dr. McLoughlin, the chief factor at Vancouver, who had received them with the utmost interest and cordiality, persuaded them that the Willamette Valley would be a more promising field. Its advantages were obvious. It was directly on water navigation to the sea, and within easy distance of it. It was so near the chief entrepôt of the Hudson's Bay Company as to be comparatively safe and accessible to all mails. The valley was of extraordinary scenic charm and salubrious climate. The natives, moreover, seemed more tractable and peaceful than those of the upper valley. Accordingly the Methodist brethren ascended the Willamette to a point near a group of farms which had been located by French employees of the Hudson's Bay Company on what is known now as French Prairie. One of these Frenchmen was Joseph Gervais, and from him the subsequent town of Gervais was named. The mission was located on the Willamette near Chemawa, the present site of the United States Indian School. It was ten miles north of Chemeketa, which was the great Indian Council Ground, or Peace Ground, from which fact the missionary applied to it the name of Salem,—a change of name more commendable for piety than for taste.

Jason Lee set to work at once with zeal, patience, and intelligence, to inaugurate the work to which he had consecrated his life. At times his efforts seemed to be well rewarded. Then pestilence would attack the Indians, followed by suspicion and excitement, as a result of which all the gains would be lost. The work among the whites and their half-breed families was more encouraging than that with the Indians. At the best, Indians have been inconstant and unreliable in respect to religious instruction.

In 1837 a strong reinforcement arrived, among whom were Dr. Elijah White, destined to become a man of note as Superintendent of Indian Affairs.

In 1838, Rev. Daniel Lee and Rev. H. K. W. Perkins established a new station at Wascopum, now the location of The Dalles. In the same year Jason Lee returned East to secure an addition to the mission. His efforts were crowned with success. Five missionaries, one physician, six mechanics, four farmers, one steward, and four female teachers, with a number unclassified,—in all thirty-six adults and seventeen children,—reached the Columbia River on the good ship *Lausanne*, under charge of Captain Spalding, on May 21, 1840. This was the most notable company that had yet reached our Great River. Among them were men and women who contributed in a great degree to the subsequent growth of Oregon. Of the number were Revs. Gustavus Hines, Alvin Waller, J. P. Richmond, and J. H. Frost; Dr. Ira L.

Babcock, George Abernethy, afterwards governor of the territory, J. L. Parrish, and L. H. Judson. All the men were accompanied by their wives, and most of them had children. They were, in short, the advance guard of the American home-builders in Oregon, and as such they deserve a special place on the roll of honour.

With this added force, it was possible to enlarge the work, in both secular and religious lines, both among the whites and the Indians. A mission was started at Clatsop on the south side of the mouth of the Columbia under Mr. Parrish, one at the falls of the Willamette, and another on Tualatin Plains, under Mr. Hines, while still another was located by Mr. Richmond at Nisqually on Puget Sound.

As time passed on, it became more and more evident that this work was to become less for Indians and more for the incoming whites. The whole aspect of it changed. The Methodist Board in New England decided that they were not justified in maintaining the missions, and these were discontinued during the decade of the forties.

Out of the mission at Chemeketa grew Willamette University, one of the most prominent educational institutions of Oregon.

Jason Lee returned to the East and died in Canada in 1845. His life, though short, was heroic and influential. He looms large on the background of the history of the Columbia. In brief retrospect, it may be said of him that he combined religious zeal with shrewd common sense and capacity to see and adapt himself to the business and political conditions of his time and place. This capacity is illustrated by his shrewd management of a bold and enterprising character named Ewing Young. This man was about starting a distillery in the Willamette Valley. Knowing the ruinous effects of intoxicants on Indians, the missionaries strongly opposed the enterprise. But knowing also that Young was a man of force and capacity and much more valuable as a friend than as an enemy, Mr. Lee accomplished the abandonment of the distillery by indirection, and at the same time gained one of the most important steps in the development of the country. For he induced Young to undertake the great work of driving into the Willamette Valley a large herd of cattle from California. To the settlers beginning to locate on the fat pasture land along the Willamette and its tributaries, this was a stage in history of priceless moment. Up to that time the only cattle in the country belonged to the Hudson's Bay Company and it was not their policy to encourage American settlers.

Another fact in connection with Jason Lee constitutes a landmark in the history of American acquisition of Oregon. This was a memorial prepared by him, with the assistance of P. L. Edwards and David Leslie, and signed by practically all the adult men then accessible in the Willamette Valley, thirty-six in number, addressed to the United States Congress and praying that the Government would consider the importance of the Columbia River country and the question of acquisition. This memorial was dated March 16, 1838, and was taken by Mr. Lee to the East and given to Senator Linn of Missouri, in January, 1839. Senator Linn was so aroused over the boundless possibilities offered to westward expansion that he introduced a bill in the Senate calling for the establishment of Oregon Territory and the occupation of it by the military forces of the United States. Though this bill did not become a law, it constituted a rallying cry for the friends of American possession, which had results of utmost importance.

In short, to Jason Lee, more than to any other one, unless we except Dr. Marcus Whitman, of whom we shall speak later, must be attributed the inauguration of that remarkable chain of causes and effects, a long line of sequences, by which Oregon and our Pacific Coast in general became American possessions, and the international destiny of our nation was secured.

From the Methodist missions of Lower Columbia we turn to the Presbyterian and Congregational missions of the upper River and its tributaries. The American Board of Foreign Missions was at that time under the joint control of three religious bodies, Presbyterian, Congregational, and Dutch Reformed. At the instance of the last named body, the Board in 1835 commissioned Rev. Samuel Parker of Ithaca, N. Y., and Marcus Whitman, M.D., of Rushville, N. Y., to make a reconnaissance of the country of the Columbia, with the view of a mission. Under the protection of the American Fur Company, the two spiritual prospectors journeyed as far as Green River. There deciding that what they learned of the land beyond the Rocky Mountains warranted the carrying out of the missionary project, they determined to part company, Dr. Whitman returning to the "States" for reinforcements, and Dr. Parker going onward through Oregon to the mouth of the Columbia, and proceeding thence by ship to Honolulu, whence he returned by water to his home. Dr. Parker was an elderly man, somewhat pedantic and notional in his ways, but withal full of energy and zeal in the cause. He was not so popular with trappers and frontiersmen as his companion. For Whitman was a young, athletic man, capable of any degree of fatigue, very ready in proffering his professional or other services to those in need. There was a bonhommie and general disregard of the conventionalities in Whitman that caused the rough spirits of the border to "take to" him at once, while they rather looked askance at the more straight-laced ecclesiastic. But Parker was a man worthy of all respect for his qualities both of mind and purpose. He was a keen observer, and has left us, as his contribution to history, his *Travels beyond the Rocky Mountains*, one of the most readable and valuable books of travel in our western literature. His journey was, in fact, the first one across the continent, after that of Lewis and Clark, which produced a book of high standard.

Dr. Whitman made his way at once to his home in New York, accompanied by two Nez Percé Indians. Arriving late on Saturday night he stopped with his brother, and no one else of the village knew of his arrival, until at the hour of service the next morning, he appeared in the aisle followed by his two Indians. His appearance was so like that of an apparition that his usually staid and proper mother lost her head entirely, and leaped to her feet, shouting "Why, there is Marcus!" The equilibrium of the meeting was for the time almost destroyed.

Within a few months, Dr. Whitman was married to Narcissa Prentiss. He persuaded Rev. H. H. Spalding and wife, who had hitherto planned to go as missionaries to the Osage Indians, to join them for Oregon. W. H. Gray was secured to go with the party as secular manager.

And now began the famous "Wedding Journey" from New York to the banks of the Columbia. It included within itself the romance, the pathos, the devotion, the heroism, and at the last, the tragedy of missions.

The History of Oregon, by W. H. Gray, is the chief original authority for this journey, though the women of the party kept journals which are of great value. It would seem that all the members of the party were of marked personality. Dr. Whitman was a tall, spare man, with deep blue eyes, wide mouth, iron-grey hair, of inflexible resolution, and very set when his mind was once made up, though flexible and even variable till that point had been reached. He was of enormous physical strength and endurance, with a constitution, as one who knew him later told the writer, "like a saw-mill."

Mrs. Whitman was a woman of liberal education for those times, large, fair-haired, blue-eyed, dignified, and somewhat reserved (rather "starchy," the mountain men thought her), very ladylike, refined, and attractive. One of the pathetic and interesting things about her is related by Mrs. Martha J. Lamb in the *Magazine of American History*, in 1884. This relates the fact that the church of which Miss Prentiss (Mrs. Whitman) was a member in Plattsburg, N. Y., held a farewell service for her, and in the course of it the minister gave out the hymn:

> Yes, my native land, I love thee,
> All thy scenes, I love them well;
> Friends, connections, happy country,
> Can I bid you all farewell.

The entire congregation joined heartily in singing, but before the hymn was ended voice after voice was choked with sobs, and in the last words the clear, sweet soprano voice of Miss Prentiss was heard alone, unwavering, like a peal of triumph.

Mr. Spalding was a very different man from Dr. Whitman and has not been so well treated by historians. He is said to have been more nervous and crotchety, though of remarkable industry and intense likes and dislikes, which he never scrupled to express in vigorous fashion. The fact remains, however, that his mission was altogether the most successful of all those founded in Oregon.

Mrs. Spalding was tall, dark, rather coarse featured, and of fragile health. It is truly wonderful that with such a handicap she should have been able to accomplish the arduous journey to Oregon. She was less fastidious and reserved than Mrs. Whitman and adopted the policy of taking the habits and manners of the Indians in greater degree, whereas her more dignified sister believed in the policy of trying to raise the Indians to her own level. The Indians therefore understood Mrs. Spalding better. The Indians always desired the privilege of entering Mrs. Whitman's private room unannounced, and, if possible, of seeing her at her bath or toilette. Her natural objection to such intrusion was a chronic grievance which resulted in the suspicion by the Indians that she was conspiring against them.

W. H. Gray, the secular agent, was a young, fine-looking, daring, and athletic man, very skilful in making and handling boats, teams, waggons, and anything else of a practical nature. He was so positive and even violent in his views as to alienate many with whom he came in contact. Yet he was one of the manliest men that ever came to Oregon, and was intimately connected with nearly every important event in the history of the Columbia River, navigation included. His four sons, all born in Oregon, became steamboat captains and pilots, and without question, no one family has been so intimately associated with the River as has the Gray family. If any one group of people could be said to have filed a claim on the River, it is the family of W. H. Gray. Gray's history is of high value, yet so intense was his hatred of the Hudson's Bay Company and of the British in general, as well as of Roman Catholics, that his book has been subjected to unsparing criticism by later writers.

The little missionary band of five, accompanied by the two Nez Percé Indians who had gone East with Whitman the year before, joined the westbound caravan of the American Fur Company, and journeyed with them the greater part of the way. One of the most thrilling and suggestive moments in their journey was when they stood on the summit of the Rockies at South Pass. There they looked down the westward maze of mountains and valleys drained by the Snake River and its tributaries as these swept west to join the Columbia and thence proceed to the Pacific. With that vision before them, they spread the Stars and Stripes to the breeze and kneeling upon the turf, they took possession of the great unknown to the westward in the name of God and the American Union. Nobly was the claim maintained, though with it came the crown of martyrdom.

Whitman desired above all other things to demonstrate the feasibility of a waggon road to the Pacific. He therefore insisted on taking his waggon,—"*Chick-chick-shaile-kikash,*" the Indians called it, in attempted onomatopœia. His demonstration was successful, though the trouble was infinite. He was compelled to leave the waggon at the Hudson's Bay Fort on the Boisé, near the present site of Boisé City, with the intention of getting it the next year. The Hudson's Bay people used every effort to discourage Whitman in his waggon enterprise, though according to Gray, they made much use of the vehicle in their fort.

On September 2, 1836, the mission party reached the Hudson's Bay Company's fort at the mouth of the Walla Walla, a little more than four months and two thousand two hundred miles from the banks of the Missouri to those of the Columbia.

But the journey was not complete, for their definite location must yet be selected. They proceeded now in bateaux down the Great River to Vancouver, the headquarters of the Hudson's Bay Company's empire. There Dr. McLoughlin, the chief factor, met them with his own peculiar cordiality, and yet with the dignity befitting the head of so great an establishment. He was a noble man, and though business considerations and the orders of the directors of the company would have led him to "freeze out" the Americans, yet humanity and his own genial nature forbade him to withhold the cordial hand from the mission band. The fort and two ships in the river were arrayed in gala attire in honour of the event. Dr. McLoughlin did the honours of his spacious hall to Mrs. Whitman and Mrs. Spalding in a style that would have graced a baronial mansion.

By Dr. McLoughlin's advice, since the Methodist mission had been located in the Willamette Valley, Whitman decided to establish himself among the Cayuses in the beautiful and fertile valley of the Walla Walla, at Waiilatpu, the "Place of the Rye-grass." Spalding accepted the urgent appeal of the Nez Percés to go a hundred and twenty-five miles eastward to Lapwai on the Clearwater, near the modern site of Lewiston. Both stations were fair to look upon, with every natural advantage. It proved, however, that the Cayuses were fierce and intractable, while the Nez Percés, though warlike and manly, were also docile, ambitious to learn, and predisposed to friendly relations with the Americans.

In 1838, the American Board of Foreign Missions sent a reinforcement to the field, consisting of Revs. Elkanah Walker, Cushing Eells, A. B. Smith, and their wives. Mr. Gray, who had returned the previous year in order to organise this reinforcement, had found a wife, and with her was now accompanying this second missionary band to Oregon.

Messrs. Walker and Eells located at Tshimakain, on what is now called Walker's Prairie, near Spokane. Mr. Smith went to Kamiah up the Clearwater, about sixty miles from Mr. Spalding's station at Lapwai.

Time fails to speak of the many interesting events marking each of the missions. They were all located in singularly attractive spots, and every one of the missionaries made great progress in cultivating the ground, building mills, houses, and fences, and interesting the Indians in the arts of peace. It is true that when the novelty of the white man's ways had passed, many of the natives lost all interest. Yet upon the Spokanes and the Nez Percés, lasting influences were wrought. The Nez Percés in particular, under the influence of their noble and intelligent chief, Hal-hal-tlos-sot, or Lawyer, almost decided the fate of American institutions in the upper Columbia River region for years.

One of the especially interesting events in connection with the Nez Percé mission was the acquisition by Mr. Spalding of the first printing-press used west of the Rocky Mountains. This was donated by the church of Rev. H. Bingham at Honolulu in 1839. The indefatigable Spalding, with the assistance of his wife, who had unusual powers as a linguist, began at once reducing the Nez Percé language to a written form and printing in it translations of hymns and portions of the Bible. Some of these first books of the Columbia River are still in existence. The venerable printing-press is in the museum of the Oregon Pioneer Society at Portland.

The most dramatic and influential event in connection with the missions of the Columbia, one of the most so in all American history, was Dr. Whitman's mid-winter ride in 1842-43 from Waiilatpu to St. Louis. Dr. Whitman, in common with Jason Lee, soon began to perceive that the Columbia Valley possessed resources and a location which would inevitably make it the seat of a civilised population. The corollary of this was that the mission must conform to the movements of the whites and in time cease to be simply an Indian mission. He perceived another thing. That was the purpose of the Hudson's Bay Company to hold Oregon under English possession and keep it a wilderness for the sake of the fur-trade. The corollary of that was that, if American families could be induced to locate in Oregon, they would in time topple the scale in favour of American ownership.

The value of Oregon was then but dimly understood among the Americans.

Webster, Benton, and others of the great statesmen are on record in the *Congressional Globe* with many disparaging remarks upon "that worthless Columbia River country."

Whitman watched all signs with anxious eye. Negotiations between England and the United States indicated a probable surrender to the former. The American Board was considering the abandonment of the mission. Looking over the broad field of the future of the American nation with a statesman's vision, Dr. Whitman readily saw that the interests of his country and of Christian civilisation demanded the acquisition of Oregon. Those interests were in jeopardy. He made the great resolution to proceed at once to the "States" with the threefold aim: confer with the officers of the American Board on the retention of the mission, confer with President Tyler, Secretary Webster, and such others of the officers of government as he could see at Washington, and finally help organise and lead back to Oregon an American immigration. His fellow-missionaries strongly opposed his purpose. They felt that it was abandoning the religious aims of the mission to take up political questions. But he declared that he had not expatriated himself by becoming a missionary. Go he would. The undertaking seemed chimerical, even desperate. But Whitman was bold, athletic, persistent, possessing all the qualities of a hero.

With a single white companion, A. L. Lovejoy, and one or more Indian guides, he left Waiilatpu on October 3, 1842. His journey through snow, ice, wind, hunger, peril, and deprivation of every sort, has been ofttimes described. The extent of his influence in securing the adoption by our Government of the policy of retaining Oregon has become the theme of earnest, even acrimonious discussion. The simple fact remains that Oregon was "saved" to the American Union. The missionaries Lee and Whitman bore, each his part, and a great one, in the great final result. It is not too much to say that of the various lines of influence by which the valley of the Columbia became American territory, that of missions was one of the strongest.

The Catholic missions of the Columbia Valley have found several chroniclers, of whom the most valuable are Rev. F. N. Blanchet and Rev. Pierre J. De Smet. The former in his book, *The Catholic Church in Oregon*, gives a clear and circumstantial account of the founding and carrying on of the work in the Willamette Valley. The latter in his *Oregon Missions*, and *Western Missions and Missionaries*, has given a singularly graphic and interesting report on religious progress, and with it many charming descriptions of the scenery and other natural conditions of the country.

Father Blanchet, in company with Rev. Modest Demers, went from Montreal to Vancouver, a journey of over four thousand miles, in 1837. At the Little Dalles of the Columbia, near the present Northport, a lamentable disaster cost the lives of twelve of the company with whom they were travelling. Reaching Vancouver on November 24, 1837, they received from Dr. McLoughlin, who had himself been brought up a Catholic, a most cordial welcome, though apparently not more cordial than the good man had given Lee, the Methodist, and Whitman, the Presbyterian. The fact that there were so many French Canadians in the country made the way of the Catholic Fathers easier than that of the other missionaries. For the French, with their gayety, sociability, and usual habit of intermarriage with the Indians, were much more popular with them than were the more harsh and reserved

British and Americans. In fact the Catholic Fathers found a building all ready for their use at the historic town of Champoeg on the Willamette, thirty miles above Portland. There in 1836, the French settlers had built a log church, the first church building in Oregon. It is rather sad to relate that petty dissensions and jealousies marred the relations between the Catholics and the Methodists. But both alike were zealous and indefatigable in promoting the secular and religious interests of both red men and white men.

While Fathers Blanchet and Demers and their associates were busily engaged in the Willamette Valley, Father de Smet had come in 1840 into the Flathead country, in what is now Northern Idaho. His first mission was St. Mary's, on the Flathead River, founded by the planting of the cross on September 24, 1841. Other missions were soon established on Cœur d'Alene Lake and Pend Oreille Lake. Branching out from them were missions in Colville, and ultimately in the Walla Walla, Yakima, Wenatchee, and Chelan valleys.

De Smet greatly overestimated the number of Indians, reckoning those in Oregon at one hundred and ten thousand. He numbered his converts by the thousands. So pressing seemed the needs that in 1843, he went to Europe for reinforcements. He was very successful in his quest, returning the following year in the ship *L'Indefatigable*, from Antwerp, accompanied by four fathers, six sisters, and several lay brothers. He gives a thrilling account of his entrance of the Columbia River on July 31, 1844. He vividly portrays the terrors of the bar with the mighty surges dashing across the entrance. The captain did not understand the channel and became diverted from the true course, which was then by the north channel, and got into the south. The latter is now the main channel, but then was dangerous. De Smet piously regards their escape from wreck as due to the special interposition of divine providence, and to the favour extended to them because of its being the day sacred to St. Ignatius Loyola, founder of their order. De Smet's brilliant and poetical descriptions of the grandeur of the river and its forests denote a keen appreciation of nature and a facile pen.

Demers, De Smet, and Blanchet entered upon their work with such energy that by the time of De Smet's report in 1844 there had been established four dioceses in the region tributary to the Columbia; viz., Oregon City, Walla Walla, Fort Hall, and Colville. Oregon City was the Metropolitan See and in charge of Rev. F. N. Blanchet. Walla Walla was under the direction of Rev. Magloire Blanchet, who at that date had charge also of Forts Hall and Colville. Eleven chapels had been erected at different points; five in the Willamette Valley, one at Vancouver, one on the Cowlitz, one on Cœur d'Alene Lake, one on Pend Oreille Lake, one at Kettle Falls on the Columbia near Colville, and one near Calispell among the Flatheads. There were three schools; one being St. Mary's among the Flatheads, while at St. Paul's on the Willamette, there were two, a college for boys, still the site of a college, and a girls' academy. Twelve clergymen were engaged at that time in the work, and the number was soon increased to twenty-six by another reinforcement from Europe. With the reinforcement were also seven female teachers.

Each of these three chief groups of missions had its special aims, methods, and results. The Catholic was more exclusively religious, while the Protestants passed over readily from their initial religious aims to the domain of political and educational interest. The net result was tremendous in the history of the country.

Among the educational institutions growing directly out of the labours of the missionaries we may mention Willamette University at Salem, the direct successor of the Methodist mission at Chemeketa; Whitman College at Walla Walla, founded by Cushing Eells as a memorial to Marcus Whitman; Pacific University at Forest Grove, Oregon, founded by a later set of Congregational Home Missionaries; and the Catholic College at St. Paul's, the successor of the school founded in 1839 by Blanchet.

They rest from their labours and their works do follow them.

CHAPTER VII

THE ERA OF THE PIONEERS:
THEIR OX-TEAMS AND THEIR FLATBOATS

Events and Men who led the Way to the Pioneer Age—Kelley, Wyeth, and Bonneville—Ewing Young—Farnham, Shortess, and the "Oregon Dragoons"—The Wilkes Expedition—The *Star of Oregon*, and the Cattle Enterprise—Dr. John McLoughlin and the Americans—Dr. Marcus Whitman and his Winter Ride, and the Immigration of 1843—Retrospect of J. W. Nesmith—Features of the Journey across the Plains—Whitman's Services—Getting the Waggons across the Plains—Reaching the River and Building Boats—Delights and then Distress of the Descent of the River—Battle with the River—Condition in which they Reached Vancouver, and their Reception by Dr. McLoughlin—Subsequent Immigrations—The Barlow Road—The Donation Land Law—Quotation from Jesse Applegate.

THE pioneer era was ushered in by the coming to Oregon of fur-hunters, missionaries, and little bands of adventurers, who together composed the nucleus of that American community which formed the Provisional Government of 1843. There were certain individuals, too, whose agency in leading the way to the immigration movement was so unique as to deserve mention.

One of these was Hall J. Kelley of Boston. He was a native of New Hampshire and a Harvard graduate. As early as 1815, when seventeen years old, he conceived the idea of the colonisation of Americans in Oregon. He was a man of high scholarship, philanthropic spirit, and patriotic purpose. He was a dreamer and idealist, planning to form a community on the Columbia, as one of the Utopias which minds of that stamp, from Plato down, have been fond of locating somewhere in the unexplored West. After making a great effort, with partial success, to enlist Congress in his schemes, he succeeded in organising a company of several hundred, and by 1828 shaped the definite plan of going to St. Louis and following the route of the fur companies across the plains to the River of Oregon. But opposition by those same fur companies, and adverse criticism by the press broke up his enterprise for that time. In 1832 he started with a small party for the land of his dreams by the route through Mexico and California. In California, he met with Ewing Young, an American of great natural abilities and some education. Young and Kelley, brainy and original men, the former from shrewd commercial instinct and the latter from philanthropic dreams, formed a little company, and proceeded overland from California to Oregon. This was in the autumn of 1834. When, after some disasters, the company of eleven reached the Columbia, Young took up a great tract of land in the Chehalem Valley, where he devoted himself to stock-raising. Kelley, having become an invalid, went in distress to Fort Vancouver, where Dr. McLoughlin treated him with kindness, though the exclusive "Britishers" would not admit him to "social equality." The other members of the company were scattered in various directions, but some of them remained till American occupancy became an accomplished fact.

This company of 1834,—the same year that the Methodist missionaries under Jason Lee arrived—may be considered the advance guard of American immigration. Kelley, upon his return to New England by way of the Sandwich Islands, disseminated much useful information about Oregon. To him, without doubt, is to be attributed much of the subsequent wave of interest which swept on toward American immigration. As first a New England college man, educator, and social theoriser, and then a leader of the pioneer movement to Oregon, Hall J. Kelley is worthy of permanent remembrance.

Ewing Young became distinguished for leading the party which in 1837 drove a band of seven hundred cattle from California to Oregon. This even marked an epoch in preparing for immigration and subsequent American possession. One of the peculiarly noteworthy facts in connection with Young's enterprise, is that Dr. McLoughlin, the Hudson's Bay Company's magnate, who had at first discountenanced Young on account of a charge of stealing brought against him from California, and who frowned upon the cattle enterprise for fear of American influence, became reconciled to both Young and the cattle, and subscribed liberally to the enterprise.

Nearly contemporary with Kelley and Young were Bonneville and Wyeth.

Bonneville was a well-educated French-American, a West Pointer, and holding the commission of captain in the United States Army. His ardent and imaginative disposition became fired with the thought of a far western expedition, and in 1832 he organised a fur-traders' company of a hundred and ten men. Though not realising his dreams of a fortune in furs, Bonneville made many interesting and valuable observations upon the Salmon, Clearwater, Snake, and Columbia rivers. He became thoroughly imbued with the romance and scenic grandeur of the far West. Upon his return to New York, he had the good fortune to meet Washington Irving at the home of John Jacob Astor. Irving had already felt the irresistible fascination which the River of Oregon has wrought upon all poetical natures, and the result of this meeting was one of Irving's most charming volumes, *Bonneville's Adventures*, a volume which became another potent force in turning toward the Pacific slope the thoughts of the eager, restless people of the frontier.

Still another in the group of men who led the way to immigration was Nathaniel Wyeth. He was a talented, well-educated, and energetic Bostonian. So distinguished a personage as James Russell Lowell has said of him: "He was a very remarkable person, whose conversation I valued highly. A born leader of men, he was fitly called Captain Nathaniel Wyeth as long as he lived."

Wyeth conceived the idea of a great trading company on the Columbia, whose operations would necessarily create rivalry with the British. His design was to send companies across the continent to the Columbia head-waters and to maintain also ship connection by way of Cape Horn. He believed that a ship load of salmon from the Columbia River to the Atlantic sea-board would be a paying venture. On so large a scale did he lay out his enterprise that he expected soon to have a business of two hundred thousand dollars a year. But he looked beyond the fur and salmon business to American possession and settlement, at least south of the River to the California line. He therefore embraced in his view the building of enterprises which should lead up to and then profit by American immigration. Wyeth spent five years in Oregon, having many interesting adventures, and as many business reverses. As was the case with Astor, the British fur-traders proved too powerful for the Yankee. Among other undertakings, he built a fort on Sauvie's Island at the mouth of the Willamette, which he called Fort William. He desired to make this the basis of his trade, and he expected the Indians to go there to trade. But such was the influence of the Hudson's Bay people and their employees with the Indians that Wyeth's fort had no trade. It was during those years that a frightful pestilence swept the natives away like flies, and there was great fear among them that Wyeth's fort might harbour the scourge. The period of Wyeth's enterprise in Oregon extended from the spring of 1832 to the autumn of 1836. Though not a business success, it had a great bearing on the creation of an interest in Oregon, and on preparing for immigration a few years later. It opened the eyes of many Americans to the attractions of Oregon and to the tremendous power and profits of the Hudson's Bay Company.

The next movement may be called a real immigration to Oregon. It consisted of a party of nineteen, commonly known as the "Peoria party," since they went from Peoria, Ill. Jason Lee, the missionary of Chemeketa, delivered a lecture at that place in 1838, and so much interest in Oregon was aroused that in the year following, the Peoria party, the first regular party from the Mississippi Valley, set forth for the River of the West. Their leader, T. J. Farnham, christened his followers the "Oregon Dragoons" and Mrs. Farnham gave them a flag with the inscription, "Oregon or the Grave." Farnham declared his purpose to seize Oregon for the United States.

The Peoria party had the good fortune to have two writers in the number, whose accounts possess rare interest. These writers were the leader Farnham, and Robert Shortess. The party went to pieces at Bent's Fort on the Arkansas, but its members reached Oregon somewhat in driblets during that year, and the one following. Shortess reached the Whitman Mission at Walla Walla in the fall of 1839, and there he remained until the following spring, when he went down the River to The Dalles. From The Dalles, he made his way over the Cascade Mountains to the Willamette Valley, and there he lived many years. Farnham also finally reached Oregon, but his avowed mission was unfulfilled. Shortess says of him: "Instead of raising the American flag and turning the Hudson's Bay Company out-of-doors, he accepted the gift of a suit of clothes and a passage to the Sandwich Islands, and took a final leave of Oregon." But upon his return to the "States," Farnham published a *Pictorial History of Oregon and California*, a book of many interesting features, and one which played a worthy part in waking the people of the Mississippi Valley to the attractions of the Pacific Coast.

Soon after the close of Wyeth's enterprise, there were two notable government expeditions to the Columbia River. One was commanded by Sir Edward Belcher of the British Navy, and the other by Lieutenant Charles Wilkes of the American Navy. The Wilkes expedition was one of the most interesting and important ever undertaken by the United States Government. The squadron consisted of two sloops-of-war, the *Peacock* and the *Vincennes*, the store ship, *Relief*, the brig, *Porpoise*, and the schooners, *Sea Gull* and *Flying Fish*. This fine squadron took up its principal station on Puget Sound, from which extensive surveys were made, one across the mountains to Fort Okanogan; another of the Cowlitz Valley and the Columbia River as far as Wallula.

One of the most important results of this elaborate Wilkes expedition was to establish in the minds of officers of the Government the essential unity of all parts of the Pacific Coast and the boundless opportunities offered to American immigration. Wilkes and his intelligent officers readily grasped, and conveyed through an elaborate report to the government, the idea that Puget Sound was an inherent and integral part of Oregon and that the Columbia Basin was essential to the proper development of American commerce upon the Pacific. They may also have forecast the time when California with her girdles of gold and chaplets of freedom would spring, Athena-like, from the Zeus brain of American enterprise. The control of the River was the key to the control of the entire coast from San Diego to the Straits of Fuca;—and American ownership should have extended to Sitka.

A memorable calamity occurred to the squadron upon its entrance to the River, and that was the loss of the *Peacock* on the Columbia River bar. The oft-depicted terrors of the River were realised at that time, and yet it was not the River's fault for the *Peacock* was out of the channel. The spit is known as "Peacock Spit" to this day.

Among the many episodes connecting Wilkes with the early immigration was the building of the schooner *Star of Oregon* and her voyage to California for cattle. This was in 1842. It will be remembered that Ewing Young had made a successful trip from California with cattle. But as the population of the Columbia had increased, there was a great desire among the settlers to obtain a larger number of cattle to let loose upon the rich pasture lands of the Willamette Valley. A little group of Americans conceived the adventurous project of building a schooner of Oregon timber, sailing with her to California, exchanging her there for stock, and driving the band across the country home again. The schooner was built by Felix Hathaway, Joseph Gale, and Ralph Kilbourne. The oak and fir timber of which the vessel was built was cut on Sauvie's Island, at the mouth of the Willamette, and in due time she was launched and taken to Willamette Falls for fitting. A difficulty arose. Dr. McLoughlin refused to sell sails, cordage, and other materials. He had the only supply in Oregon. In despair the enterprising ship-builders appealed to Lieutenant Wilkes. He felt a keen interest in their laudable undertaking and made a visit to McLoughlin to try to change his resolution. By assuring the Doctor that he would be responsible both for all the bills, as well as for the good conduct of the party, he induced him to allow the requisition for all materials necessary to complete the gallant craft. Gale was the only sailor in the party. Having satisfied Wilkes that he was qualified to command a ship, and having received from him a present of a flag, an ensign, a compass, kedge-anchor, hawser, log line, and two log glasses, the captain flung the flag to the Oregon breeze and turned the prow of the *Star of Oregon* toward the River's mouth. She may be remembered as the first sea-going vessel built of Oregon timber. Crossing the Bar in a storm, she sped southward in a spanking breeze, all hands seasick except Gale. He held the wheel thirty-six hours continuously, and in five days "dashed through the portals of the Golden Gate like an arrow, September 17, 1842."

As it was too late to get the cattle back to Oregon that fall, the party sold their schooner for three hundred and fifty cows, wintered in California, and the next spring drove to the Columbia twelve hundred and fifty head of cattle, six hundred head of mules and horses, and three thousand sheep. This was an achievement which made the way for immigration clearer than ever before, and in a most effective manner united the American settlers with the American government. Some of the Hudson's Bay Company people could begin to see the handwriting on the wall. Dr. McLoughlin saw most quickly and most clearly, and as elsewhere narrated, began to transfer his interests to the American side. This fine old man was big-brained, big-bodied, and big-souled, a natural American, though compelled to work for the British fur monopolists for the time. He admired the independent spirit of the incoming Yankee immigrants, even when the joke was on him. He afterwards told with much gusto of an American named Woods crossing the Columbia to Vancouver to try to get goods. He found his credit shaky, and somewhat piqued, he exclaimed: "Well, never mind, I have an uncle back East rich enough to buy out the whole of your old Hudson's Bay Company!" "Well, well, Mr. Woods," demanded the autocrat, "who may this very rich uncle of yours be?" "Uncle Sam," was the unabashed and characteristic American reply. "Old Whitehead" also appreciated, though he was obliged to manifest a dignified disapproval, when two young men from New York, having reached the fort on the River, were asked about their passports. Laying their hands on their rifles they replied, "These are an American's passports."

These small miscellaneous immigrations were in continuance from about 1830 to 1842. In the latter year a hundred came. In 1843, as elsewhere related, the Provisional Government was instituted. At the very same time, the immigration of 1843 was on its way to the River.

This immigration of 1843 was in many respects the most remarkable of all. It was the first large one, and it was a type of all. It will be remembered that Dr. Marcus Whitman had made his great winter ride in 1842-43 across the Rockies to St. Louis, with a double aim. First he wished to see the officers of the American Board of Missions, and then to enlist the American government and people in the policy of holding Oregon against the manifest aims of the British. There was already a tremendous interest felt in Oregon among the people of Missouri, Illinois, and the other great prairie States. Whitman's opportune arrival and his announced purpose to guide an immigration to the Columbia became widely known, and brought to a focus many vaguely-considered plans.

J. W. Nesmith, subsequently one of the most prominent pioneers and a member of each House of Congress from Oregon, has given a humorous account of the manner of starting this immigration of 1843, of which he was a member, which is so characteristic that we quote it here.

> Mr. Burnett, or as he was more familiarly styled, "Pete," was called upon for a speech. Mounting a log the glib-tongued orator delivered a glowing florid address. He commenced by showing his audience that the then western tier of states and territories were crowded with a redundant population, who had not sufficient elbow room for the expansion of their enterprise and genius, and it was a duty they owed to themselves and posterity to strike out in search of a more expanded field and a more genial climate, where the soil yielded the richest return for the slightest amount of cultivation, — where the trees were loaded with perennial fruit, — and where a good substitute for bread, called La Camash, grew in the ground; where salmon and other fish crowded the streams; and where the principal labour of the settlers would be confined to keeping their gardens free from the inroads of buffalo, elk, deer, and wild turkeys. He appealed to our patriotism by picturing forth the glorious empire we should establish upon the shores of the Pacific, — how with our trusty rifles we should drive out the British usurpers who claimed the soil, and defend the country from the avarice and pretensions of the British Lion, — and how posterity would honour us for placing the fairest portion of the land under the Stars and Stripes.... Other speeches were made full of glowing descriptions of the fair land of promise, the far-away Oregon, which no one in the assemblage had ever seen, and about which not more than half a dozen had ever read any account. After the election of Mr. Burnett as captain, and other necessary officers, the meeting, as motley and primitive a one as ever assembled, adjourned with "three cheers" for Captain Burnett and Oregon.

Peter Burnett to whom Nesmith here refers, was the same who became the first governor of California.

By the walnut hearth-fires in many a home of the prairie States and at the corn-huskings and quilting bees the talk of Oregon and the forests of the Columbia, and the rich pasture lands of the Willamette, and the salmon and game, and genial climate and majestic mountains, went the rounds. Interest grew into enthusiasm, enthusiasm waxed hot, and in the early spring the great immigration of 1843 set forth from Westport, Missouri, for the Columbia waters. Though the immigration of 1843 was the earliest of any size and the first with any number of women and children, it had perhaps the least trouble and misfortune and the most romance and gayety and enthusiasm of any. The experience of crossing the plains was one which nothing else could duplicate;—the hasty rising in the chill damp of the morning, the preparing the cattle and horses for the long, hard drive, the rounds of the waggons to strengthen bolts and tires and tongues, the loading of the rifles for possible hostile Indians or buffalo, the setting forth of the scouts on horseback, the long train strung across the dusty plain, the occasional bands of wild Indians emerging like a whirlwind from the broad expanse, and then the approaching cool of night with its hurried rest on the rough prairie sod. Sometimes there were nights of storm and stampede and darkness. Sometimes savage beasts and savage men startled the train, or one of the stupendous herds of buffalo went thundering across the prairie. Then came the first glimpse of snowy heights, then of deep cañons, and then the summit was attained, and far westward stretched the maze of plains and mountains through which the Snake River, the greatest of the tributaries of the Columbia, took its swift way.

During most of the journey, Dr. Marcus Whitman was guide, physician, and friend. While severe controversy has arisen as to the extent of his services in organising the immigration, the testimony is unvarying as to the value of his presence with the train. Last to bed at night and first up in the morning, attending both people, cattle, and horses in their sicknesses and accidents, ahead of the train on horseback to find the passes of the hills and the fords of the rivers, the watcher by night and the pilot by day, the missionary doctor was the veritable "Mr. Greatheart" of the immigration.

Great was the astonishment of Captain Grant, commandant of the Hudson's Bay Fort Hall on Snake River, near the present Pocatello, when the long train filed past the enclosure. Grant had known Whitman before and was aware of his stubborn determination and patriotic purpose. But Grant attempted just the same to dissuade the immigrants of 1843 from going farther with their waggons, declaring the Blue Mountains to be impassable. The doughty doctor simply laughed quietly and told the immigrants to push on, and he would see them through. But just as they were entering the rough defiles of the Blue Mountains, a band of Indians from Waiilatpu, headed by Sticcus, came to meet the train, searching for Whitman, telling him that his medical services were in great demand at Lapwai. The much-needed guide turned over the pilotage of the train to Sticcus, and he himself hastened on to minister to the sick at Lapwai. As he passed through Waiilatpu he learned that the threatening conduct of the Indians had led Mrs. Whitman to go to Vancouver, and that during his absence the Indians had burned his mill and committed other depredations. But it was his lot to labour and suffer. He had become accustomed to it.

The event proved that Sticcus was a thoroughly capable guide. For, though not speaking a word of English, he made his directions so well understood by pantomime that, as Mr. Nesmith has said, he led them safely over the roughest mountain road that they ever saw. And so in due time the train emerged from the screen of timber on the Blue Mountains. Stretched wide before them, lay the plains of Umatilla and Walla Walla, while in the far distance the River of the West poured through the arid waste. Yet farther the snow summits of the Cascades ridged the western sky. After a brief pause at Waiilatpu, the train reached the banks of the River. The immediate vicinity of the section of the River first reached is very dry in autumn. Aside from the River itself, the immediate scene is desolate and forbidding. But probably those immigrants of '43 gazed upon the blue flood, a mile wide and hastening to the western ocean, with feelings almost akin to those which swelled the hearts of the Pilgrims landing from the *Mayflower*. This was another epic of state-making, and one generation after another of the Americans who have wrought such achievement may well turn back to join hands with those before.

Doubtless the immigrants, as they stood by the River in the pleasant haze of the October afternoon, felt as though their journey was substantially at an end. Being now at Fort Walla Walla on the river of that name, they paused to make ready for the last stage of the journey, little realising what perils and sufferings it would entail. Dr. Whitman and Archibald McKinley, the chief factor at the fort, advised them to leave their cattle and waggons to winter on the Walla Walla, while they pursued their way down the stream on flatboats. Part of the company accepted the advice, but a number determined to keep all their belongings together and to take their road along the bank of the River to The Dalles, and there make their flatboats.

To those who remained on the Walla Walla now fell the difficult task of constructing flatboats. Huge, uncouth, structures they were, made of timber gathered on the river bank. But when loaded and pushed out into the swift current, steered with immense sweeps in the stern, these flatboats afforded to the footsore and exhausted immigrants a delightful change. Out of the dust, off the rocks, away from the sage-brush, with more of laugh and song than they had had for many a day, they swept gaily on. For a hundred miles or more the elements were propitious. With the bright sunshine, the clear, cool water, the majestic snow-peaks in the distance, the easily gliding boats, — this seemed the pleasantest part of the entire journey. But after The Dalles had been reached and the two divisions of the company were again united and on their way down the River to the Cascades, disaster began to haunt them. At the Cascades, a boat with several members of the Applegate family, one of the most prominent in the immigration as well as afterwards, was overturned in the rapids, and three of the party drowned in the boiling surge. Two were saved in a way that seems almost miraculous. One of these was a young boy, the other a young man. The boy was very active and an excellent swimmer. After the overturning of the boat he was carried two miles in the current, part of the time being entirely sucked under by the whirling under-current. After being tossed with violence betwixt rock and wave till it seemed that he must expire, he was suddenly spewed forth upon a ledge of slippery rock, to which he clung desperately till he had recovered breath. Then he drew himself up on a narrow shelf, and at the same instant saw the young man swept by. Reaching forth, the brave boy managed to bring the struggling man to the same shelter with himself. But when they had regained sufficient strength to examine their surroundings, they discovered that they were on a rocky niche from which they could find no ascent of the ragged precipitous cliff. They were in a trap. Looking across the River, they could see that the bank was smooth and that on that side lay the trail. Young Applegate saw that a reef extended a considerable part of the way across the River, and desperate as the attempt seemed, he resolved to pick his way along the reef to a point whence he might swim to the other shore. It was his only chance for life. Fearful as were the odds, the daring lad accomplished his aim. He emerged on the further end of the reef. Looking around, he discovered that his comrade had not possessed the nerve to follow. And then,—most wonderful of all,—back he went to assist his more timid fellow. In this, too, he succeeded, and after a return in which they should have been drowned a dozen times, they both reached the farther end of the reef. There casting themselves again into the inhospitable flood, they buffeted their way to shore. Battered, bruised, exhausted, they yet recovered and lived to a good old age to tell the tale of their fight with the Columbia River.

From the Cascades to Vancouver, the company suffered more than in all the rest of their journey. The fall rains were at hand, and it poured with an unremitting energy such as no one can realise who has not seen a rain storm on the lower River. Food had become almost exhausted. Clothing was in rags. Tired, hungry, wet, cold, disheartened, the immigrants who had so jauntily descended the River to this "Strait of Horrors," presented a most woful appearance. It actually seemed that many must perish. But in the crisis, help came. One of the party managed to procure a canoe and hastened down the River to Fort Vancouver. As soon as Dr. McLoughlin learned that nearly nine hundred men, women, and children were beleaguered in the mist and chill, he equipped boats with flour, meat, and tea, and in his choleric excitement, waving his huge cane, bade the boatman hurry to the rescue. It was not business for the good Doctor to thus aid and abet American immigrants, and the directors of the Hudson's Bay Company and the cold-blooded Sir George Simpson, Governor-in-chief, disapproved. But it was humanity, and that ever predominated in the mind of "Old Whitehead." The next night he caused vast bonfires to be alight along the bank, and gathered all the eatables and blankets that the place afforded. When the boat loads of the battered, but rescued Americans drew near, the Doctor was on the bank to meet them, to hand out the women and children, to administer the balm of cheery words and warmth and food. Few were the travellers on the River, none were the immigrants of '43, who would not rise up and call him blessed.

After this happy pause at Vancouver, the immigration passed on to the Willamette Falls, then the centre of operations in Oregon, and there they were soon joined by the chosen men who had driven their thirteen hundred head of cattle by the trail over the Cascade Mountains, a task toilsome and even distressing, but one that was accomplished. After an inactive winter in the mild, muggy, misty Oregon climate, the immigrants of '43 spread abroad in the opening spring to secure land, each his square mile, as the Provisional Government provided, and as the American government was contemplating.

Such was the coming of the immigrants to the River. Subsequent immigrations bore a general resemblance to that of 1843. Each had its special feature. That of 1845 was conspicuous for its size. It was three thousand strong. It was also illustrious for the laying out of the road across the Cascade Mountains near the southern flank of Mt. Hood. This noble and difficult undertaking was carried through by S. K. Barlow and William Rector. It was a terrific task, and was not completed the first year. Cañons, precipitous rocks, morasses, sand-hills, tangled forests, fallen trees, criss-crossed and interlaced with briars and vines and shrubbery of tropical luxuriance, such as no one can appreciate who has not seen an Oregon jungle,—these were the obstructions to the Barlow Road. But they were vanquished and in 1846 and thence onward the immigrants made this the regular route to the Willamette Valley. So steep was Laurel Hill on the western slope that waggons had to be let down by ropes from level to level. The marks of the ropes or chains are still seen on the trees of Laurel Hill. The immigration of 1852 was sadly conspicuous for the devastations of cholera. Many a family was broken in sunder and some even were entirely eliminated by the dreadful plague. The immigrations of 1854 and 1855 were notable for the Indian outbreaks, and especially for the atrocious butchery of the Ward family near Boisé in the earlier year, the most pitiless Indian outrage in Oregon history.

From 1850 onward for some years the Donation Land Law of Congress was a great lure to immigrants, for by it a man and wife could obtain a section of land. A single man could take up half a section. That situation encouraged early marriages. Girls were in great demand. It was not uncommon to see fourteen-year-old brides. Some narrators relate having found married women in the woods of the Columbia who were playing with their dolls! But though the immigrations varied in special features, they were all alike in their mingling of mirth and melancholy, of toil and rest, of suffering and enjoyment, of heroism, and self-sacrifice. They embodied an epoch of American history that can never come again. To have been an immigrant from the Missouri to the Columbia was an experience to which nothing else on earth is comparable. It confers a title of American nobility by the side of which the coronets of some European dukes are tawdry and contemptible. Perhaps no one ever better phrased the spirit of Oregon immigration than Jesse Applegate of the train of '43, one of the foremost of Oregon's builders, long known as the "Sage of Yoncalla." So fitting do we deem his language that we quote here an extract from one of his addresses.

> The Western pioneer had probably crossed the Blue Ridge or the Cumberland Mountains when a boy and was now in his prime. Rugged, hardy, and powerful of frame, he was full to over-flowing with the love of adventure, and animated by a brave soul that scorned the very idea of fear. All had heard of the perpetually green hills and plains of Western Oregon, and how the warm breath of the vast Pacific tempered the air to the genial degree and drove winter back to the North. Many of them contrasted in imagination the open stretch of a mile square of rich, green, and grassy land, where the strawberry plant bloomed through every winter month, with their circumscribed clearings in the Missouri bottoms. Of long winter evenings neighbours visited each other, and before the big shell-bark hickory fire, the seasoned walnut fire, the dry black-jack fire, or the roaring dead elm fire, they talked these things over; and as a natural consequence, under these favourable circumstances, the spirit of emigration warmed up;

and the "Oregon fever" became as a household expression. Thus originated the vast cavalcade, or emigrant train, stretching its serpentine length for miles, enveloped in vast pillars of dust, patiently wending its toilsome way across the American continent.

How familiar these scenes and experiences with the old pioneers! The vast plains, the uncountable herds of buffalo; the swift-footed antelope; the bands of mounted, painted warriors; the rugged snow-capped mountain ranges; the deep, swift, and dangerous rivers; the lonesome howl of the wild wolf; the midnight yell of the assaulting savage; the awful panic and stampede; the solemn and silent funeral at the dead hour of night, and the lonely and hidden grave of departed friends,—what memories are associated with the Plains across!

CHAPTER VIII

CONFLICT OF NATIONS
FOR POSSESSION OF THE RIVER

The Six Nations at First Engaged in the Conflict—The Three Left in
it—Claims by Sea of Spain, England, and the United States—
Claims by Land—Rivalries of the Great Fur Companies—Capture
of Astoria by the English—Its Restoration to the United States—
Appearance of Fort George in 1818—Joint Occupation Treaty of
1818—Florida Treaty of 1819—Treaty with Russia in 1825—Forces on the Side of England and those on the side of the United
States—American Triumph Inevitable—Policy of the Hudson's
Bay Company in Contrast with that of the American Immigration—Indifference of the American Government—Utterances of
Some American Statesmen—Doings of the American People—
Gathering of the Little American Colony in the Willamette Valley—Need of Government—First Meeting at Champoeg—Advice
of Commodore Wilkes that they Delay—The "Wolf Meetings"—
Second Meeting at Champoeg, and Establishment of the Provi-
sional Government—Its Chief Provisions—Thornton's Account
of the "Hall" at Champoeg—Peter H. Burnett—Dr. McLoughlin's Position—Triumphs of the American Immigrant over the
Great Fur Company—McLoughlin and Whitman—Movements
of Diplomacy between England and the United States—Webster,
Linn, Benton, and Calhoun—Inconsistent Positions of the Democratic Party—Polk and the Platform of 54 Degrees 40 Minutes, or
Fight—Near Approach of War—Compromise on the Line of 49
Degrees—Momentous Nature of the Issue—Triumph of American Home-builders.

EARLIER chapters of this volume have already developed some of the essential
elements in the complicated strife of the maritime nations of the world for possession of the land of the Oregon. This brief chapter will endeavour to recapitulate
and group those steps, and to trace the course of events by which the line finally
was drawn on the parallel of 49 degrees.

As we have seen, the many-named river, and the fact that it was the key to a
vast region and that the shores of the ocean contiguous to it seemed to abound in
the finest of furs, was a lure to Portuguese, Frenchman, Russian, Spaniard, En-

glishman, and American. The first three became early eliminated from the conflict, and the last three fought the triangular battle to its ending with the final result that Uncle Sam inserted his broad shoulders between Mexico and the 49th parallel, and thus controls the choicest land of the sunset slope of the continent.

Spain, England, and the United States each had a valid claim to Oregon. Spain, by the partial discovery of the River by Heceta in 1775, by the voyages of Bodega and Arteaga in the same year and again in 1779, and by the voyage of Valdez and Galiano around Vancouver Island in 1792, together with many other voyages of a less definite nature by illustrious navigators, as Malaspina, Bustamente, Elisa, and others, had a strong position. Yet she had failed to clinch her discoveries or to take effective possession.

Great Britain could point to the elaborate examinations of Cook and Vancouver. The latter had made a minute investigation of the noble group of waters whose outlet preserves the name of the old Greek pilot of Cephalonia, Juan de Fuca; and his Lieutenant Broughton had entered the Columbia River and proceeded over a hundred miles up the stream. The nomenclature given to both the River and the Sound regions by Vancouver had been the first in any sense complete. So England, too, had a strong claim.

And what were the claims of the United States? First and foremost was the discovery by Robert Gray of the River and his actual twenty-five-mile ascension of it in May, 1792. He had gone much farther than Heceta, who had only looked in, but he had not gone so far as Broughton. The latter indeed, claimed, and his government followed him in the claim, that Gray had not really been in the River at all, but was only in an estuary of the sea into which the River flowed. But that, to any one who has seen the River, is too much of a forced construction to stand serious examination. Moreover, Gray antedated Broughton by some months.

Turning from sea claims to land claims, England could point to Alexander Mackenzie as having crossed the continent in 1792, and as having reached the veritable ocean at Cascade Inlet. But it again was a very strained construction to extend that claim so far as to include the lower Columbia Valley. The United States could justly advance as a sufficient offset, the expedition of Lewis and Clark in 1804. In 1811 David Thompson had traversed the entire length of the Columbia for the British flag, only to find the Astor Company already established under the Stars and Stripes at the mouth of the River. From these essential facts out of many, we can easily draw the conclusion that no one of these three contestants could justly be too arrogant and exclusive. Some degree of modesty was befitting each.

We have already seen the rivalries of the great fur companies, the Hudson's Bay and the North-western of the British, and the Pacific of the Americans, and the effect of the War of 1812 on their fortunes. As a result of that war the Pacific Fur Company sold out to the North-westers, and a few years later the North-westers united with the Hudson's Bay Company under the name of the latter. To all appearance the Yankee was worsted, and the Briton in possession of the River.

But the Treaty of Ghent in 1815, closing the War of 1812, provided that all territory taken by either party should be restored. The boundary line west of the

Lake of the Woods was left undrawn. John Jacob Astor now applied to the Government to restore his captured property on the Columbia, stating that if again in possession, he would resume his former operations. The United States Government accordingly notified Great Britain of its intention to re-occupy the fort at the Columbia's mouth. For two years the communication lay unanswered. In September, 1817, the sloop-of-war, *Ontario*, Captain J. Biddle, was despatched to the Columbia with Mr. J. B. Provost as special agent, under instructions to assert the claim of the United States to the territory of the River. This decisive move compelled Great Britain to come out from under cover. A long and tedious diplomatic warfare ensued. Meanwhile the *Ontario* was pursuing her long journey around Cape Horn. In 1818, an agreement was reached to the effect that Astoria should be formally restored to the United States, but that the North-western Fur Company should be allowed to remain in actual possession. Captain Biddle of the *Ontario* had left Mr. Provost in Chile and had proceeded to the Columbia to take possession. Captain Sheriff, commandant of the British ships in the Pacific, being in Valparaiso, in H. M. S. *Blossom*, learning of Mr. Provost's presence there, conceived the happy thought that it would be an international courtesy to invite Mr. Provost to accompany him to Astoria. Accordingly on October 1, 1818, the *Blossom* pushed her bow across the Bar, and on the 6th the formal ceremony of transfer from the Union Jack to the Stars and Stripes took place. Captain J. Hickey of the *Blossom* represented Great Britain, Mr. J. Keith acted for the North-west Fur Company, while Mr. Provost stood for the United States. It seems to have been a very good-natured affair throughout. Placards were posted at the capes on both sides of the River declaring the change of sovereignty. Fort George was quite a powerful structure at that time, consisting of a strong stockade of fir logs twelve feet high, enclosing a parallelogram one hundred and fifty by two hundred and fifty feet, having within it dwellings, shops, store houses, and magazines. On the walls were two eighteen-pound cannon, six six-pounders, four four-pound carronades, two six-pound cohorns, and seven swivels. The day of transfer must have been a very picturesque day among the many such in Astoria's history. We can imagine the soft October haze floating over Cape Hancock, and the long, lazy swell of six thousand miles of sea, thundering across Point Adams.

One interesting feature of Mr. Provost's presence at Astoria was his observation of the bar at the entrance of the River. This had generally been represented to the world as something frightful. It is often so represented at the present time. Mr. Provost in a letter to Secretary of State, John Quincy Adams, says that there is a spacious bay, by no means so difficult of ingress as has been represented. He states that there is a bar across the mouth of the River, at either extremity of which there are sometimes appalling breakers; but that there is a channel of nearly a league in width with a depth of twenty-one feet at the lowest tides. He thinks, therefore, that with proper buoys the access to vessels of almost any tonnage may be rendered secure. This statement in regard to the Bar is of much interest as furnishing a basis for comparison with the present conditions. The depth at low tide now is about twenty-six feet, the increase probably being due to the jetty.

The logic of the restoration of Astoria to the United States, while at the same time the British Fur Company was left in practical possession, was realised in the Joint Occupation Treaty of 1818. By this singular arrangement it was agreed that any country on the north-west coast of America that may be claimed by either power shall be open for ten years to the vessels, citizens, and subjects of the two powers.

In 1819 another very important step was taken; viz.: the Florida Treaty with Spain. By this, Spain retired to the line of 42 degrees, ceding to the American Republic all her rights above that line. With her own claims joined to those of Spain, the Republic would seem to be able to snap her fingers at England. But, with characteristic tenacity, the latter power made ready to insist all the more strenuously upon her claims. In 1825 England and the United States agreed with Russia upon the line of 54 degrees 40 minutes, as the southern line of Russian claims. With Spain and Russia out of it, Oregon was left for England and the United States to fight over. The Joint Occupation Treaty was to last ten years, with the privilege of renewal. Meanwhile what were the factors in the struggle for possession? There was on the side of England the Briarean monopoly of the Hudson's Bay Company, supported by a disciplined and intelligent government. But the English people were not in it. On the American side the Government was strangely indifferent. There were several ambitious attempts to control the situation by American trading and fur companies. But the essential forces were the American immigrant, the American missionary, the Declaration of Independence, and the ox-team. Those were the champions of America. They were the Davids against the Goliaths of British monopoly. At first thought it seemed that Goliath would have a "walk-over." The case seemed hopeless for the Americans.

But to the deeper observer, American triumph was inevitable. It was the Age of Democracy. The conception both of popular government and of individual ownership of land, with which went the corollary of "equal opportunities for all men and special privileges for none," was graven deep upon American character. With these things there went, of necessity, the disapproval of slavery and the support of free labour. Still further there went, by the same logic, the doctrine of unity and continental expansion. These various influences have constituted the broad foundation on which were reared the towers and battlements of American nationality.

In previous chapters we have outlined the operations of the Hudson's Bay Company, the coming of the missionaries, and the immigrations of Americans. The policy of the Hudson's Bay Company was to keep the country a wilderness, to maintain amicable relations with the Indians, and to depend mainly on the fur-trade for the great profits of their enterprise. The policy of the American immigrants was to build homes, cities, roads, steamboats, mills, develop the country, crowd out the natives, and depend on mining, farming, stock-raising, lumbering, for their profits; not profits of a monopoly located in a distant money centre, but profits of the individual worker on his own land. The difference was world-wide. It represented two different conceptions of government and of life itself.

But though the American people had the manifest destiny of expanding to the Pacific, the Government was strangely supine. We say "strangely," but it was not so strange after all. Congress was dominated by the South in the interest of slavery, and by the East in the interest of the tariff. Calhoun usually led the South, and he weighed everything in the scales of slavery. Webster governed Eastern sentiment largely, and he spoke for New England manufacturers. It is true that Clay was at all times a power in the councils of the nation, and Clay's constant word was nationalisation and expansion. But even Clay was so committed to the tariff that he did not always appreciate the possibilities of the "West-most West." The Presidents of the period from 1819 to 1846 were from the South or the Atlantic seaboard and not usually inclined to regard the far West with special interest.

The American people were away ahead of the American government in the struggle for possession of Oregon. A few of the utterances of leading statesmen of that period as significant of their conception of Oregon, may be given here. Benton, who became later the greatest champion of Oregon, was so imperfectly informed in 1825 that he spoke thus: "The ridge of the Rocky Mountains may be named as a convenient, natural, and everlasting boundary. Along this ridge the western limit of the Republic should be drawn, and the statue of the fabled god Terminus should be erected on its highest peak, never to be thrown down." But Benton improved, for later referring to the Columbia, he said, "That way lies the Orient." Webster said of Oregon: "What do we want of this vast, worthless area, this region of savages and wild beasts, of shifting sands and whirlwinds of dust, of cactus and prairie dogs. To what use could we ever hope to put these great deserts or these great mountain ranges, impenetrable and covered to their base with eternal snow? What can we ever hope to do with the western coast, a coast of three thousand miles, rock-bound, cheerless, and uninviting, and not a harbour on it? What use have we of such a country? Mr. President, I will never vote one cent from the public treasury to place the Pacific Coast one inch nearer Boston than it is now." And that was "God-like Dan!" Dayton expressed himself thus: "God forbid that the time should ever come when a State on the shores of the Pacific, with interests and tendencies of trade all looking toward the Asiatic nations of the East, shall add its jarring claims to our distracted and already overburdened confederacy." The *National Intelligencer* doubtless expressed a common sentiment in the following: "Of all the countries upon the face of the earth, Oregon is one of the least favoured by nature. It is almost as barren as Sahara and quite as unhealthy as the campagna of Italy."

Such an estimate by American statesmen was all right to the Hudson's Bay Company. They wished such an estimate and had taken pains to foster it. But while the gullible American statesmen were thus accepting just the version which their rivals were disseminating, the hard-handed and hard-headed, though not hard-hearted frontiersmen of Missouri and Illinois and Iowa were packing their ox-teams and starting across the desert for that Sahara on the Columbia River. Also one Marcus Whitman, a missionary physician of the Walla Walla, was floundering in the snows of the Sierra Madre and crossing the Arkansas through broken ice, in order to tell the benighted statesmen what the land of the Oregon really was like. The American people were busy, and the statesmen looked askance. And so, a few here and a few there, by trail or ship, adventurers, missionaries, sailors, trappers, there was formed a gathering in the Willamette of the advance guard of

American home-builders. They began to call out of the wilderness to Uncle Sam.

As a result of the coming of the missionaries and of the small immigrations of the thirties and early forties, together with the settlement in the Willamette Valley of various French-Canadian employees of the Hudson's Bay Company, there was enough of a population to demand some sort of organised society.

W. H. Gray made a summary of population in 1840 to consist of two hundred persons, of whom a hundred and thirty-seven were American and sixty-three Canadian. Up to 1839 the only law was the rules of the Hudson's Bay Company. In that year the Methodist missionaries suggested that two persons be named as magistrates to administer justice according to the ordinary rules of American law. This was the first move looking to American political organisation. In 1839 and 1840 memorials were presented to the Senate by Senator Linn of Missouri at the request of American settlers praying for the attention of Congress to their needs. But, not content with lifting their voices to the home land, they proceeded to organise for themselves.

At that time, Champoeg, a few miles above the falls of the Willamette and located pleasantly on the west bank of that river, was the chief settlement. There, on the seventh of February, 1841, a gathering of the settlers was held "for the purpose of consulting upon steps necessary to be taken for the formation of laws, and the election of officers to execute them." Jason Lee, the Methodist missionary, was chairman of the meeting, and he outlined what he deemed the needed method of establishing a reign of law and order. The meeting proved rather a conference than an organisation and the people dispersed to meet again at the call of the chairman.

A week later an event occurred which brought most forcibly to the minds of the settlers the need of better organisation. This was the death of Ewing Young, one of the most prominent men of the little community. He left considerable property, with no known heirs and no one to act as administrator. It became clear that some legal status must be established for the settlement. Another meeting was held, in which it was determined that a government be instituted, having the officers usual in an American locality. The work of framing a constitution was entrusted to a committee, in which the five different elements, the Methodist missionaries, the Catholics, the French Canadians, the independent American settlers, and the English, had representation. The committee was instructed to confer with Commodore Wilkes of the American Exploring Squadron, just at that time in the River, and Dr. McLoughlin, the Hudson's Bay magnate. Wilkes advised the settlers to wait for added strength and for the United States Government to throw its mantle over them. The committee decided that his advice was sound and indefinitely adjourned. Constitution building rested for a time along the shores of the Willamette.

In 1841 and 1842, two hundred and twenty Americans reached Oregon, doubling the population.

The Americans were ill at ease without a government and kept agitating the question of another meeting. But the English and the Catholic influences opposed this. Some diplomacy was needed. The irrepressible Yankees were equal to it. They determined to draw the settlers together under the announcement of a meeting for the purpose of discussing the means of protecting themselves against the ravages of the numerous wild beasts of the valley. W. H. Gray was the leading spirit in this enterprise. In a most picturesque and valuable account of it, John Minto has developed the thought that the founding of the Oregon State bore a striking resemblance to that stage in the Roman state, subsequently celebrated in the festival of Lupercalia, wherein the first organisation was for defence against the wild beasts. So the Willamette witnessed again the gathering of the clans, Americans, English, French, half-breeds, Catholics, Protestants, Independents, all coming together to protect themselves against the bears, cougars, and wolves. The meetings were usually known thereafter as the "wolf meetings."

James O'Neil was made chairman of this historic gathering. With the astuteness characteristic of American politicians, a previous understanding had been made between Mr. O'Neil and the little coterie of which Mr. Gray was the manager, that everything should be shaped to the ultimate end of raising the question of a government. As soon, therefore, as the ostensible aim of the meeting had been attained, W. H. Gray arose and broached the all-important issue. After declaring that no one could question the wisdom and rightfulness of the measures looking to protecting their herds from wild beasts, he continued:

> How is it, fellow-citizens, with you and me, and our wives and children? Have we any organisation on which we can rely for mutual protection? Is there any power in the country sufficient to protect us and all that we hold dear, from the worse than wild beasts that threaten and occasionally destroy our cattle? We have mutually and unitedly agreed to defend and protect our cattle and domestic animals; now, therefore, fellow-citizens, I submit and move the adoption of the two following resolutions, that we may have protection for our lives and persons, as well as our cattle and herds: *Resolved* that a committee be appointed to take into consideration the propriety of taking measures for the civil and military protection of this colony; *Resolved* that this committee consist of twelve persons.

There spoke the true voice of the American state-builder, the voice of the Declaration of Independence and the Constitution. The resolutions were passed and the committee of twelve appointed, mainly Americans. The committee met at the Falls of the Willamette, which by that time was becoming known as Oregon City. Unable to arrive at a definite decision, the committee issued a call for a general meeting at Champoeg on May 2d.

Pending the meeting, there was a general policy of opposition developed among the French Canadians in the interest of the Hudson's Bay Company and England. This opposition threatened the overthrow of the entire plan. It was, however, checkmated in an interesting fashion. George W. Le Breton was one of the leading settlers and occupied a peculiar position. He was of French origin, from Baltimore to Oregon, and had been a Catholic. His existing affiliations were with the Americans. He was keen, facile, and well educated. He discovered that the Canadians had been drilled to vote "No" on all questions, irrespective of the bearing which such a vote might have on the leading issue. Le Breton accordingly proposed that measures be introduced upon which the Canadians ought to vote "Yes." These tactics were carried out. The Canadians were confused thereby. Le Breton watched developments carefully and, becoming satisfied that he could command a majority, rose and exclaimed, "We can risk it, let us divide and count!" Gray shouted, "I second the motion!" Jo Meek, famous as one of the Mountain Men, stepped out of the crowd and said, "Who is for a divide? All in favour of an organisation, follow me!" The Americans speedily gathered behind the tall form of the erstwhile trapper. A count followed. It was a close vote. Fifty-two voted for, and fifty against. The Americans would have been outvoted had it not been that Le Breton, with two French Canadians, François Matthieu and Étienne Lucier, voted with them. The defeated Canadians withdrew, and the Indians, who lined the banks of the River to discover what strange proceedings the white men were engaged in, perceived from the loud shouts of triumph that the "Bostons" had won. Though the victory was gained by so scanty a margin, it was gained, and it was decisive. It was one of the most interesting events in the history of Oregon or the United States, for it illustrates most vividly the inborn capacity of the American for self-government.

The new government went at once into effect. The constitution formulated by the committee and adopted by the meeting at Champoeg provided that the people of Oregon should adopt laws and regulations until the United States extended its jurisdiction over them. Freedom of worship, habeas corpus, trial by jury, proportionate representation, and the usual civil rights of Americans were guaranteed. Education should be encouraged, lands and property should not be taken from Indians without their consent. Slavery or involuntary servitude should not exist.

The officers of government consisted of a legislative body of nine persons, an executive body of three, and a judiciary of a supreme judge and two justices of the peace, with a probate court and its justices, and a recorder and treasurer. Every white man of twenty-one years or more could vote. The laws of Iowa were designated to be followed in common practice. Marriage was allowed to males at sixteen and females at fourteen. One of the most important provisions was the land law. This permitted any individual to claim a mile square, provided it be not on a town site or water-power, and that any mission claims already made be not affected, up to the limit of six miles square. This land law was framed upon the general conception of the proposed Linn bill already brought before Congress. The land law allowed land to be taken in any form, but since there was no existing survey, each man had to make his own survey.

The first elected executive committee consisted of David Hill, Alanson Beers, and Joseph Gale. Within a year an amendment was made to the constitution providing for a governor. George Abernethy, a former member of the Methodist mission, was chosen to fill the place.

Outer things were pretty crude in the little colony on the Willamette, though brains and energy were there in abundance. J. Quinn Thornton expressed himself as follows on the "Oregon State House," which he says was in several respects different from that in which laws are made at Washington City:

The Oregon State House was built with posts set upright, one end set in the ground, grooved on two sides, and filled in with poles and split timber, such as would be suitable for fence rails, with plates and poles across the top. Rafters and horizontal poles, instead of iron ribs, held the cedar bark which was used instead of thick copper for roofing. It was twenty by forty feet and therefore did not cover three acres and a half. At one end some puncheons were put up for a platform for the president; some poles and slabs were placed around for seats; three planks, about a foot wide and twelve feet long, placed upon a sort of stake platform for a table, were all that was believed necessary for the use of the legislative committee and the clerks.

There are several facts in connection with the inauguration of this Provisional Government of Oregon which are almost equal to itself in interest. One of these is that Peter H. Burnett, a lawyer and the most notable member of the emigration of 1843, rendered the opinion that, by the spirit of American institutions, the Provisional Government might be regarded as possessing valid authority. Going in a few years to California, Mr. Burnett incorporated the same principles into the government of that State and became its first governor.

Another most significant fact was the attitude of the Hudson's Bay Company. That great organisation was of course opposed to American ownership and to the Provisional Government. At first, the management under Sir James Douglas (Dr. McLoughlin had been superseded by Douglas because of his supposed leaning toward the Americans) affected to ignore the government framed at Champoeg, declaring loftily that the company could protect itself. Dr. McLoughlin, in his very interesting account of this, says that the Americans adopted in 1845 a provision in the constitution that no one should be called to do any act contrary to his allegiance. This provision struck him as designed to enable British subjects to join the organisation. Dr. McLoughlin was so pleased with the wise and liberal spirit which this evinced that he prevailed on Douglas to join the Provisional Government. The family was now complete. The American farmers and immigrants and missionaries had triumphed over the autocratic government of the great fur company. The American idea—government of the people, by the people, and for the people—was vindicated. The local battle was won for the Yankee.

Before leaving this great epoch of the history of the River, it will interest the reader to know that Dr. McLoughlin, so conspicuous in the story thus far, removed to Oregon City, and became an avowed American citizen, living on the claim on which he filed at the Falls. Much trouble subsequently arose between him and the Methodist mission people represented by Rev. A. F. Waller. Harder yet, Congress was led by Delegate Thurston of Oregon, to exclude him from the benefit of the Donation Land Law. The final result was that the great-hearted ex-king of the Columbia lost the most of his claim on the ground that he was an alien at the time of taking it. The Hudson's Bay Company directors chose to disapprove his acts in bestowing provisions upon the weary and hungry and ragged American immigrants, and they charged him personally with the cost. This, in addition to the loss of his claim, rendered him almost penniless and sadly embittered his old age. He said that he supposed he was becoming an American, but found that he was neither American nor British, but was without a country. It is pleasant to be able to record the fact that the Oregon Legislature restored his land in so far as the State controlled it, but this was only just before his death.

Of all the brave and big-souled men who bore their part in redeeming Oregon and the Columbia from the wilderness, John McLoughlin has stood at the head of the column, side by side with Marcus Whitman, the American physician and missionary. Though identified at first with rival interests and conflicting aims, McLoughlin and Whitman had many traits in common, and the story of their lives and life-work in Oregon should be written in one chapter. No one that ever knew or sympathised with Oregon history has failed to give his meed of praise to both Whitman and McLoughlin. No one ever stood on the hill at Waiilatpu and viewed the mission home of Whitman in the fertile vale of the Walla Walla, the scene of martyrdom and anguish, without joining it in mind with the expanse of the Columbia at Vancouver and recalling "Old Whitehead," and his large-minded and humane lordship for twenty years of the land of the Oregon. Nor can one withhold the thrill of indignation at the cold-blooded commercialism of the Hudson's Bay Company, and at the petty ingratitude of some Americans, which together brought darkness to the old hero's last days.

But though American Democracy was winning a bloodless triumph on the Columbia, it seemed by no means certain that American diplomacy would win on the Potomac. Webster, as Secretary of State under Harrison and during part of Tyler's administration, represented the conservative councils of the New England seaboard, and was inclined to yield to England in respect to the Oregon boundary.

Senator Linn of Missouri was the most steadfast friend of American occupancy. He was the one to frame land bills to encourage American immigration, and in his hands the memorials of the settlers on the Columbia had been placed. But in 1843, he died, with his work undone. Benton, his colleague, had meanwhile become fully as pronounced, and he pursued the same policy with uncompromising and volcanic energy.

But a curious and anomalistic alignment of interests and parties now arose. The Oregon question became entangled with those of Texas and slavery. Calhoun became Tyler's Secretary of State upon Webster's resignation. While the Democrats in general were more inclined to western expansion than the Whigs, yet the slaveholders of the South were much more interested in Texas than in Oregon. The Provisional Government of Oregon had prohibited slavery. Calhoun was ready to fight Mexico for the possession of Texas, but he did not want to fight England for possession of Oregon. Nevertheless, he did not dare to offend the West by a square back-down on Oregon. He therefore adopted a policy of "masterly inactivity." He believed that if war arose with England, we would lose "every inch of Oregon," for England could hurry a fleet to the Columbia River from China in six weeks, whereas American ships would have to double Cape Horn, and an American army would have to cross the continent under every disadvantage of transportation. But time, he believed, would win all for the Americans.

In this conception, Von Holst thinks Calhoun was wise. Roosevelt in his *Life of Benton*, thinks that the war, if there had been war, would have been fought out in Canada, and that, while Calhoun was not wrong in desiring delay, he should never have abated one jot in demanding all of Oregon up to 54 degrees 40 minutes.

The Democratic platform on which Polk was elected President, demanded "54 degrees 40 minutes," and, in popular clamour, the words, "or fight," were added. Oregon, Texas, and slavery were practically the issues on which Polk was elected. His inaugural address declared our title to Oregon to be "clear and unquestionable." Great excitement ensued, for if Congress stood by the President, war was almost inevitable, unless England yielded. To the surprise of the world, however, James Buchanan, the yielding, not to say shifty, Secretary of State under the new administration, now announced the willingness of our Government to compromise on the line of 49 degrees. But here another complication ensued. Pakenham, the British envoy, declined, in almost insulting terms, to accept 49 degrees. Polk thereupon withdrew the proposition and in his next message stated that "no compromise which the United States ought to accept can be effected." At the same time he advised the cancellation of the Joint Occupation Treaty. It seemed now that the conflict between the nations for the possession of the River would surely eventuate in war. Senator Cass of Michigan fanned the flame by a speech declaring that "War is almost upon us." The committees on Foreign Relations in both House and Senate proposed resolutions to notify England at once of the close of the Joint Occupation Treaty. Excitement rose to fierce heat, and the standing of marine risks and commercial ventures at once showed the popular sentiment. "Fifty-four, forty, or fight!" was the spirit of Congress.

But now Calhoun found himself betwixt the devil and the deep sea. He did not really wish to get all of Oregon, for fear of the effect on slavery. Yet he dared not throw cold water on the tremendous spirits of patriotism and ambition in the West demanding Oregon. A compromise was the only recourse. Powerful men of the "Moderates" in both England and the United States brought their influence to bear. Calhoun caused Lord Aberdeen, Foreign Secretary of England, to understand that the President would again take up the line of 49 degrees. Lord Aberdeen directed Pakenham to revive the negotiations which had been somewhat rudely broken off. The Senate reconsidered the situation more calmly and opened the way to a new treaty. This was consummated and signed by President Polk on June 15, 1846, and confirmed by the Senate on June 19th. The line of 49 degrees was accepted. The Great River was divided by that line nearly equally between the two nations, there being about seven hundred and fifty miles in American territory and six hundred and fifty in British.

The decision of the ownership of the River was one of the most momentous in American history. If we had not got Oregon, we probably would not have got California. And without the Pacific Coast, the history of the Great Republic would be essentially different, and the history of the world would be essentially different.

The Oregon Question owed much of its interest to its very complicated nature. It was at first a question between the governments of five different nations, England, France, Russia, Spain, and the United States. In time it became a question between England and the United States. Then it was a question between Oregon immigrants and British Fur Company. Then it became a question between slavery and freedom. This was still further complicated by the fact that it was also a question between West, East, and South. Different factions of different parties still further complicated it. It was in truth a manifold question, and in its final solution we read some of the most vital of American traits and movements. Out of it all the settlers of the River may justly be said to have emerged with highest credit. The American home-builder, the great Democracy of the West, the inborn impulse to expand and to nationalise,—these were the essential factors in the triumph. The settlers on the Willamette, the constitution-makers of Champoeg, the immigrants and the missionaries, had already gained the day before diplomacy took it up.

CHAPTER IX

THE TIMES OF TOMAHAWK AND FIREBRAND

Extent of Indian Troubles in the Region of the Columbia—Destruction of the *Tonquin*—Conflicting Policies of the British and the Americans in Regard to the Fur-trade—Advances in Settlement by Americans, and Indian Opposition—The Whitman Mission and its Relations to the Indians, and to the Hudson's Bay Company—The Pestilence of 1847—The Whitman Massacre—Mr. Osborne's Reminiscences—Saving of the Lapwai and Tshimakain Missions—The Cayuse War—Great War of 1855-56—Kamiakin and Peupeumoxmox—Governor I. I. Stevens of Washington Territory and his Efforts to Make Treaties—The Walla Walla Council and the Division among the Indians—Pearson and his Ride—Outburst of Hostilities and the Destruction that Followed—Conflict between the Regulars and the Volunteers—Battles of Walla Walla, Cascades, and Grande Ronde—Second Walla Walla Council—An Unsatisfactory Peace—Continued Incoming of Prospectors and Land-seekers—Third Indian War—Disastrous Steptoe Campaign—Garnett's Campaign in the Yakima—Wright's Campaign to Spokane and Overthrow of Indian Power—Peace Proclaimed and the Country Thrown Open to Settlement—Nez Percé War of 1877—Hallakallakeen, or Joseph, the Indian Warchief—His Melancholy Fate—The Bannock War.

COLUMBIA RIVER history has had its full share of Indian wars. To narrate these in full would transcend the limits of this chapter. Even during the era of discovery desperate affrays with the natives were a common experience of explorers. Captain Gray of the *Columbia* lost a boat's crew of seamen at Tillamook. The ship *Boston* was seized in 1803 by the wily old chief Maquinna at Nootka.

In 1812 the *Tonquin*, the first vessel of the Pacific Fur Company, in command of Captain Thorn, was captured at some point to the north of the Columbia River, variously known as Eyuck Whoola on Newcetu Bay, or Newity Bay, or Newcetee. She was, as a result of the capture, blown up by the explosion of her own powder magazine. Gabriel Franchère and Alexander Ross, of the Astoria party, are the original authorities for this dramatic story. Irving has made the event a leading feature of his charming *Astoria*. H. H. Bancroft has discussed it at length in his history of the Pacific Coast. In recent years Major H. M. Chittenden in his valuable book, *History of the American Fur Trade,* presents new testimony of much interest. But whatever discrepencies existed in the records, the general truth remains that the ship and all her crew, with the exception of one Indian, disappeared, and great was the loss to the traders at Astoria as a result.

For more than three decades after the destruction of the *Tonquin* there were no serious Indian conflicts. The Hudson's Bay Company carried out consistently the general policy of harmony with the natives. Most of the employees were of French Canadian origin, and, with their general sociability, they were more popular with the Indians than the Americans usually have been. But with the incoming of American missionaries, trappers, explorers, and immigrants, the situation changed. Conflicts of interests, ambitions, and national aims led both Americans and British to be somewhat more ready to encourage the hostile and suspicious disposition of the natives. Chiefly, however, the cause of the changing attitude of the natives must be attributed to the perception by the more intelligent of the fact that the actual occupation of the country by white farmers, home builders, and land owners, meant their own destruction. Though this truth dawned on them only vaguely and gradually, they had begun to be somewhat familiar with it by the decade of the thirties.

The founding of American missions during that decade, as narrated earlier, at Chemeketa, Walla Walla, Lapwai, and Tshimakain, and, during the years following, the obvious intent of the Americans to draw immigration to the country, prepared the way for the first and perhaps the most ferocious, though by no means the greatest, of the four principal wars which we plan to consider. This first one was the war connected with the Whitman massacre.

We have already described the founding of the Whitman Mission at Waiilatpu, six miles from the present site of Walla Walla, and twenty-six miles from the Hudson's Bay fort on the Columbia, known as Fort Walla Walla. We have also told of Whitman's journey across the continent in the mid-winter of 1842-43, of his efforts to secure the attention of Congress and of the Executive to the importance of the Oregon country, and of his return to Walla Walla in 1843, with the first large immigration of American settlers.

After the incoming of this immigration, it became more than ever clear to the more intelligent Indians that this movement of settlers portended a change in their whole condition. Their wild life could not co-exist with farming, houses, and the fixed and narrowed limits of the white man's life. Moreover, since they saw the antagonism between the Americans and the Hudson's Bay Company, and since the latter was obviously more favourable to perpetuating the life of the wilderness, the natives were naturally drawn into sympathy with the latter. Still further, since the Americans were Protestants and naturally affiliated with the Whitman Mission and its associated missions, and since the Hudson's Bay people were mainly Catholics and interested in maintaining the missionary methods adapted to the régime of the fur-traders, there became injected into the situation the dangerous element of religious jealousy.

Dr. Whitman perceived that he was standing on the edge of a powder magazine, and, during the summer of 1847, he arranged to acquire the mission property of the Methodists at The Dalles, a hundred and sixty miles down the River, intending to remove thither in the spring. But meanwhile, the explosives being all ready, the spark was prepared for igniting them.

During the summer of 1847 measles became epidemic among the Indians. Their method of treating any disease of which fever was a part was to enter a pit into which hot rocks had been thrown, then casting water on the rocks, to create a dense vapour, in which, stripped of clothing, they would remain until thoroughly steamed. Thence issuing, stark naked and dripping with perspiration, they would plunge into an icy cold stream. Death was the almost inevitable result in case of measles. Whitman, who was, it should be remembered, a physician, not a clergyman, was skilful and devoted in his attentions, yet many died. Now just at that time a renegade half-breed known as Jo Lewis seems to have become possessed with the diabolical mania of massacre. He made the Indians think that Whitman was poisoning them. Istickus or Sticcus, a Umatilla Indian and a warm friend of Whitman, had formed some impression of the plot and suggested the danger. Whitman's intrepid spirit laughed at this, but Mrs. Whitman, though equally intrepid, seems to have felt some premonition of the swift coming doom, for the mission children found her in tears for the first time since the death of her beloved little girl eight years before. The Doctor tried to soothe her by declaring that he would arrange to go down the River at once. But on that very day, November 28, 1847, the picturesque little hill rising a hundred feet above the mission ground, now surmounted by the granite shaft of the Whitman monument, was observed to be black with Indians. It was evident from various sinister aspects that something was impending.

On the next day, November 29th, at about one o'clock, while Dr. Whitman sat reading, a number of Indians entered the room. Having gained his attention by the usual request for medicines, one of them, afterwards said by some to have been Tamahas, and by others have been Tamsaky, rushed suddenly upon the Doctor and struck his head with a tomahawk. Another wretch named Telaukait, to whom the Doctor had been the kindest friend, then cut and hacked the noble face of the philanthropist. The work of murder thus inaugurated went on with savage energy. The men about the mission were speedily slain, with the exception of a few who were in remote places and managed by special fortune to elude observation. Mrs. Whitman, bravely coming forward to succour her dying husband, was shot in the breast and sank to the floor. She did not die at once, and it is said by some of the survivors, then children, that she lingered some time, being heard to murmur most tender prayers for her parents and children. Mrs. Whitman was the only woman killed. The other women and girls were cruelly outraged and held in captivity for several days.

William McBean was at that time in charge of the fort at Walla Walla, and with a strange disregard of humane feelings, he shut the door of the fort in the face of one of the escaped Americans, and a little later served the Osborne family in the same manner. McBean sent a courier down the River to convey the tidings to Vancouver, but this courier did not even stop at The Dalles to warn the people, though they were not attacked. James Douglas was then chief factor at Vancouver, as successor to Dr. McLoughlin. As soon as he was apprised of the massacre, he sent Peter Skeen Ogden with a force to rescue the survivors. Ogden acted with promptness and efficiency, and by the use of several hundred dollars' worth of commodities ransomed forty-seven women and children. Thirteen persons had been murdered.

One of the most distressing experiences was that of the Osborne family. Of this Mr. Osborne says:

> As the guns fired and the yells commenced I leaned my head upon the bed and committed myself and family to my Maker. My wife removed the loose floor. I dropped under the floor with my sick family in their night clothes, taking only two woollen sheets, a piece of bread, and some cold mush, and pulled the floor over us. In five minutes the room was full of Indians, but they did not discover us. The roar of guns, the yells of the savages, and the crash of clubs and knives and the groans of the dying continued till dark. We distinctly heard the dying groans of Mrs. Whitman, Mr. Rogers, and Francis, till they died away one after the other. We heard the last words of Mr. Rogers in a slow voice calling "Come, Lord Jesus, come quickly." Soon after this I removed the floor and we went out. We saw the white face of Francis by the door. It was warm as we laid our hand upon it, but he was dead. I carried my two youngest children, who were sick, and my wife held on to my clothes in her great weakness. We had all been sick with measles. Two infants had died. She had not left her bed in six weeks till that day, when she stood up a few minutes. The naked, painted Indians were dancing the scalp dance around a large fire at a little distance. There seemed no hope for us and we knew not which way to go, but bent our steps toward Fort Walla Walla. A dense cold fog shut out every star and the darkness was complete. We could see no trail and not even the hand before the face. We had to feel out the trail with our feet. My wife almost fainted but staggered along. Mill Creek, which we had to wade, was high with late rains and came up to the waist. My wife in her great weakness came nigh washing down, but held to my clothes. I braced myself with a stick, holding a child in one arm. I had to cross five times for the children. The water was icy cold and the air freezing some. Staggering along about two miles, Mrs. Osborne fainted and could go no farther, and we hid ourselves in the brush of the Walla Walla River, not far below Tamsukey's (a chief) lodges, who was very active at the commencement of the butchery. We were thoroughly wet, and the cold fog like snow was about us. The cold mud was partially frozen as we crawled, feeling our way, into the dark brush. We could see nothing, the darkness was so extreme. I spread one wet sheet down on the frozen ground; wife and chil-

dren crouched upon it. I covered the other over them. I thought they must soon perish as they were shaking and their teeth rattling with cold. I kneeled down and commended us to my Maker. The day finally dawned and we could see the Indians riding furiously up and down the trail. Sometimes they would come close to the brush and our blood would warm and the shaking would stop from fear for a moment. The day seemed a week. Expected every moment my wife would breathe her last. Tuesday night, felt our way to the trail and staggered along to Sutucksnina (Dog Creek), which we waded as we did the other creek, and kept on about two miles when my wife fainted and could go no farther. Crawled into the brush and frozen mud to shake and suffer on from hunger and cold, and without sleep. The children, too, wet and cold, called incessantly for food, but the shock of groans and yells at first so frightened them that they did not speak loud. Wednesday night my wife was too weak to stand. I took our second child and started for Walla Walla; had to wade the Touchet; stopped frequently in the brush from weakness; had not recovered from measles. Heard a horseman pass and repass as I lay concealed in the willows. Have since learned that it was Mr. Spalding. Reached Fort Walla Walla after daylight; begged Mr. McBean for horses to get my family, for food, for blankets, and clothing to take to them, and to take care of my child till I could bring my family in, should I live to find them alive. Mr. McBean told me I could not bring my family to his fort.

Mr. Hall came in on Monday night, but he could not have an American in his fort, and he had put him over the Columbia River; that he could not let me have horses or anything for my wife and children, and I must go to Umatilla. I insisted on bringing my family to the fort, but he refused; said he would not let us in. I next begged the priests to show pity, as my wife and children must perish and the Indians undoubtedly would kill me, with no success. I then begged to leave my child who was not safe in the fort, but they refused.

There were many priests in the fort. Mr. McBean gave me breakfast, but I saved most of it for my family. Providentially Mr. Stanley, an artist, came in from Colville, narrowly escaped the Cayuse Indians by telling them he was "Alain" H. B. He let me have his two horses, some food he had left from Rev. Eells and Walker's mission; also a cap, a pair of socks, a shirt, and handkerchief, and Mr. McBean furnished an Indian who proved most faithful, and Thursday night we started back, taking my child, but with a sad heart that I could not find mercy at the hands of the priests of God. The Indian guided me in the thick darkness to where I supposed I had left my dear wife and children. We could see nothing and dared not call aloud. Daylight came and I was exposed to Indians, but we continued to search till I was about to give up in despair when the Indian discovered one of the twigs I had broken as a guide in coming out to the trail. Following these he soon found my wife and children still alive. I distributed what little food and clothing I had, and we started for the Umatilla, the guide leading the way to a ford.

Mr. McBean came and asked who was there. I replied. He said he could not let us in; we must go to Umatilla or he would put us over the river, as he had Mr. Hall. My wife replied she would die at the gate but she would not leave. He finally opened and took us into a secret room and sent an allowance of food for us every day. Next day I asked him for blankets for my sick wife to lie on. He had nothing. Next day I urged again. He had nothing to give, but would sell a blanket out of the store. I told him I had lost everything, and had nothing to pay; but if I should live to get to the Willamette I would pay. He consented. But the hip-bones of my dear wife wore through the skin on the hard floor. Stickus, the chief, came in one day and took the cap from his head and gave it to me, and a handkerchief to my child.

The Whitman massacre was a prelude to the Cayuse War. It should be remembered that, the year before the massacre, the Oregon country had, by treaty with Great Britain, become the property of the United States. No regular government had yet been inaugurated, but the Provisional Government already instituted by the Americans met on December 9th and provided for sending fourteen companies of volunteers to the Walla Walla. These were immigrants who had come to seek homes and their section of land, and it was a great sacrifice for them to leave their families and start in mid-winter for the upper Columbia. But they bravely and cheerfully obeyed the call of duty and set forth, furnishing mainly their own equipment, without a thought of pecuniary gain or even reimbursement. Cornelius Gilliam, an immigrant of 1845 from Missouri, was chosen colonel of the regiment. He was a man of great energy and courage, and though not a professional soldier,—none of them were,—had the frontier American's capacity for warfare. The command pushed rapidly forward, their way being disputed at various points. At Sand Hollows the Indians, led by Five Crows and War Eagle, made an especially tenacious attempt to prevent the crossing of the Umatilla River. Five Crows claimed to have wizard powers by which he could stop all bullets, and War Eagle declared that he could swallow all balls fired at him. But at the first onset the wizard was so badly wounded that he had to retire and "Swallow Ball" was killed. Tom McKay had levelled his rifle and said, "Let him swallow this."

The way was now clear to Waiilatpu, which the command reached on March 4th. The mangled remains of the victims of the massacre had been hastily interred by the Ogden party, but coyotes had partially exhumed them. The remains were brought together by the volunteers and reverently, though rudely, buried at a point near the mission, a place where a marble crypt now encloses the commingled bones of the martyrs. A lock of long, fair hair was found near the ruined mission ground which was thought surely to be from the head of Mrs. Whitman. It was preserved by one of the volunteers and is now one of the precious relics in the historical museum of Whitman College.

Grave of Marcus Whitman and his Associate Martyrs at Waiilatpu.

Photo. by W. D. Chapman.

Cayuse Babies 1.
Copyright by Lee Moorehouse, 1898.

Cayuse Babies 2.
Copyright by Lee Moorehouse, 1898.

The Cayuse War dragged along in a desultory fashion for nearly three years. The refusal of the Nez Percés and Spokanes and the indifference of the Yakimas to join the Cayuses made their cause hopeless, though there were several fierce fights with them and much severe campaigning. In 1850 a band of friendly Umatilla Indians undertook to capture the chief band of the Cayuses under Tamsaky, which had taken a strong position about the head waters of the John Day River. After a savage battle Tamsaky was killed and most of the warriors captured. Of these, five, charged with the leading part in the Whitman massacre, were hanged at Oregon City on June 3, 1850. It remains a question to this day, however, whether the victims of the gallows were really the guilty ones. The Cayuse Indians were quite firm in their assertion that Tamahas, who, by one version, struck Dr. Whitman the first blow, was the only one of the five concerned in the murder.

Thus ended the first principal war in the Columbia Basin. It was quickly followed by another, which was so extensive that it may be well called universal. This was the War of 1855-56. This was the greatest Indian war in the entire history of the Columbia River.

As we have seen, the American home-builders had outmatched the English fur-traders in the struggle for possession. On the 3d of March, 1853, Washington Territory, embracing the present States of Washington and Idaho, with parts of Wyoming and Montana, was created by Act of Congress, and Isaac I. Stevens was appointed governor. This remarkable man entered with tremendous energy upon his task of organising the chaos of his great domain. The Indian problem was obviously the most dangerous and pressing one. There were at that time two remarkable chiefs of the mid-Columbia region, natural successors of Philip, Pontiac, Black Hawk, and Tecumseh, possessing those Indian traits of mingled nobleness and treachery which have made the best specimens of the race such interesting objects of study. These Indians were Kamiakin of the Yakimas, and Peupeumoxmox of the Walla Wallas.

In 1855 the great war broke out almost simultaneously at different points. There were six widely scattered regions especially concerned. Four of these, the Cascades, the Yakima Valley, the Walla Walla, and the Grande Ronde, were on or adjacent to the River. The others were the Rogue River region and Puget Sound. So wide was the area of this war that intelligent co-operation among the Indians proved impracticable. This, in fact, was the thing that saved the whites. For there were probably not less than four thousand Indians on the war-path, and if they had co-operated, the smaller settlements, possibly all in the country except those in the Willamette Valley, might have been annihilated.

The first efforts of Governor Stevens were to secure treaties with the Indians. Having negotiated several treaties in 1854 with the Puget Sound Indians, the governor passed over the Cascade Mountains to Walla Walla in May, 1855. There during the latter part of May and first part of June, he held a great council with representatives of seventeen tribes. Lieutenant Kip, U. S. A., has preserved a vivid account of this great gathering, one of the most important ever held in the annals of Indian history. According to Lieutenant Kip, there were but about fifty men in the escort of the daring governor, and if he had been a man sensible to fear he might well have been startled when there came an army of twenty-five hundred Nez Percés under Halhaltlossot, known as Lawyer by the whites. Two days later three hundred Cayuses, those worst of the Columbia River Indians, surly and scowling, led by Five Crows and Young Chief, made their appearance. Two days later a force of two thousand Yakimas, Umatillas, and Walla Wallas came in sight under Kamiakin and Peupeumoxmox. The council was soon organised. Governor Stevens and General Palmer, the latter the Indian Agent for Oregon, set forth their plan of reservations, all their speeches being translated and retranslated until they had filtered down among the general mass of the Indians. Then there must be a great "wawa," or discussion by the Indians. It soon became apparent that there were two bitterly contesting parties. One was a large faction of Nez Percés led by Lawyer, who favoured the whites. The other faction of the Nez Percés, with all the remaining tribes, were set against any treaty. With remarkable skill and patience, Governor Stevens, with the powerful assistance of Lawyer, had brought the Indians to a point of general agreement to the creation of a system of reservations. But suddenly there was a commotion. Into the midst of the council there burst the old chief Looking Glass (Apashwahayikt), second only to Lawyer in influence among the Nez Percés. He had made a desperate ride of three hundred miles in seven days, following a buffalo hunt and a raid against the Blackfeet, and as he now burst into the midst, there dangled from his belt the scalps of several slaughtered Blackfeet. As quoted in Hazard Stevens's *Life of Governor Stevens*, he began his harangue thus: "My people, what have you done? While I was gone you sold my country. I have come home and there is not left me a place on which to pitch my lodge. Go home to your lodges. I will talk with you." Lieutenant Kip declares that though he could understand nothing of the speech of Looking Glass to his own tribe, which followed, the effect was tremendous. All the evidence showed that Looking Glass was a veritable Demosthenes. The work of Governor Stevens was all undone.

But later the Governor and Lawyer succeeded in rallying their forces and gaining the acquiescence of the Indians to the setting aside of three great reservations, one on the Umatilla, one on the Yakima, and the third on the Clearwater and the Snake. These reservations still exist, imperial domains in themselves, though now divided into individual allotments. The acquiescence of the Indians in this treaty, as the sequel proved, was feigned by a number of them, but for the time it seemed a great triumph for Governor Stevens. From Walla Walla the Governor departed to the Cœur d'Alene, the Pend Oreille, and the Missoula regions to continue his arduous task of negotiating treaties.

This great Walla Walla Council cannot be dismissed without brief reference to an event, not fully known at the time, but which subsequent investigation made clear, and stamped as one of the most dramatic in the entire history of Indian warfare. This event was the conspiracy of the Cayuses and Yakimas to kill Governor Stevens and his entire band, and then exterminate the whites throughout the country. While the acceptance of the treaty was still pending, Kamiakin and Peupeumoxmox were framing the details of this wide-reaching plot, which was indeed but the culmination of their great scheme of years. Kamiahkin was the soul of the conspiracy. He was a remarkable Indian. He was of superb stature, and proportions, over six feet high, sinewy and active. Governor Stevens said of him: "He is a peculiar man, reminding me of the panther and the grizzly bear. His countenance has an extraordinary play, one moment in frowns, the next in smiles, flashing with light and black as Erebus the same instant. His pantomime is great, and his gesticulation much and characteristic. He talks mostly in his face and with his hands and arms." He was withal a typical Indian in treachery and secretiveness. Peupeumoxmox was similar in nature, but was older and less capable.

Exactly opposite to these was Halhaltlossot, or Lawyer, the Solon of the Nez Percés. Lawyer became convinced of the existence of this conspiracy and went by night to the camp of Governor Stevens and revealed it. He concluded his revelation by saying: "I will come with my family and pitch my lodge in the midst of your camp, that those Cayuses may see that you and your party are under the protection of the head chief of the Nez Percés." When it became clear to the conspiring Cayuses and Yakimas that Lawyer's powerful division of the Nez Percés was sustaining the little band of whites, they did not execute their design. Lawyer and his Nez Percés saved the day for the whites.

And yet the sequel is one of the most lamentable examples of the miscarriage of justice in Indian affairs that we have any record of. The friendly Nez Percés saved the whites. The unfriendly faction of the Nez Percés, led by Joseph and Looking Glass, finally yielded and accepted the treaty. But they did this with certain expectations in regard to their reservation. This was set forth to the author by William McBean, a half-breed Indian, son of the McBean who was the commandant of the Hudson's Bay post at Wallula. McBean the younger was a boy at the time of the council at Walla Walla. He was familiar with all the Indian languages spoken at the council and in appearance was so much of an Indian that he could pass unquestioned anywhere. Governor Stevens asked him to spy out the situation and learn what the Nez Percés were going to decide. The result of his investigations was to show that the whole decision hinged on the understanding by Joseph's faction that, if they acquiesced in the treaty and turned their support to the whites, they might retain perpetual possession of the Wallowa country in North-eastern Oregon as their special allotment. Becoming finally satisfied that this would be granted them, they yielded to the Lawyer faction and thus the entire Nez Percé tribe made common cause with the whites, rendering the execution of the great plot of Kamiakin and Peupeumoxmox a foredoomed failure. But now for the sequel. Though it was thus clear in the minds of Joseph and his division of the Nez Percés that the loved Wallowa (one of the fairest regions that ever the sun shone on and a perfect land for Indians) was to be their permanent home, yet the stipulation, if indeed it were intended by Governor Stevens, never became definitely set down in the "Great Father's" records at Washington. The result was that when, twenty years later, the manifold attractions of the Wallowa country began to draw white immigration, the Indians, now under Young Joseph, son of the former chief, stood by their supposed rights and the great Nez Percé War of 1877 ensued.

And now, to resume the thread of our discourse, we may note that Governor Stevens proceeded on his laborious mission to the Flatheads in the region of the Cœur d'Alene and Pend Oreille lakes in what is now Northern Idaho. After protracted and at times excited discussion, a treaty was accepted by which an immense tract of a million and a quarter acres was set apart for a reservation. From Pend Oreille, Governor Stevens with his little force, now reduced to twenty-two, crossed the Rockies to Fort Benton.

But what was happening on the Walla Walla? No sooner was the governor fairly out of sight across the flower-bespangled plains which extended two hundred miles north-east from Walla Walla, than the wily Kamiakin began to resume his plots. So successful was he, with the valuable assistance of Peupeumoxmox, Young Chief, and Five Crows, that the treaties, just ratified, were torn to shreds, and the flame of savage warfare burst forth across the entire Columbia Valley.

Hazard Stevens, in his invaluable history of his father, gives a vivid picture of how the news reached them in their camp thirty-five miles up the Missouri from Fort Benton. Summer had now passed into autumn. A favourable treaty had been made with the Blackfeet. On October 29th, the little party were gathered around their campfire in the frosty air of fall in that high latitude, when they discerned a solitary rider making his way slowly toward them. As he drew near they soon saw that it was Pearson, the express rider. Pearson was one of the best examples of those scouts whose lives were spent in conveying messages from forts to parties in the field. He usually travelled alone, and his life was always in his hand. He seemed to be made of steel springs, and it had been thought that he could endure anything. "He could ride anything that wore hair." He rode seventeen hundred and fifty miles in twenty-eight days at one time, one stage of two hundred and sixty miles having been made in three days. But as he slowly drew up to the party in the cold evening light, it was seen that even Pearson was "done." His horse staggered and fell, and he himself could not stand or speak for some time. After he had been revived he told his story, and a story of disaster and foreboding it was, sure enough.

All the great tribes of the Columbia plains west of the Nez Percés had broken out, the Cayuses, Yakimas, Palouses, Walla Wallas, Umatillas, and Klickitats. They had swept the country clean of whites. The ride of Pearson from The Dalles to the point where he reached Governor Stevens is one of the most thrilling in the annals of the River. By riding all day and night, he reached a horse ranch on the Umatilla belonging to a noted half-breed Indian, William McKay, but he found the place deserted. Seeing a splendid horse in the bunch near by, he lassoed and saddled him. Though the horse was as wild as air, Pearson managed to mount and start on. Just then there swept into view a force of Indians who, instantly divining what Pearson was trying to do, gave chase. Up and down hill, through vale, and across the rim-rock, they followed, sending frequent bullets after him, and yelling like demons, "Whupsiah si-ah-poo, Whup-si-ah!" ("Kill the white man!") But the wild horse which the intrepid rider bestrode proved his salvation, for he gradually outran all his pursuers. Travelling through the Walla Walla at night Pearson reached the camp of friendly Nez Percé Red Wolf on the Alpowa the next day, having ridden two hundred miles from The Dalles without stopping except the brief time changing horses. Snow and hunger now impeded his course. Part of the way he had to go on snowshoes without a horse. But with unflinching resolution he passed on, and so now here he was with his dismal tidings.

The despatches warned Governor Stevens that Kamiakin with a thousand warriors was in the Walla Walla Valley and that it would be impossible for him to get through by that route, and that he must therefore return to the East by the

Missouri and come back to his Territory by the steamer route of Panama. That meant six months' delay. With characteristic boldness, Governor Stevens at once rejected the more cautious course and went right back to Spokane by the Cœur d'Alene Pass, deep already with the winter snows, suffering intensely with cold and hunger, but avoiding by that route the Indians sent out to intercept him. With extraordinary address, he succeeded in turning the Spokane Indians to his side. The Nez Percés, thanks to Lawyer's fidelity, were still friendly, and with these two powerful tribes arrayed against the Yakimas, there was still hope of holding the Columbia Valley.

After many adventures, Governor Stevens reached Olympia in safety. Governor Curry of Oregon had already called a force of volunteers into the field. The Oregon volunteers were divided into two divisions, one under Colonel J. W. Nesmith, which went into the Yakima country, and the other under Lieutenant-Colonel J. K. Kelley, which went to Walla Walla. The latter force fought the decisive battle of the campaign on the 7th, 8th, 9th, and 10th of December, 1855. It was a series of engagements occurring in the heart of the Walla Walla Valley, a "running fight" culminating at what is now called Frenchtown, ten miles west of the present city of Walla Walla. The most important feature of it all was the death of the great Walla Walla chieftain, Peupeumoxmox. But though defeated and losing so important a chief, the Indians scattered across the rivers and were still unsubdued.

In March, 1856, the sublime section of the Columbia lying between The Dalles and the Cascades became the scene of a series of atrocities the most distressing in the entire war. The Klickitats swooped down upon the defenceless settlers and massacred them with revolting cruelty. They vanished like a whirlwind, but men whom the writer has known have related to him how the volunteers, returning to the scenes of desolation, found all houses destroyed and the carcasses of cattle thrown into the springs and wells. They found the naked bodies of the girls and women with stakes driven through, and those of men horribly mutilated. In savage humour, the Indians had killed the hogs and left parts of human bodies in their mouths. One interesting fact connected with the campaign at the Cascades is that General Phil Sheridan fought his first battle there. The old Block House on the north side of the River, nearly opposite the present Cascade Locks, existed until a few years ago, and there was Sheridan's first battle.

Meanwhile Governor Stevens had organised a force of Washington volunteers. As the year 1856 progressed, it seemed more plain that the discord which developed between the regulars under command of General John E. Wool and the volunteers would result in fatal weakness. Nevertheless Governor Stevens and Governor Curry kept pressing the movements of their backwoods soldiers with unflagging energy. They were at last rewarded with a measure of success. For Colonel B. F. Shaw, commanding the Washington volunteers, learning that the hostiles were camped in force in the Grande Ronde Valley, made a rapid march from Walla Walla across the western spur of the Blue Mountains and struck the collected force of Indians a deadly blow, scattering them in all directions and ending the war in that quarter.

But the end had not yet come in Walla Walla. Governor Stevens determined to hold another great council at the site of the first. Leaving The Dalles on August 19th, he pressed on to Shaw's camp, two miles above the present location of Walla Walla. On September 5th, Colonel E. J. Steptoe, with four companies of regulars, arrived at the same place and made camp on the site of the present fort.

Col. B. F. Shaw, who Won the Battle of Grande Ronde in 1856.

By Courtesy of Major Lee Moorehouse.

And now came on the second great Walla Walla council. The tribes were gathered as before, and were aligned as before. The division of Nez Percés under Lawyer stood firmly by Stevens and the treaty. The others did not. The most unfortunate feature of the entire matter was that Colonel Steptoe, acting under General Wool's instructions, thus far kept secret, refused to grant Stevens adequate support and subjected him to humiliations which galled the fiery Governor to the limit. In fact, had it not been for the vigilance of the faithful Nez Percés of Lawyer's band, Stevens and his force would surely have met the doom prepared for them at the first council. The debt of gratitude due Lawyer is incalculable. Spotted Eagle ought to be recorded, too, as of similar devotion and watchfulness. Governor Stevens afterward declared that a speech by him in favour of the whites was equal in feeling, truth, and courage to any speech that he ever heard from any orator whatever.

But in spite of oratory, zeal, and argument, nothing could overcome the influence of Kamiakin, Owhi, Quelchen, Five Crows, and others of the Yakimas and Cayuses. Nothing was gained. They stood just where they were a year before. The fatal results of divided counsels between regulars and volunteers were apparent.

The baffled Governor now started on his way down the River, but not without another battle. For, as he was marching a short distance south of what is now Walla Walla city, the Indians burst upon his small force with the evident intention of ending all scores then and there. But Colonel Steptoe came to the rescue, and with united forces the Indians were repulsed.

That was the last battle on the Walla Walla. Colonel Steptoe established a rude stockade fort on Mill Creek in what is now the heart of the present Walla Walla city, and went into winter quarters there in 1856-57. Governor Stevens returned to Olympia and launched forth a bitter arraignment against Wool. The latter, however, was in a position of vantage and issued a proclamation commanding all whites in the upper country to go down the River and leave the Cascade Mountains as the eastern limit of the white settlement. Thus ended for a time this unsatisfactory and distressing war. To all appearances Kamiakin and his adherents had accomplished all they wanted.

But this was not the end. Gold had been discovered in Eastern Washington. Vast possibilities of cattle raising were evident on those endless bunch-grass hills. Although there was as yet little conception of the future developments of the Inland Empire in agriculture and gardening, yet the keen-eyed immigrants and volunteers had scanned the pleasant vales and abounding streams of the Walla Walla and the Umatilla and the Palouse, and had decided in their own minds that, Wool or no Wool, this land must be opened. In 1857 the Government decided on a change of policy and sent General N. S. Clarke to take Wool's place. General Clarke opened the gates, and the impatient army of land hunters and gold hunters began to move in. Meanwhile, Colonel Wright and Colonel Steptoe, though formerly they had closely followed Wool's policy, now began to experience a change of heart. Out of these conditions the third Indian war, in 1858, quickly succeeded the second, being indeed its inevitable sequence.

Fort Sheridan on the Grande Ronde, Built by Philip Sheridan in 1855.

By Courtesy of Major Lee Moorehouse.

Three campaigns marked this third war. The first was conducted by Colonel Steptoe against the Spokanes and Cœur d'Alenes, and ended in his humiliating and disastrous defeat. The second was directed by Major Garnett against the Yakimas, resulting in their permanent overthrow. The third was conducted by Colonel Wright against the Spokanes and other northern tribes who had defeated Steptoe. This was the Waterloo of the Indians, and it ushered in the occupation and settlement of the upper Columbia country.

The Steptoe expedition was the most ill-starred event in the whole history of the North-west, unless we except that of the destruction of the *Tonquin*. Colonel Wright was then in command of the new Fort Walla Walla, located in 1857 on the present ground. Perceiving his former error in giving the turbulent and treacherous natives undisputed sway, he ordered Colonel Steptoe to go with two hundred dragoons to the Spokane region and subject the restless tribes centring there. Steptoe's force was well equipped in every way except one. The pack train was heavily laden, and an inebriated quartermaster conceived the brilliant idea of lessening the burden by *leaving out the larger part of the ammunition*. Even aside from this fatal blunder, Colonel Steptoe seems to have had no adequate conception of the vigour and resources of the Indians.

As before, the Nez Percés were the faithful friends of the whites. Timothy, a Nez Percé chief living on Snake River at the mouth of the Alpowa, put them across the wicked stream, then running high with the May freshet, and went on with them as guide.

On May 16, 1858, the force reached a point near four lakes, probably the group of which Silver Lake and Medical Lake are the chief ones, a few miles west of Spokane. Here was gathered a formidable array, Spokanes, Pend Oreilles, Cœur d'Alenes, Okanogans, and Colvilles, the hosts of the upper country. Steptoe was soldier enough to perceive that it was time for caution, and he halted for a parley. Saltese, a brawny chief of the Cœur d'Alenes, declared to him that the Indians were ready to dispute his farther progress, but that if the white men would retire the Indians would not molest them. A friendly Nez Percé, seeing the duplicity of Saltese, struck his mouth, exclaiming, "You speak with a double tongue."

The force turned back and that night all seemed well. But at nine o'clock the next morning, while the soldiers were descending a cañon to Pine Creek, near the present site of Rosalia, a large force of Indians burst upon them like a cyclone. As the battle began to wax hot, the terrible consequences of the error of lack of ammunition began to become manifest. Man after man had to cease firing. Captain O. H. P. Taylor and Lieutenant Gaston commanded the rear-guard. With extraordinary skill and devotion they held the line intact and foiled the efforts of the savages to burst through. Meanwhile the whole force was moving as rapidly as consistent with formation on their way southward. Taylor and Gaston sent a messenger forward, begging Steptoe to halt the line and give them a chance to load. But the commander felt that the safety of the whole force depended on pressing on. Soon a fierce rush of Indians followed, and, when the surge had passed, the gallant rear-guard was buried under it. One notable figure in the death-grapple was De May, a Frenchman, trained in the Crimea and Algeria, and an expert fencer. For some time he used his gun barrel as a sword and swept the Indians down by dozens with his terrific sweeps. But at last he fell before numbers, and one of his surviving comrades relates that he heard him shouting his last words, "O, my God, my God, for a sabre!"

But the lost rear-guard saved the rest. For they managed to hold back the swarm of foes until nightfall, when they reached a somewhat defensible position a few miles from the towering cone of what is now known as Steptoe Butte. There they spent part of a dark, rainy, and dismal night, anticipating a savage attack. But the Indians, sure of their prey, waited till morning. Surely the first light would have revealed a massacre equal to the Custer massacre of later date, had not the unexpected happened. And the unexpected was that old Timothy, the Nez Percé guide, knew a trail through a rough cañon, the only possible exit without discovery. In the darkness of midnight the shattered command mounted and followed at a gallop the faithful Timothy on whose keen eyes and mind their salvation rested. The wounded and a few footmen were dropped at intervals along the trail. After an eighty-mile gallop during the day and night following, the yellow flood of Snake River suddenly broke before them between its desolate banks. Saved! The unwearied Timothy threw out his own warriors as a screen against the pursuing foe, and set his women to ferrying the soldiers across the turbulent stream.

Thus the larger part of the command reached Fort Walla Walla alive.

One of the most extraordinary individual experiences connected with the Steptoe retreat, was that of Snickster and Williams. Some of the survivors question the correctness of this, and others vouch for its accuracy. It perhaps should not be set down as proven history. Snickster and Williams were riding one horse, and could not keep up with the main body. The Indians, therefore, overtook and seized them before they reached the Snake River. In a rage because of having been balked of their prey, the Indians determined to have some amusement out of the unfortunate pair, and told them to go into the river with their horse and try to swim across. Into the dangerous stream, two thousand feet wide, almost ice-cold, and with a powerful current, they went. As soon as they were out a score of yards, the Indians began their fun by making a target of them. The horse was almost immediately killed. Williams was struck and sank. Snickster's arm was broken by a ball, but diving under the dead horse, and keeping himself on the farther side till somewhat out of range, and then boldly striking across the current, which foamed with Indian bullets, he reached the south side of the river and was drawn out, almost dead, by some of Timothy's Nez Percé Indians.

With the defeat of Steptoe, the Indians may well have felt that they were invincible. But their exultation was short-lived. As already noted, Garnett crushed the Yakimas at one blow, and Wright a little later repeated Steptoe's march to Spokane, but did not repeat his retreat. For in the battle of Four Lakes on September 1st, and that of Spokane Plains on September 5th, Wright broke for ever the power and spirits of the northern Indians.

The treaties were thus established at last by war. The reservations, embracing the finest parts of the Umatilla, Yakima, Clearwater, and Cœur d'Alene regions, were set apart, and to them after considerable delay and difficulty the tribes were gathered.

With the end of this third great Indian war and the public announcement by General Clarke that the country might now be considered open to settlement, immigration began to pour in, and on ranch and river, in mine and forest, the well-known labours of the American state-builders and home-builders became displayed. The ever-new West was repeating itself.

**Tullux Holiquilla, a Warm Springs Indian Chief,
Famous in the Modoc War as a Scout for U. S. Troops.**

By Courtesy of Major Lee Moorehouse.

The Valley of the Columbia now rested from serious strife for a number of
years. But in 1877, an echo of the war of 1855 suddenly startled the country, and
provided an event to which lovers of the tragic and romantic in history have ever

since turned with deep interest. This was the "Joseph War" in the Wallowa. Our readers will recall that the so-called Joseph band of Nez Percés opposed the Walla Walla Treaty at first, but finally acquiesced, with what they understood was the stipulation that they should possess the Wallowa country as their permanent home. The Joseph of that time was succeeded by his son, whose Indian name was Hallakallakeen, "Eagle Wing." He was the finest specimen of the native red man ever produced in the Columbia Valley. Of magnificent stature and proportions, with a rare dignity and nobility, which wider opportunities would have made remarkable, and with a career of mingled light and shade, pathos and tragedy, Hallakallakeen will go down into history with a record of passionate devotion from his followers and unstinted encomiums from most of his opponents.

Joseph loved the Wallowa with a passionate affection, and made at first every effort to maintain amity with his white neighbours. But when the Government violated what he had regarded its sacred pledge and permitted entrance upon the lands which he claimed, he refused to abide by the decision and led out his warriors to battle. The Nez Percés, though few in number, could fight face to face with white men, and could use white men's weapons and white men's tactics. At a desperate battle at White Bird Cañon they routed the detachment in command of Colonel Perry. The result was to put arms, ammunition, and provisions in abundance into the hands of the Indians and hope into their hearts.

General O. O. Howard, then commanding the department of the Columbia, now assumed command and began so vigorous a campaign against Joseph that the Indian chief plainly saw that with all his activity he could not avoid being seized in the closing arms of Howard's command. The interesting details of the marches, countermarches, desperate encounters, sometimes favourable to white man and sometimes to red, are to be found in General Howard's own book. At last, with marvellous skill and good fortune, Joseph eluded capture and adopted the desperate resolution of crossing the Bitter Root Mountains by the Lolo trail, descending the Missouri, and ultimately reaching the Canadian line beyond the land of the Sioux. Encumbered as he was with his women, children, and entire movable possessions, obliged to forage and hunt on the way, and avoiding pursuers in rear as well as forces coming to meet him in front, fighting frequent and some of the time successful battles,—the Nez Percé chieftain exhibited qualities of leadership and resources of mind and body which offer materials for a historical romance equal to De Quincey's *Flight of the Kalmuck Tartars*.

Howard's tireless pursuit in the rear and the active and intelligent co-operation of Gibbon and Miles, who ascended the Missouri to meet the fleeing Nez Percés, resulted at last in their capture at Bear Paw Mountain on the Milk River in Montana.

General Howard says that the campaign from the beginning of the Indian pursuit across the Lolo trail until the embarkation on the Missouri for the homeward journey, including all stoppages and halts, extended from July 27th to October 10th, during which time his command marched one thousand three hundred and twenty-one miles. He says that Joseph, encumbered with women, children, and possessions, traversed even greater distances, "for he had to make many a loop in his skein, many a deviation into a tangled thicket, to avoid or deceive his enemy." Howard pays the highest tribute to his Indian foe and declares that some of his operations are not often equalled in warfare.

Hallakallakeen (Eagle Wing) or Joseph, the Nez Percé Chief.

By T. W. Tolman.

Joseph's subsequent career was a melancholy one. Transported with his band to Oklahoma, the wild eagle of the Wallowa so pined away on the flat prairie and begged so piteously to be allowed to return to the waters of the Columbia, that his request was granted. But so intense was the feeling among the people who had suffered from their dangerous enemy that this poor fragment of the Nez Percés was placed on the Colville Reservation in Northern Washington. There the restless heart of the Nez Percé Bonaparte was eaten out by bitter yearnings for his loved Wallowa.

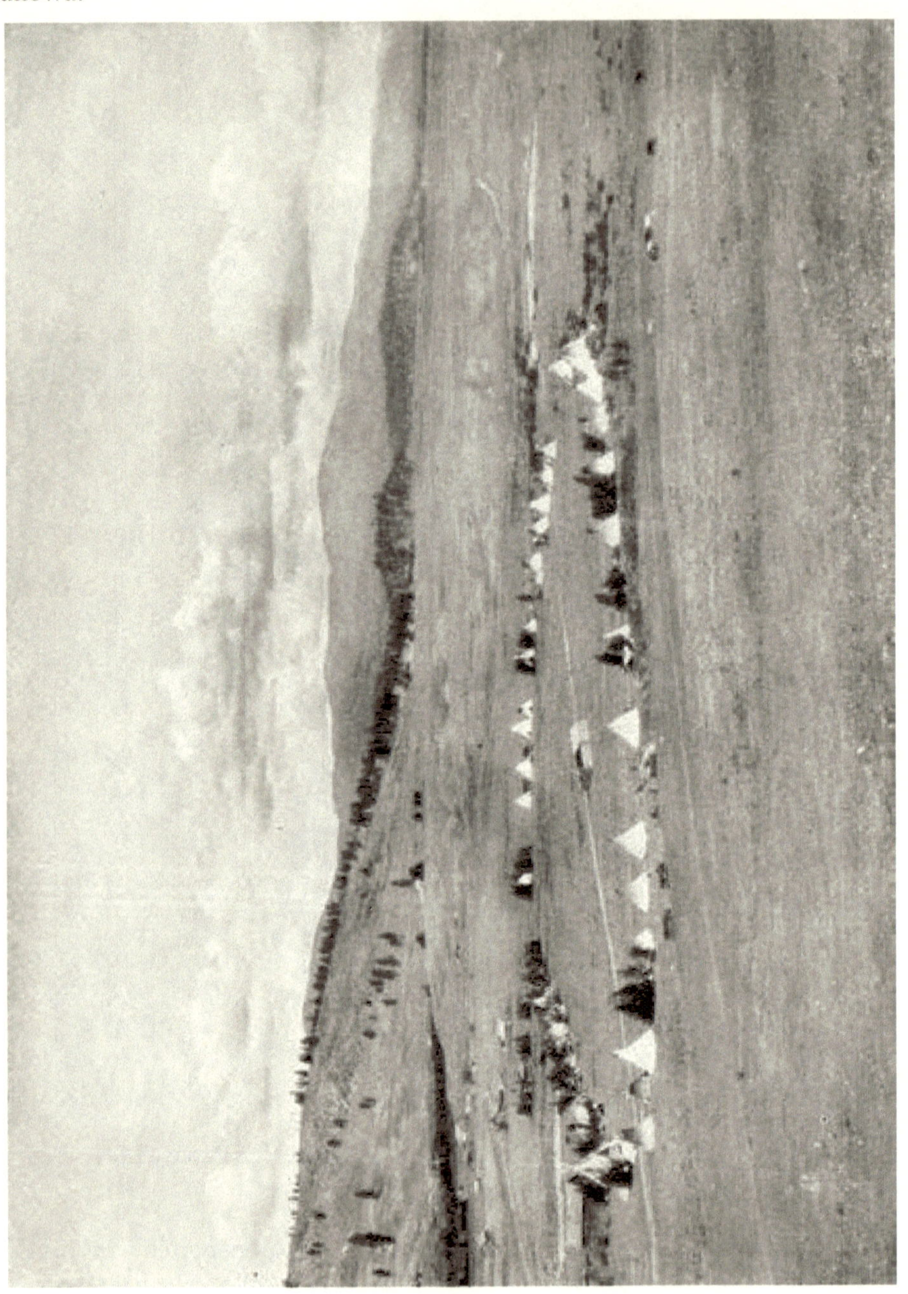

Camp of Chief Joseph on the Nespilem, Wash.

Photo. by T. W. Tolman, Spokane.

He had an occasional proud and interesting hour. At the time of General Grant's obsequies at New York, Joseph was in Washington to see the "Great Father" about his reservation. General Miles, who greatly admired the hero of the Lolo trail, asked him to ride with himself at the head of the funeral procession. Mounted on a magnificent charger, Joseph rode solemnly through the streets of the metropolis by the side of the conqueror of Bear Paw Mountain, and there were not wanting those who said that the Indian was the finer horseman and the finer-looking man.

But Joseph died at his camp on the Nespilem without ever seeing Wallowa. His last request was that he be buried there. He remained an Indian to the last, not ordinarily living in a house or wearing civilised costume or even speaking English, though perfectly able to do so. His life might have been happier had he never been known to fame.

The next year after the Joseph War, or in 1878, occurred the Bannock War, the scene of which was mainly Umatilla County in Oregon and other parts adjoining the River. Though at first, as has happened so many times, the Indians met with successes, the end was their inevitable defeat.

With the close of the Bannock War it may be said that Indian warfare practically ended. The war-whoop ceased to be heard and the tomahawk was brandished no more along the Columbia.

CHAPTER X

WHEN THE "FIRE-CANOES" TOOK THE PLACE OF THE LOG-CANOES

Variety of Craft that have Navigated the Columbia—The *Beaver*, *Carolina*, *Columbia*, and *Lot Whitcomb*—Beginning of Steamboating above the Cascades—Steamboats above The Dalles—Rival Companies on the River—The Oregon Steam Navigation Company—Great Business Developments of the Decade of the Sixties—Specimen Shipments in 1862—The Steamboat Ride from Portland to Lewiston—Some of the Steamboat Men of the Period—Story of W. H. Gray and his Sailboat on the Snake River—Descending The Dalles—Captain Coe's Account of the First Steamboat Ride on the Upper Columbia and the Snake—Navigation above Colville and on the Lakes—The Locks and Prospects of Future Navigation—Remarkable Trips on the River—Some Steamboats of the Present.

WE have learned that our River has been navigated by boats of almost every description. At one time it was the hollowed cedar-log canoes of the aborgines. Again, the bateaux of the trappers were the chief craft to cut the blue lakes and the white rapids. At yet other times it was the flat-boats of the immigrants. Sailing ships of every sort—frigates, galleons, caravels, men-of-war, full-rigged ships, barks, brigs, schooners, and sloops—crowded early to the silver gate of the River.

In due process of time the "Fire-canoes," as the natives called steamers, let loose their trails of smoke amid the tops of the "continuous woods." The *Beaver*, a small steamship belonging to the Hudson's Bay Company and sent from England, entered the River in 1836, the first steamer to ply these waters. The Company afterwards sent her to Puget Sound, and, if we are correctly informed, she is still afloat on the Gulf of Georgia. In 1850 the first American steamship, the *Carolina*, crossed the Bar. In the same year a little double-ender, called the *Columbia*, began running between Portland and Astoria.

The first river steamer of any size to ply upon the Willamette and Columbia was the *Lot Whitcomb*. This steamer was built by Whitcomb and Jennings. J. C. Ainsworth was the first captain, and Jacob Kamm was the first engineer. Both these men became leaders in every species of steamboating enterprise. In 1851 Dan Bradford and B. B. Bishop inaugurated a movement to connect the up-river region with the lower river by getting a small iron propeller called the *Jason P. Flint* from the East and putting her together at the Cascades, whence she made the run to Portland. The *Flint* has been named as first to run above the Cascades, but the author has the authority of Mr. Bishop for stating that the first steamer to run above the Cascades was the *Eagle*. That steamer was brought in sections by Allen McKinley to the upper Cascades in 1853, there put together, and set to plying on the part of the river between the Cascades and The Dalles. In 1854, the *Mary* was built and launched above the Cascades, the next year the *Wasco* followed, and in 1856 the *Hassalo* began to toot her jubilant horn at the precipices of the mid-Columbia. In 1859 R. R. Thompson and Lawrence Coe built the *Colonel Wright*, the first steamer on the upper section of the River. In the same year the same men built at the upper Cascades a steamer called the *Venture*. This craft met with a curious catastrophe. For on her very first trip she swung too far into the channel and was carried over the upper Cascades, at the point where the Cascade Locks are now located. She was subsequently raised, rebuilt, and rechristened the *Umatilla*.

Tirzah Trask, a Umatilla Indian Girl — Taken as an Ideal of Sacajawea.

Photo. by Lee Moorehouse, Pendleton.

This part of the period of steamboat building was cotemporary with the Indian wars of 1855 and 1856. The steamers, *Wasco, Mary*, and *Eagle* were of much service in rescuing victims of the murderous assault on the Cascades by the Klickitats.

While the enterprising steamboat builders were thus making their way up-river in the very teeth of Indian warfare, steamboats were in course of construction on the Willamette. The *Jennie Clark* in 1854 and the *Carrie Ladd* in 1858 were built for the firm of Abernethy, Clark & Company. These both, the latter especially, were really elegant steamers for the time.

The close of the Indian wars in 1859 saw a quite well-organised steamer service between Portland and The Dalles, and the great rush into the upper country was just beginning. The *Señorita*, the *Belle*, and the *Multnomah*, under the management of Benjamin Stark, were on the run from Portland to the Cascades. A rival steamer, the *Mountain Buck*, owned by Ruckle and Olmstead, was on the same route. These steamers connected with boats on the Cascades-Dalles section by means of portages five miles long around the rapids. There was a portage on each side of the River. That on the north side was operated by Bradford & Company, and their steamers were the *Hassalo* and the *Mary*. Ruckle and Olmstead owned the portage on the south side of the River, and their steamer was the *Wasco*. Sharp competition arose between the Bradford and Stark interests on one side and Ruckle and Olmstead on the other. The Stark Company was known as the Columbia River Navigation Company, and the rival was the Oregon Transportation Company. J. C. Ainsworth now joined the Stark party with the *Carrie Ladd*. So efficient did this reinforcement prove to be that the Transportation Company proposed to them a combination. This was effected in April, 1859, and the new organisation became known as the Union Transportation Company. This was soon found to be too loose a consolidation to accomplish the desired ends, and the parties interested set about a new combination to embrace all the steamboat men from Celilo to Astoria. The result was the formation of the Oregon Steam Navigation Company, which came into legal existence on December 20, 1860. Its stock in steamboats, sailboats, wharf-boats, and miscellaneous property was stated at $172,500.

Such was the genesis of the "O. S. N. Co." In a valuable article by Irene Lincoln Poppleton in the *Oregon Historical Quarterly* for September, 1908, to which we here make acknowledgments, it is said that no assessment was ever levied on the stock of this company, but that from the proceeds of the business the management expended in gold nearly three million dollars in developing their property, besides paying to the stockholders in dividends over two million and a half dollars. Never perhaps was there such a record of money-making on such a capitalisation.

The source of the enormous business of the Oregon Steam Navigation Company was the rush into Idaho, Montana, and Eastern Oregon and Washington by the miners, cowboys, speculators, and adventurers of the early sixties. The up-river country, as described more at length in another chapter, wakened suddenly from the lethargy of centuries, and the wilderness teemed with life. That was the great steamboat age. Money flowed in streams. Fortunes were made and lost in a day.

When first organised in 1860, the Oregon Steam Navigation Company had a nondescript lot of steamers, mainly small and weak. The two portages, one of five miles around the Cascades and the other of fourteen miles from The Dalles to Celilo Falls, were unequal to their task. The portages at the Cascades on both sides of the River were made by very inadequate wooden tramways. That at The Dalles was made by teams. Such quantities of freight were discharged from the steamers that sometimes the whole portage was lined with freight from end to end. The portages were not acquired by the company with the steamboat property, and as a result the portage owners reaped the larger share of the profits. During high water the portage on the Oregon side at the Cascades had a monopoly of the business, and it took one-half the freight income from Portland to The Dalles. This was holding the whip-hand with a vengeance, and the vigorous directors of the steamboat company could not endure it. Accordingly, they absorbed the rights of the portage owners, built a railroad from Celilo to The Dalles on the Oregon side, and one around the Cascades on the Washington side. The company was reorganised under the laws of Oregon in October, 1862, with a declared capitalisation of two million dollars.

Business on the River in 1863 was something enormous. Hardly ever did a steamer make a trip with less than two hundred passengers. Freight was offered in such quantities at Portland that trucks had to stand in line for blocks, waiting to deliver and receive their loads. New boats were built of a much better class. Two rival companies, the Independent Line and the People's Transportation Line, made a vigorous struggle to secure a share of the business, but they were eventually overpowered. Some conception of the amount of business may be gained from the fact that the steamers transported passengers to an amount of fares running from $1000 to $6000 a trip. On April 29, 1862, the *Tenino*, leaving Celilo for the Lewiston trip, had a passenger load amounting to $10,945, and a few trips later reported receipts of $18,000, for freight, passengers, meals, and berths. The steamships sailing from Portland to San Francisco showed equally remarkable records. On June 25, 1861, the *Sierra Nevada* conveyed a treasure shipment of $228,000; July 14th, $110,000; August 24th, $195,558; December 5th, $750,000. The number of passengers carried on The Dalles-Lewiston route in 1864 was 36,000 and the tons of freight were 21,834.

It was a magnificent steamboat ride in those days from Portland to Lewiston. The fare was sixty dollars; meals and berths, one dollar each. A traveller would leave Portland at five A.M. on, perhaps, the *Wilson G. Hunt*, reach the Cascades sixty-five miles distant at eleven A.M., proceed by rail five miles to the upper Cascades, there transfer to the *Oneonta* or *Idaho* for The Dalles, passing in that run from the humid, low-lying, heavily timbered West-of-the-mountains, to the dry, breezy, hilly East-of-the-mountains. Reaching The Dalles, fifty miles farther east, he would be conveyed by another portage railroad, fourteen miles more, to Celilo. There the *Tenino, Yakima, Nez Percé Chief,* or *Owyhee* was waiting. With the earliest light of the morning the steamer would head right into the impetuous current of the River, bound for Lewiston, two hundred and eighty miles farther yet, taking two days, sometimes three, though only one to return. Those steamers were mainly of the light-draught, stern-wheel structure, which still characterises the Columbia River boats. They were swift and roomy and well adapted to the turbulent waters of the upper River.

The captains, pilots, and pursers of that period were as fine a set of men as ever turned a wheel. Bold, bluff, genial, hearty, and obliging they were, even though given to occasional outbursts of expletives and possessing voluminous repertoires of "cuss-words" such as would startle the effete East. Any old Oregonian who may chance to cast his eyes upon these pages will recall, as with the pangs of childhood homesickness, the forms and features of steamboat men of that day; the polite yet determined Ainsworth, the brusque and rotund Reed, the bluff and hearty Knaggs, the frolicsome and never disconcerted Ingalls, the dark, powerful, and nonchalant Coe, the patriarchal beard of Stump, the loquacious "Commodore" Wolf, who used to point out to astonished tourists the "diabolical strata" on the banks of the River, the massive and good-natured Strang, the genial and elegant O'Neil, the suave and witty Snow, the tall and handsome Sampson, the rich Scotch brogue of McNulty, and dozens of others, whose combined adventures would fill a volume. One of the most experienced pilots of the upper River was Captain "Eph" Baughman, who has been running on the Snake and Columbia rivers for fifty years, and is yet active at the date of this publication. W. H. Gray, who came to Waiilatpu with Whitman as secular agent of the mission, became a river man of much skill. He gave four sons, John, William, Alfred, and James, to the service of the River, all four of them being skilled captains. A story narrated to the author by Captain William Gray, now of Pasco, Washington, well illustrates the character of the old Columbia River navigators. W. H. Gray was the first man to run a sailboat of much size with regular freight up Snake River. That was in 1860 before any steamers were running on that stream. Mr. Gray built his boat, a fifty-ton sloop, on Oosyoos Lake on the Okanogan River. In it he descended that river to its entrance into the Columbia. Thence be descended the Columbia, running down the Entiat, Rock Island, Cabinet, and Priest Rapids, no mean undertaking of itself. Reaching the mouth of the Snake, he took on a load of freight and started up the swift stream. At Five-mile Rapids he found that his sail was insufficient to carry the sloop up. Men had said that it was impossible. His crew all prophesied disaster. The stubborn captain merely declared, "There is no such word as fail in my dictionary." He directed his son and another of the crew to take the small boat, load her with a long coil of rope, make their way up the stream until they got above the rapid, there to land on an islet of rock, fasten the rope to that rock, then pay it out till it was swept down the rapid. They were then to descend the rapid in the small boat. "Very likely you may be upset," added the skipper encouragingly, "but if you are, you know how to swim." They were upset, sure enough, but they did know how to swim. They righted their boat, picked up the end of the floating rope, and reached the sloop with it. The rope was attached to the capstan, and the sloop was wound up by it above the swiftest part of the rapid to a point where the sail was sufficient to carry, and on they went rejoicing. Any account of steamboating on the Columbia would be incomplete without reference to Captain James Troup, who was born on the Columbia, and almost from early boyhood ran steamers upon it and its tributaries. He made a specialty of running steamers down the Dalles and the Cascades, an undertaking sometimes rendered necessary by the fact that more boats were built in proportion to demand on the upper than the lower River. These were taken down the Dalles, and sometimes down the Cascades. Once down, they could not return. The first steamer to run down the Tumwater Falls was the *Okanogan*, on May 22, 1866, piloted by Captain T. J. Stump.

The author enjoyed the great privilege of descending the Dalles in the *D. S. Baker* in the year 1888, Captain Troup being in command. At that strange point in the River, the whole vast volume is compressed into a channel but one hundred and sixty feet wide at low water and much deeper than wide. Like a huge mill-race this channel continues nearly straight for two miles, when it is hurled with frightful force against a massive bluff. Deflected from the bluff, it turns at a sharp angle to be split in sunder by a low reef of rock. When the *Baker* was drawn into the suck of the current at the head of the "chute" she swept down the channel, which was almost black, with streaks of foam, to the bluff, two miles in four minutes. There feeling the tremendous refluent wave, she went careening over and over toward the sunken reef. The skilled captain had her perfectly in hand, and precisely at the right moment, rang the signal bell, "Ahead, full speed," and ahead she went, just barely scratching her side on the rock. Thus close was it necessary to calculate distance. If the steamer had struck the tooth-like point of the reef broadside on, she would have been broken in two and carried in fragments on either side. Having passed this danger point, she glided into the beautiful calm bay below and the feat was accomplished. Captain J. C. Ainsworth and Captain James Troup were the two captains above all others to whom the company entrusted the critical task of running steamers over the rapids.

In the *Overland Monthly* of June, 1886, there is a valuable account by Captain Lawrence Coe of the maiden journey of the *Colonel Wright* from Celilo up what they then termed the upper Columbia.

This first journey on that section of the River was made in April, 1859. The pilot was Captain Lew White. The highest point reached was Wallula, the site of the old Hudson's Bay fort. The current was a powerful one to withstand, no soundings had ever been made, and no boats except canoes, bateaux, flatboats, and a few small sailboats, had ever made the trip. No one had any conception of the location of a channel adapted to a steamboat. No difficulty was experienced, however, except at the Umatilla Rapids. This is a most singular obstruction. Three separate reefs, at intervals of half a mile, extend right across the River. There are narrow breaks in these reefs, but not in line with each other. Through them the water pours with tremendous velocity, and on account of their irregular locations a steamer must zigzag across the River at imminent risk of being borne broadside on to the reef. The passage of the Umatilla Rapids is not difficult at high water, for then the steamer glides over the rocks in a straight course.

In the August *Overland* of the same year, Captain Coe narrates the first steamboat trip up Snake River. This was in June, 1860, just at the time of the beginning of the gold excitement. The *Colonel Wright* was loaded with picks, rockers, and other mining implements, as well as provisions and passengers. Most of the freight and passengers were put off at Wallula, to go thence overland. Part continued on to test the experiment of making way against the wicked-looking current of Snake

River. After three days and a half from the starting point a few miles above Celilo, the *Colonel Wright* halted at a place which was called Slaterville, thirty-seven miles up the Clearwater from its junction with the Snake. There the remainder of the cargo was discharged, to be hauled in waggons to the Oro Fino mines. The steamer *Okanogan* followed the *Colonel Wright* within a few weeks, and navigation on the Snake may be said to have fairly begun. During that same time the city of Lewiston, named in honour of Meriwether Lewis, the explorer, was founded at the junction of the Snake and Clearwater rivers.

While parts of the Columbia and it chief tributary, the Snake, were thus opened to navigation by 1860, no "fire-canoe" had yet appeared on that magnificent stretch of navigable water from Colville into the Arrow Lakes. From contemporary files of the *Daily Mountaineer* of The Dalles, we learn that Captain Lew White launched the *Forty-nine* in November, 1865, at Colville. In December the *Forty-nine* ascended the Columbia one hundred and sixty miles, nearly to the head of lower Arrow Lake, whence, meeting floating ice, she returned. From the *Mountaineer* we learn also that in the early months of 1866 a steamer was constructed at the mouth of Boisé River for navigation of the far upper Snake. At the same time also the steamer *Mary Moody* was constructed by Z. F. Moody, on Pend Oreille Lake, the first steamer on any of the lakes except the Arrow Lakes of the Columbia.

With the close of the decade of the sixties, it may be said that the Columbia and its tributaries had fairly entered upon the steamboat era. While many steamers were added within the succeeding years, the steamboat business was never so active on the upper River as during that early age. After the building of the railroads along the River and into interior valleys and eastward, it became apparent that the heavy handicap of rehandling freight at two portages would forbid the steamers from competing with the railroads. In 1879 the Oregon Steam Navigation Company sold out to the Villard interests for $5,000,000, and the Oregon Railroad and Navigation Company was the result.

Since that time there have been few steamboats on that part of the River above The Dalles. The section between The Dalles and the Cascades was joined to the tide-water section by the opening of the Government locks at the Cascades in 1896, and since that time many of the finest steamers on the River do an immense tourist business between The Dalles and Portland. It is only a question of a few years till the locks at Celilo will be completed, and then the whole vast Inland Empire, with its enormous production, will be thrown open to the sea. Then there will come on a new age of steamboat navigation, and with it the electric railroad. The steamer and the trolley car will set the whole Columbia Basin next door to tide-water. When improvements now in view by Government are completed, our River will be one of the most superb steamer courses in the world. That may truthfully be said already of the two hundred and twenty miles from The Dalles to the Ocean, as well as of the three hundred miles from Kettle Falls, Washington, to Death Rapids, B. C.

The Government engineers in Senate Document, 344, February, 1890, name the amount of navigable water on the Columbia and its tributaries at 1664 miles. This may, perhaps, be an underestimation, since President Roosevelt has recently referred to it as twenty-five hundred miles, in which he probably included the lakes. Generally speaking, the rivers of the Pacific slope descend from high altitudes in comparatively short distances, and are necessarily swift. Hence we can expect no such vast extent of navigable water on them as the Mississippi and its affluents offer. Aside from the Columbia itself, the main streams, east of the Cascade Mountains offering steamboat transportation, are the Snake, Okanogan, and Kootenai, together with Lakes Pend Oreille, Chelan, Cœur d'Alene, Flathead, Okanogan, Kootenai, Arrow, Christina, and Slocan. On the west side are the Willamette, Cowlitz, and Lewis rivers.

It would fill a volume to narrate even a tithe of the thrilling tales of daring and tragedy which gather around the subject of boating in all its forms on the Columbia.

One of the most remarkable steamboat journeys was that elsewhere described in this work, under command of Captain F. P. Armstrong, of the *North Star*, from Jennings, Montana, on the Kootenai to Canal Flats and thence through the canal to Lake Columbia. With that should be coupled as equally daring and more difficult, the trip down Snake River, from the Seven Devils to Lewiston, in a steamer piloted by Captain W. P. Gray.

Undoubtedly the most remarkable journey in any other sort of craft than a steamboat was that undertaken by a party of eighteen miners in 1865. They built a large sailing boat at Colville and in her ran up the entire course of the River, never having their boat entirely out of water, though our informant says that they must have had her on skids part of the way. They reached the very head of the Columbia, over seven hundred miles above their starting point, hauled their boat across Canal Flats, launched her again on the Kootenai, and so descended that furious stream to Fort Steele on Wild Horse Creek. The full history of that journey would be deserving of a place in any record of daring exploration.

In concluding this chapter, it may be said that there are now upon the lower Columbia some of the swiftest and most beautiful "fire-canoes" in the world. These ply on the two great scenic routes, one from Portland to Astoria, and the other from Portland to The Dalles. The most noted of these swift steamers at present writing are the *Hassalo* (No. 2), the *T. J. Potter*, the *Charles D. Spencer*, and the *Bailey Gatzert*.

CHAPTER XI

ERA OF THE MINER, THE COWBOY, THE FARMER, THE BOOMER, AND THE RAILROAD BUILDER

Early Gold-hunters—Gold in California—Effects of that Discovery
on the Columbia River Country—Growth of Towns on the Columbia—Discovery of Gold in the Colville Country—Gold on
the Clearwater—Stampede to the Idaho Mines—Cowboys Rush
in with the Miners—Sudden Development of Industries at Walla
Walla, Lewiston, and Other Towns—Profits and Fare in the Mines
in 1861—The Hard Winter—Development of the Farming Industry—The Boomers—The Hard Times—The Railroad Age—Beginning of Railroading in the Willamette Valley—Ben Holladay—
Transcontinental Railways—Henry Villard—His Great Building
and his Downfall—The Present Railroads on the River—Dr. D. S.
Baker and the Pioneer Railroad on the Upper River.

THE age of gold in the Columbia pressed hard upon that of the trappers. But it
dawned first far south.

The Spaniards had sought the precious metals with boundless energy. Richly
had the treasures of the Montezumas and the Incas rewarded their reckless cupid-
ity. But as they moved northward they met with nothing but disappointment. The
El Dorados of their ardent fancy had vanished as they turned toward Oregon and
California.

In 1848 the guns of Stockton and Fremont thundered the salvos of American
occupation over the Sierras. Just as the sovereignty of Uncle Sam was acknowl-
edged, the long-sought discovery of gold startled the world.

In 1838 a gay, mercurial Switzer, Captain Sutter, had made his way with a
band of trappers across the plains to Oregon, and thence had gone to California.
A dashing adventurer, without money, but with boundless *sang-froid* and *bonhommie*, Sutter had marvellously interested all whom he met and in some inexplicable
manner had got money and credit sufficient to build a fort and start an immense
ranch on the Sacramento, almost on the site of the present capital of the Golden
State. "Sutter's fort" became one of the most notable places in California. In 1844
James W. Marshall went to the Columbia, but after only a year's stay made his way
to California. In 1847 he entered into partnership with Sutter in a sawmill enterprise at Coloma on the south fork of the American River. There, while at work in

the mill-race on the 19th of January, 1848, Marshall discovered shining particles. Gold!

The discovery was made, and soon the secret was out. And then—! There never was anything quite comparable to what followed. The first and greatest of the great stampedes for gold took place.

When the tidings reached Oregon it was as though a prairie fire were running over the country. Men went fairly mad. Throngs, hardly stopping to take their ploughs from the furrow, mounted their horses, galloped off up the Willamette, through the lonely valleys of the Umpqua and the Rogue River, over the Siskiyou, and down the Sacramento, where a fortune could be had for the digging.

All the stress and strain of American life and history reached the utmost intensity in the fever strife for gold on the Sacramento. The Willamette and Columbia were almost equally stirred. During the first two years of the gold excitement homes on the Columbia were well-nigh deserted. Then the Oregonians began to drift back again. Some came with gold-bricks in their pockets and sacks of gold-dust in their packs. Some came broken in health and spirits, sick with disappointment. Some did not come at all, and their bones found unmarked graves in the pestilential ditches of the Sacramento.

But the shrewder Oregonians perceived that they had better than a gold mine in the trade with California. Grain, fruit, eggs, lumber,—these were in such demand that frequently twenty ships at a time were moored by the dense forests of the lower Willamette waiting for cargoes. Gold-dust was the universal medium, and it seemed to be cheaper than anything else. Four bushels of Oregon apples brought five hundred dollars in gold-dust in San Francisco. Tons of eggs were sold for a dollar apiece in the gold mines.

Portland, the lonely little village on the Willamette, with just enough of a foothold by the edge of the forest to keep from rolling into the River, sprang at a bound into the rank of a city. The huge firs were dug out, and wharves went in. The face of nature, even, as well as that of industry and politics, was transformed by that gold-dust in Marshall's mill-race on the Sacramento.

But, most of all, the disposition of the people was changed. The serene, idyllic, pastoral age passed, and the fierce lust for wealth, the boundless imagination, the fever in the veins, came on. Why should there not be gold as well by the Columbia as by the Sacramento! The men who had come down the Columbia in search for homes and grass-land for cattle, now began to retrace their steps and turn again up the River in search of the precious metals. Nor was it long before discovery of gold in the region tributary to Colville was made known. The first discovery was at the mouth of the Pend Oreille River. A regular stampede ensued. Other discoveries on a greater scale were soon to follow. During the early days of the gold excitement of California, a Nez Percé Indian had wandered on to the Sacramento. He made acquaintance with a group of miners, who became impressed with his general force and dignity. Among these miners was E. D. Pearce, and to him the Indian gave a vivid account of his home in the wilds of what is now Idaho. He told also a tale of how he with two companions were once in the high mountains, when they beheld in the night a light of dazzling brilliance, with the appearance of a refulgent star. The Indians looked at this with awe as the eye of the Great Spirit. But in the morning they summoned courage sufficient to investigate, and found a glittering ball that looked like glass. It was so embedded in the rock that they could not dislodge it. It was clear to them that this was some great "tomanowas." On hearing this fantastic story, the mind of Pearce was kindled with the idea that perhaps the Indians had found an immense diamond. He determined to seek it. After several years he made his way up the Columbia and reached Walla Walla. From that point he ranged the mountains of Idaho, but for a long time met no success. With a company of seven men, he entered upon an elaborate search, which finally so much aroused the suspicion of the Indians that they ordered him from the country. Nothing daunted, however, he induced a Nez Percé woman to guide the party from the Palouse to the Lolo trail, from which they reached an unfrequented valley on the north fork of the Clearwater. There one of the party, W. F. Bassett, tried washing a pan of dirt, with the result that he got a "colour." This was the first discovery of gold in Idaho, and the spot was where Oro Fino afterwards stood.

Fall was coming on, and after digging out a small amount of dust, the party deemed it wise to return to the settlements for a more thorough outfitting. Accordingly, they went to Walla Walla and located with J. C. Smith, to whom they imparted their secret. So impressed was Mr. Smith with the tidings that he organised a party of fifteen, with whom he returned just at the opening of the winter of that same year, 1860. Soon shut in by deep snows in inaccessible mountains, the little company built five rude huts, and in the intervals of the storms they dug for gold along the streams, meeting with such success that in March Mr. Smith made his way to Walla Walla with $800 in gold-dust. The dust was sent to Portland. Now ensued another gold excitement and stampede almost equal to that of '49 in California.

As the miners rushed into Idaho, every other species of industry rushed up the River with them. The cowboy came side by side with the miner. In fact, already following close on the heels of the Indian war, had come an inrush of cattle, horses, and sheep. During the last years of the decade of the fifties, stockmen had driven from the Willamette Valley thousands of head of stock to the rich pasture lands of the Walla Walla, Umatilla, and Yakima. When the gold discoveries of 1860 and 1861 became known, the activities of the cowboys were multiplied, added bands of stock were driven in, all the wild and extravagant features of a combined cowboy and mining age, vendors of "chain-lightning and forty-rod," gamblers, prostitutes, murderers,—and with them missionaries and teachers,—became reproduced again on the shores of the Columbia, Snake, Clearwater, Salmon, Walla Walla, and other rivers of the Inland Empire. It was another of those wild eras in which the worst and the best that are in human nature jostled each other at every turn.

Transportation problems followed close upon the cowboy and the miner. The Oregon Steam Navigation Company, organised in 1860, began within a year to run steamboats from Portland to Lewiston, with portage railroads around the Cascades and the Dalles. Stage lines were started from Umatilla, Walla Walla, and Lewiston, within a year or two after the gold discoveries of Oro Fino. Prairie-schooners, huge waggons, sometimes three in tandem fashion, drawn by a team of twenty mules, with jingling bells, driven with a "single line," formed the approved system of hauling freight over the mountain roads. In addition to the stages and prairie-schooners, however, thousands of mules and horses were driven with pack-saddles over the trails and roads. Then was the time when "throwing the diamond hitch" became a fine art. Then was the time, too, when it behooved stage-drivers and packers to be handy with a "gun," for "road-agents" were plentiful and vigilant. Many a man with a pack-saddle loaded with gold-dust, or sometimes with whiskey or even "canned goods," "passed in his checks" under some over-shadowing tree or behind some sheltering rock.

Both the distresses and the successes of that epoch are well illustrated by extracts from some of the newspapers of the time. From issues of the *Washington Statesman* of Walla Walla, we learn that flour was at one time a dollar a pound; beef, thirty to fifty cents a pound; bacon, sixty; beans, thirty; rice, fifty; tea a dollar and a half; tobacco, a dollar and a half; sugar, fifty cents; candles, a dollar. Some of these staples could not be had at all. Physicians, when they got into the mines, would charge twenty dollars a visit. Board was from five to ten dollars a day, frequently more.

But as an offset to the expense and frequent positive suffering, we gather the following item from an issue of the *Statesman* in December, 1861:

> S. F. Ledyard arrived last evening from the Salmon River mines, and from him it is learned that some six hundred miners would winter there; that some two hundred had gone to the south side of the river, where two streams head that empty into the Salmon, some thirty miles south-east of the present mining camp. Coarse gold is found, and as high as one hundred dollars per day to the man has been taken out. The big mining claim of the old locality belongs to Mr. Weiser of Oregon, from which two thousand six hundred and eighty dollars were taken out on the 20th, with two rockers. On the 21st, three thousand three hundred and sixty dollars were taken out with the same machines.

The *Statesman* for December 13, 1861, contains the following:

> During the week past not less than two hundred and twenty-five pack animals, heavily laden with provisions, have left this city for the mines. A report in relation to a rich strike by Mr. Bridges of Oregon City seems to come well authenticated. The first day he worked on his claim (near Baboon Gulch) he took out fifty-seven ounces; the second day he took out one hundred and fifty-seven ounces; the third day, two hundred and fourteen ounces; and the fourth day, two hundred ounces in two hours.

As an ounce of gold was worth sixteen dollars, it will be seen that Mr. Bridges of Oregon City had truly "struck it rich."

Within a year, a million and a half dollars in gold-dust had been taken from those mines. Anticipated demands led cattlemen to rush still larger numbers of stock into the upper Columbia Basin, and traders brought in yet larger supplies of goods into Walla Walla and Lewiston, as well as the mining camps themselves. A considerable part of these goods, we regret to narrate, consisted of material for spirituous refreshments. That the said refreshments were of a stalwart character may be inferred from a reminiscence of a traveller to Walla Walla, who relates that upon going into one of the numerous saloons, he found the floor covered with sawdust, and upon asking for whiskey, he received with it a whisk-broom. Feeling puzzled as to the intent of the latter, and not wishing to reveal his ignorance, he waited till another man came in. Waiting for developments, he found that the object of the broom was to sweep off a place on the floor to have a fit on, for the whiskey was sure to produce one. After having got through his fit, the happy (?) purchaser would return the broom and go on his way.

An Oregon Pioneer in his Cabin.

Photo. by E. H. Moorehouse.

Just as miners, cowboys, and traders were plunging eagerly into every form of enterprise, the famous "hard winter" of '61 descended upon the country. It was almost a Minnesota winter. There was snow on the ground from December 1st to March 22d, something never known before or since in the Columbia Basin. Cattle could find no food and perished by the thousands. Miners were found frozen into the stiff crust. In the rude cabins, with wide cracks into which the snow drifted, the few women and children in the Inland Empire fought a distressing and frequently losing fight. Even in the Willamette Valley where houses were more comfortable, supplies more plentiful, and the weather less severe, the conditions were hard enough. At Portland the price of hay was eighty dollars a ton. In Eastern Oregon it could not be obtained for any price, and the maintenance of life by cattle depended entirely on their endurance.

But with the coming on of tardy spring, the rush up the River was resumed, and the game went on. Seven millions in gold was reported in 1862, besides almost as much, as was estimated, taken out in ways of which no record was reported.

At Florence in February, 1862, flour was a dollar a pound; butter, three dollars; sugar, a dollar and a quarter; coffee, two dollars; boots, thirty dollars a pair.

The enormous profits, as well as enormous expense, of developing those mines hastened the coming of the farmer. Among the throng that passed madly into the mountains for gold, and among the throng that drove the wide-horned cattle over the bunch-grass hills, there were a few keen-eyed observers who asked themselves if wheat and corn and potatoes and barley and fruit-trees might not grow on those broad prairies, and especially along the numerous watercourses descending from the Blue Mountains.

A farm here and there at some favourable point beside some favouring stream, followed in two or three years by a flour-mill, then a few apples whose bright red cheeks and fragrant smell showed that the upper Columbia lands could match those of the Willamette, then an experimental wheat-field or barley-field on the high bunch-grass prairies, — and, almost before people realised it, the farmer was standing up beside the miner and the stockman, as tall and broad and important as either. The plough and the hoe and the mowing-machine took their places beside the pick and gold-pan and quirt and schapps and spurs as symbols of Columbia River nobility.

The "boomer" was the logical result of the development of mine and range and farm and garden and orchard. If people were going to eat and travel and raise wheat and cattle, they must inevitably buy and sell. And if they were going to buy and sell, they must needs "boom." The decade of the eighties was the great age of the boom in real estate along the Columbia and its tributaries. Then, as also upon Puget Sound, cities were founded with most extravagant size and expectations— on paper. Farm lands changed hands rapidly. If a man could raise nothing else on his land, he could at least raise the price. That was the time when the boomer boomed, the promoter promoted, and the sucker sucked. It was a great age, but alas, it was followed by an awakening, similar to that which follows a night of carousal, when the next day brings a dark-brown taste in the mouth and a very heavy head. The decade of the nineties was dolorous along the River and in the mines and forests and farms and town-lots and additions and suburbs adjoining.

Old Portage Railroad at Cascades in 1860.

A Log-boom Down the River for San Francisco.

Photo. by Woodfield.

Interlocked with the days of miner, cowboy, rancher, and boomer, was another age of equal importance and one that was both result and cause of the others. This was the age of the railroad builder.

Transportation by the River was a great feature of traffic in the fifties and sixties. But, during the second of those decades, the people of Portland began to realise that the time had arrived for rails as well as sails. The first great transcontinental railroad, the Union Pacific and Central Pacific, was in active process of building between California and Omaha. A fever of railroad building spread to the Columbia River people. Railroads were projected from Portland on both sides of the Willamette, up the valley, with the view of ultimate connection with California. Surveys were made by S. G. Elliott from Marysville, California, to Portland in 1863. It was October, 1870, when the first train reached Salem, the capital of the State. The road was known as the Oregon Central Railroad, and its manager and ultimately its chief owner was Ben Holladay, the most famous railroad man of that period in Oregon. In 1871 and 1872, railroad building was extended on the west side of the Willamette. The lines on both sides were reorganised under Mr. Holladay's control as the Oregon and California Railroad.

Meanwhile the air was full of discussion of a transcontinental line to the Pacific Northwest. The conception of a Northern Pacific railroad was nothing new. Away back in 1853, Governor I. I. Stevens and Captain George B. McClellan had made a reconnaissance across the Rocky and Cascade Mountains and over the great plains of the Columbia, for the purpose of ascertaining a route for a northern line. They pronounced the route feasible, but the time had not yet come for such an undertaking. In a letter to McClellan of April 5, 1853, Governor Stevens states the route to be from St. Paul to Puget Sound by the great bend of the Missouri River. It is interesting to note that this is nearly the course afterwards followed.

Work on the Northern Pacific was begun in the vicinity of Kalama on the Columbia in 1870. The financial panic of 1873 resulted in the failure of Jay Cooke & Company, the backers of the enterprise, and for several years railroad work was at a standstill.

In 1879 there came to Oregon the greatest railroad builder of that era, Henry Villard. He was a true financial genius, daring, far-seeing, persistent, and self-reliant. With the quick grasp of a statesman, Mr. Villard perceived that the Columbia River was the key to a boundless opportunity. He saw that a central line up the Columbia with branches north, east, and south-east, might be thrust like a wedge between the Northern Pacific and the Union Pacific and control both. In pursuance of this conception he made three rapid moves. The first was the incorporation of the Oregon Railway and Navigation Company. The second was the formation of the "blind pool" and the Oregon and Transcontinental Company. The third was the acquisition of a controlling interest in the Northern Pacific Railroad. The three years up to and including 1883 were years of almost feverish activity along the River. The line of the Oregon Railroad and Navigation Company between Wallula and Portland was pushed on with tireless energy. Rock bluffs were split off by enormous charges of dynamite, or were tunnelled through. The road was indeed built so hastily and the curves were in some cases so extreme that much work had to be done over at later times.

Lumber Mill and Steamboat Landing at Golden, B. C.

Photo. by C. F. Yates.

A part of Villard's plan in pushing the work so hastily was to divert the Northern Pacific system to the River, and make Portland rather than Puget Sound the western terminus. The undertaking seemed to be crowned with success. The connection was made. A gorgeous celebration, the greatest ever held in the Columbia River country, commemorated, in October, 1883, the completion of the transcontinental railroad to tide-water on the Columbia River. But in the very hour of victory, the sceptre fell from Villard's hands. His downfall was as sudden and dramatic as his rise. By clever jobbing of the market, the Wright interests regained possession of the majority of the Northern Pacific stock, the transcontinental pool broke, and at the very time that Mr. Villard was being worshipped at Portland as the financial god of the North-west, he learned that his gigantic enterprise had fallen into the hands of the enemy. But in spite of defeat the work of Villard was assured, and his name and fame as the champion railroad builder of the Columbia River was established.

After the Wright interests had regained possession of the Northern Pacific, that great system was pushed to Puget Sound. The Oregon Short Line was carried to a connection with the Union Pacific system. Thus two independent transcontinental lines reached the River. Yet later the Southern Pacific system acquired control of the Oregon and California Railroad, and, by joining the sections, connected the Columbia River with the Golden Gate. Through connecting lines the Canadian Pacific Railroad gained access to the Columbia River. There are, therefore, four distinct transcontinental railroad systems into the valley of our River. Two more are rapidly approaching completion. As a logical result, too, many local and connecting lines have been built. The Astoria and Columbia River Railroad, on the Oregon side of the River, joins Portland to Astoria and Seaside and the other resorts of the ocean beach. The Oregon Railway and Navigation Company has continuous connection on the south side of the Columbia and Snake rivers to Riparia on the latter stream, and thence by a road on the north side, owned jointly with the Northern Pacific, to Lewiston, Idaho. The most remarkable of all these connecting and joint roads is the Portland, Seattle, and Spokane Railroad, commonly called the "North Bank Road." This is supposed to be the joint property of the Northern Pacific and Great Northern railroads. It is one of the many monuments in the West to the financial genius and tireless energy of James J. Hill. It was completed in 1908, between Pasco and Portland, and at the first of the year following, from Pasco to Spokane. It is said to be the most expensively and scientifically built road in the United States, having curves and grades reduced to a minimum, being, in fact, a continuous descent from near Spokane to tide-water. Its builders evidently expect stupendous traffic, and every feature of the line is adjusted to such expectation.

Any account of the great railroads joining the Inland Empire to the River and thence to the seaboard would be incomplete without reference to the pioneer of them all, the "Strap-iron" narrow-gauge from Walla Walla to Wallula. This line was forced by the exigencies of the times, but it commemorates the rare commercial foresight and ability of a man, who, in native business genius, ranks with the foremost in the history of the Columbia Valley. This man was Dr. D. S. Baker, a native of Illinois, an immigrant to the Columbia in 1848, and a settler in Walla Walla in 1860. Perceiving the vast latent resources of the Inland Empire, he invested in land, founded a bank, became a partner in a store, and during much of the time was also actively engaged in his profession of medicine.

A Typical Lumber Camp.

Photo. by Trueman.

In 1863, the Oregon Steam Navigation Company was running boats from Portland to Lewiston, over four hundred miles, having short railroad portages at the Cascades and The Dalles. That was the most active era of the mines in Idaho. Rates from Portland to up-river points were as follows: freight from Portland to Wallula, $50.00 per ton; to Lewiston, $90.00; fare from Portland to Wallula, $18.00;

to Lewiston, $28.00. (The rates had been much higher a year or two earlier.) From Wallula to Walla Walla, freight was hauled by prairie-schooners at from $10.00 to $12.00 a ton, thirty miles. Needless to say, the company piled up a fortune.

A Logging Railroad, near Astoria.

Photo. by Woodfield.

Dr. Baker saw the possibilities of the region and, almost unaided, with every difficulty and discouragement, constructed a narrow gauge, with wooden rails, on which strap-iron was fastened. An astonishing amount of business was soon developed, steel rails were substituted, and the business made a fortune for its builder. It was absorbed by the Oregon Steam Navigation Company. But Dr. Baker's strap-iron road may be considered the true progenitor of the railroads of the upper Columbia.

During these first years of the twentieth century, the shores of the River have echoed with the sound of whistles on many a new road, but the distinguishing mark has been the construction of electric roads. The lower Willamette Valley, centring at Portland, has become fairly swarming with electric roads. Spokane has become almost an equal centre of electric lines, while Walla Walla is following close behind her larger sisters in the procession. When lines already constructed from Spokane southward are joined to a system projected from Walla Walla northward and westward, there will be a complete system of independent electric lines from all parts of Eastern Washington and North-eastern Oregon to steamboat connections on the River, and thence to tide-water. The significance of this as a commercial fact cannot be realised as yet.

CHAPTER XII

THE PRESENT AGE OF EXPANSION AND WORLD COMMERCE

Population and Productions of the Region on the River and its Tributaries—Extent of its Navigability—Improvements Needed—Kinds of Traffic—Local Traffic—Transcontinental Traffic—World Traffic—Advantages of the River Route for these Kinds of Traffic—The Bar—The Competition of Puget Sound—The Combination of River Route and Sound Route.

WE have traced the successive eras which have brought the land of the Oregon from a wilderness to a group of powerful young American States, abounding in resources and filled to the brim with hope and enthusiasm. We have followed the River through its eras of canoe, bateau, flatboat, sail-ship, and steamboat, and we have seen railroads built along its banks. It remains only to cast a brief final glance at the River in its present age, and to forecast something of what seems its sure future.

It may be said that the population of those parts of Oregon, Washington, Idaho, Wyoming, and Montana, which are embraced in the watershed of the Columbia, is probably nearly a million and a quarter. The population of the area in British Columbia is scanty, but rapidly increasing.

The productive capacity is very great. A rough estimate of production in the valley of the Columbia for the year 1908 would probably give a grain production of seventy million bushels, a lumber output of three billion feet, a mineral output worth sixty million dollars, and a combined output of pastoral, horticultural, fishing, and miscellaneous industries of fifty millions of dollars.

Such figures indicate that the Columbia River is already a factor in world commerce. Yet its development is but begun. What is to be its part in the world commerce of the future?

Inspection of a map will show that the Columbia possesses the only water-level route from the vast productive regions of the Inland Empire to the seaboard. As has been shown in the course of this volume, the River is navigable throughout the larger part of its course from Revelstoke in British Columbia to the ocean. In that distance there is one canal, with locks. That is at the Cascades, sixty-five miles from Portland. Before the River can be continuously navigable it will be necessary that a canal be constructed to overcome the obstructions at the Dalles, a few miles above the city of that name, another at Priest Rapids, seventy miles above Pasco, and still another at Kettle Falls. The Government is already engaged in the first of these works. The second seems comparatively near of accomplishment by reason of work done and projected by a powerful irrigation company. Nothing has yet been done at Kettle Falls, but it would be comparatively a light task to provide canal and locks at that point. Besides these larger obstructions there are several rapids at points between Kettle Falls and the Dalles which impede navigation at certain stages of water. The Government has made surveys of these sections of the River, and has announced that with comparatively small outlay the rocks and reefs may be removed, the channels deepened and straightened, and the River made navigable. One thing may be emphasised in this connection, and this is that the Columbia River has mainly a rocky bed, and hence work on the channels is permanent. It will not cut and fill, nor pile up islands and bars as does the Missouri.

In view of the capability of the River to carry great water traffic, and in view of the fact that railroad traffic is seeking and will still more seek the down-hill grade to the sea, it becomes a question of great interest what the future commerce of the River will be.

It is evident that there will be three kinds of traffic: local, transcontinental, world-wide. Each is bound to be vast beyond the calculations or even the imagination of the present. The local traffic is sure to be immense, for it is estimated that there is a million acres of land immediately contiguous to the River, irrigable and adapted to intensive farming. Present experience shows that five or ten acres of such land are sufficient to support a family. Many cities and towns are sure to grow upon the banks of the River. Its banks will sometime become populated like those of ancient Nile. Besides the immediate region of the River, there are millions upon millions of acres of land more remote, the great wheat fields and stock ranges and valley lands of tributary streams, and these broad areas will seek the river route. Much of this immense local traffic of the future will be conveyed by steamboats and barges.

The second class of traffic will be the transcontinental. All the railroads across the continent, except those down the Columbia, are obliged to climb the Cascade Mountains, four thousand feet or more in height. With difficulty two powerful locomotives pull a freight train of forty cars up the grades, and at some points even a third is needed. But a single locomotive will pull eighty cars on the level grades of the River roads. In the even keener competition bound to come, this advantage of grades and curves will be a factor of immense importance.

The third class of future commerce is the world-wide. No western American can contemplate the future of the world without being persuaded that the Pacific Ocean and its shores will be the scene of the greatest problems of the twentieth century. If this prove true, that world commerce of the Pacific will seek that point of the American continent which most swiftly and cheaply communicates with the eastern side of the continent and with Europe. Granting that a large part of world commerce will pass through the Panama Canal, there will still be, without question, an immense trade between the Orient and such points in our own country as are so far from the Atlantic seaboard that a transcontinental route is a necessity. Moreover, even for our Atlantic seaboard and for Europe, there will be large amounts of products, for the transit of which time will be a great object. Hence we may be sure that there will be extensive world commerce across the American continent. If so, where will it cross? Inspection of a globe demonstrates that the Columbia River route is shortest, and, for reasons already given, it is cheapest of all.

Puget Sound is its only present competitor. But the water-grade through the Cascade Mountains, along the banks of the Columbia, constitutes an advantage beyond the reach of permanent competition. Here, however, the critic comes in and claims that the Bar at the mouth of the River forbids entrance of the largest ships. This in a measure is true, though the difficulties of the Columbia Bar have been grossly exaggerated. There are over twenty-five feet of water on the Bar at the lowest tide. The flood-tide adds from six to twelve feet. In any ordinary weather, forty feet of water is safe enough for any vessel. But if marine architecture is going to keep pace with growing commerce, we may soon have ships drawing forty or fifty feet of water. If so, the Bar may indeed seriously block the heaviest commerce. Some observers have, therefore, believed that the big freights of the future will enter the Straits of Fuca, go to some one of the Puget Sound ports, thence pass by rail across the low tract of country between the Sound and the Columbia River, and proceed thence by the River route to the interior and eastward. This would combine the advantages of the two great routes of the Pacific North-west, abundant depth of water, low altitudes, and easy grades. This would, in truth, come nearest to realising the dream of the old navigators, the Strait of Anian. In any event, the future world will look to our River as the goal of markets as well as of vision, and as a highway of nations both for freights and for tourists.

PART II
A JOURNEY DOWN THE RIVER

CHAPTER I

IN THE HEART OF THE CANADIAN ROCKIES

Extent of Navigation on the River—Attractions of a Canoe Journey—The Canadian Pacific Railroad—Banff and Lake Louise—Summit of the Rockies—The Continental Divide and its Western Descent—Field and the Wapta River—Golden and the Upper Columbia—Peculiar Interlocking of the Columbia and the Kootenai, and Professor Dawson's Explanation of this—Views of the Selkirks and the Rockies—Some Steamboat Men and their Tales—Captain Armstrong's Adventures on the Kootenai—The Picture Rocks—Lake Windermere—The Location of the Old Thompson Fort—Baptiste Morigeau and his Stories of Pioneer Days—The War between the Shuswaps and the Okanogans—Down the River from Golden—Rapids and Navigation—By the Canadian Pacific through the Selkirks—Glacier and the Illecillewaet—Revelstoke and the River again—Wise Management of the Canadian Government and the Railroad.

A JOURNEY upon the River may best begin with its source and end with the ocean. It is about fourteen hundred miles by the windings of the stream from its origin in the upper Columbia Lake to the Pacific. It descends twenty-five hundred feet in that distance. It is therefore swift in many places. Yet it would be possible to descend almost the entire length of the River in a small boat. Nor can one imagine a more fascinating journey, especially if he could conjure back the shades of the great *voyageurs* of seventy years ago, as Monique and Charlefoux, famous in Dr. McLoughlin's time, and listen to their gay song, mingling with the plash of oars:

> Rouli, roulant, ma boule roulant,
> En roulant, ma boule roulant.

The way of approach for the Eastern tourist to a journey down the Columbia is by the Canadian Pacific Railway, a magnificent road in a gallery of masterpieces. Wonders begin before he reaches the western watershed. He will see Banff, with its hot springs, its immense hotel, its Bow River and Falls and Valley. He will see the gem of the Canadian Rockies, one of the gems of the earth, Lake Louise. Imagine a glistening wall of purest white, Mts. Lefroy and Victoria, with a vast glacier descending from them, great bastions of variously tinted rock closing on either side as a frame of the snowy picture, and in front a lake, small indeed, but of perfect form, a mirror in which the snowy wall, the glacier, the rocky ramparts, find a duplication as distinct as themselves.

A few miles farther west, and the traveller will find himself at one of the most significant of all places, the Continental Divide. Eastward the water flows into the Bow, thence into the Saskatchewan, and ultimately into the Atlantic. Westward the springs find their way to the branches of the Wapta, thence to the Columbia and the Pacific. The long westward ascent which we have followed all the way from Winnipeg ends at last. The track becomes level. We are at the summit. Looking southward we can see descending the steep slope, a clear mountain stream, which is parted into two branches by a little wall of stone. One branch goes east to the Atlantic, the other west to the Pacific.

It must have been of some such place, though farther north, that Holmes was imagining when he wrote:

> Yon stream, whose sources run
> Turned by a pebble's edge,
> Is Athabasca, rolling toward the sun,
> Through the cleft mountain-ledge.
>
> The slender rill had strayed
> But for the slanting stone,
> To evening's ocean, with the tangled braid
> Of foam-flecked Oregon.

At the parting of the streams, a pretty rustic framework has been erected, bearing the words, "The Continental Divide."

We are now on the Columbia's waters. We are also in the heart of the Canadian Rockies, and in the midst of a perfect sea of mountains. It has been said that British Columbia is "fifty or sixty Switzerlands rolled into one." Here are five distinct ridges, up and down, and through and around which, the Columbia and its affluents chase each other in a dizzy dance.

The descent of the west side of the Divide is appallingly steep. From Stephen to Field is a drop of one thousand two hundred and fifty-seven feet in ten miles. In that distance are several places which reach two hundred and thirty-six feet to the mile. Most explicit directions are given to engineers in respect to handling trains on this grade. A speed of only six miles an hour is allowed, and frequent stops and tests of air-brakes and signals are required. By reason of the exceeding care, no serious accident has ever occurred. In ascending three locomotives are required for an ordinary train.

There are several splendid resorts on the line of the Canadian railroad. Banff and Lake Louise are the resorts on the east side of the Divide. The first one west of that point is Field. There, as at all the other resorts, the hotels are managed by the Canadian Pacific Railroad Company. They are conducted with great skill and elegance, and may well be regarded as a tribute to the business ability and artistic taste of the managers.

As we descend the steep grade from Stephen to Field, we catch glimpses of peak after peak, range after range, valley after valley, glacier after glacier, purple, saffron, red, dazzling white, glistening greens and blues. Mt. Stephen lifts its great wall over a mile of almost perpendicular height, and nearly opposite is the spire of Mt. Burgess. Mountain wonders and attractions of every sort lie in all directions from Field. Perhaps the finest is Yoho Valley. There are the Takkakaw Falls, twelve hundred feet high. There is the Wapta Glacier, itself a part of a prodigious ice-field, known as Wahputekh, lying between the towering heights of Mts. Gordon, Balfour, and Tralltinderne.

Leaving Field, the road runs between two chains of mountains, the Ottertail on the north and the Van Horne on the south. The former is bold and spire-like in outline, with the snow-fields and ice pinnacles of Mt. Goodwin closing the vista. The latter is less bold in contour, but has a colouring of yellow rock-slopes in beautiful contrast with the rich purple of the lower forests.

Passing between those sublime mountain chains, we soon plunge into the Wapta cañon, with its perpendicular walls of rock rising hundreds of feet on either side. The Wapta is more commonly known as the Kicking Horse. It received that name in this wise. The Palliser exploring expedition of 1858 had been seeking unsuccessfully a feasible route through the Rockies. In the progress of the search, Sir James Hector, then in charge of the party, pitched camp on the Wapta. While there a vicious horse kicked him with such effect that he was left on the ground apparently dead. The three Indians with him had, in fact, dug his grave. But while they were conveying him to it, he suddenly came to himself. Having recovered, he became curious to follow the stream where he had met with the disaster. As a result he discovered the cañon and a short route through the main chain. Upon the pass he bestowed the name of "Kicking Horse," and this has latterly been bestowed upon the river itself. The river is one of the most remarkable of the tributaries of the upper Columbia. It drains a cordon of glaciated peaks, from which it bears a vast volume of water, foaming and frothing with frequent cataracts down the steep descent, from fifty to a hundred feet to the mile.

Forty-five miles west of the Divide we reach Golden on the Columbia. It is indeed a thrilling moment to the traveller when he first sets eyes upon these head-waters of the River of the West. Golden is a pleasant little town, a hundred and fifty miles below the upper Columbia Lake and twelve hundred and fifty by the windings of the River from its destination in the Pacific.

At Golden we must pause and make ready for our first journey on the River. The greater part of the tourist travel passes by Golden, not realising that between that pretty town and the lakes lie some of the most charming scenes in all the vast play-ground of British Columbia.

We find at Golden several steamboats in command of captains who are very princes of good fellows, as Captain Armstrong of the *Ptarmigan* and Captain Blakeney of the *Isabel*, with whom we may journey from Golden to Lake Windermere. Over the hundred miles between these two points the Columbia is a slack-water stream, having a descent of but fifty feet in the distance from the extreme head waters to Golden. Over considerable part of this distance the River runs in bayous.

These bayous or channels wind their serpentine courses through low flats, flooded at high water, and exposing fair expanses of vivid green at the subsidence of the waters.

Natural Bridge Kicking Horse or Wapta River, and Mt. Stephen, B. C.
Photo. by C. F. Yates.

Sunrise on Columbia River, near Washougal.
Copyright, 1902, by Kiser Photograph Co.

Professor Dawson, the eminent Canadian geologist, made a study of this section of the River some years before his death, and as a result expressed the opinion that the section of the Columbia above the mouth of Blue River, some thirty miles below Golden, formerly united with the Kootenai. But owing to some convulsion of nature, the surface was tilted just sufficiently to turn the section of the stream from Columbia Lake toward the north instead of the south, with the result that we have this slack-water system of lagoons and lakes constituting this marvellously picturesque division of the River. Now in confirmation of this theory of Professor Dawson we have in the relations of the Columbia and Kootenai the singular geographical phenomenon already referred to in an earlier chapter. The Kootenai runs through "Canal Flats," in which the upper Columbia Lake is situated, and comes within a mile of that lake. It is nine feet higher than the lake, but there is no high land there, and at one time a canal joined the Kootenai with the lake. This canal was wrecked in the great flood of 1894, but steamboats had run through it from the Kootenai to the Columbia, and it would be entirely feasible to reconstruct it. After having thus passed within a mile of each other and evidently having once been actually connected, the two rivers part company. The Columbia flows north and the Kootenai south. Each makes a vast bend. Again they reverse directions, the Columbia flowing south and the Kootenai north, and then come together many miles from their point of separation.

Aside from the unique beauty of the lagoons and the grassy shores, the eye of the traveller is delighted with the two mountain chains which confront each other across those glassy channels throughout the entire stretch from Golden to Windermere. On the east side is the main chain of the Rockies, and on the west are the Selkirks.

As we proceed on the deep, still stream, gliding from channel to channel, we may find ourselves mightily entertained by the conversation of such a navigator as Captain Armstrong or Captain Blakeney. For each can command a fund of historical and descriptive matter of rare interest.

Captain Armstrong was one of the earliest pilots on the Kootenai. In 1894 he built the *North Star* at Jennings, Montana, ran her up the wild stream to Canal Flats, thence through the canal to the Columbia lakes, and into the River itself. A more exquisite stretch of river navigation than that through Columbia Lake, Lake Adela, and Lake Windermere, and from them into the lagoons of the River, can scarcely be found or even imagined, and it was the lot of the *North Star* to ply upon that route until her unhappy destruction by fire in 1900.

There is little danger of accident on the placid water of the uppermost Columbia, but it is far different on the Kootenai. We heard many a tale of steamboating adventure from these pilots.

One of these so well illustrates those old-time conditions that we repeat here its chief points. Captain Armstrong owned two steamers, the *Ruth* and the *Gwendoline*. Both were engaged in transporting freight by way of Jennings to Fort Steele and the various mining camps in that district. The business was enormously profitable, for the boats received two and one half cents a pound. At that particular time there were twenty-six cars on the Great Northern Railway awaiting shipments.

**Lake Windermere, Upper Columbia,
where David Thompson's Fort was Built in 1810.**

Photo. by W. D. Lyman.

From his two steamers Captain Armstrong sometimes made two thousand dollars a day in gross receipts. But though profitable, the business was also correspondingly risky. The Jennings Cañon, above Bonner's Ferry, is, perhaps, the worst piece of water that has ever been navigated on the Columbia or its tributaries. A strip of water, foaming-white, down-hill almost as on a steep roof, hardly wider than the steamboat, savage-looking rocks waiting to catch hold of any unwary craft that might venture through, — so forbidding in fact was that route that Captain Armstrong found no insurance agent that felt disposed to insure his boats and cargo. At last he induced a San Francisco agent to make the trip with him and to offer a rate. After sitting in silence on the deck while the steamer whirled down the Jennings Cañon, the agent stated that his rate would be twenty-five per cent. of the cargo. The daring captain decided to take the risk himself. He had made a number of trips with entire success and immense profit. But just at the height of the season, when the twenty-six cars were on the track and a sack full of gold was waiting for him, the captain got into too much of a hurry. He was running the *Gwendoline*; one of his best pilots, the *Ruth*. The *Ruth* was ahead. Both were making their best possible time down the cañon to get a cargo. Captain Armstrong, at the wheel of the *Gwendoline*, was whizzing down the cañon at a rate which made stopping impossible, when to his dismay he saw the *Ruth* right ahead of him in a narrow turn, lying across the channel, wedged in the rocks. To stop was impossible. To select any comfortable landing-place was equally so. The *Gwendoline* piled right on top of the *Ruth*. Both were total wrecks, without a dollar of insurance. A two-thousand-dollar cargo gone in five minutes, to say nothing of boats and business that could not be replaced and a fortune within grasp that would never be so near again.

But such were the risks of steamboating on the Kootenai.

There are two historical notes of special interest to be made in connection with the journey to Windermere. One of these is a prehistoric drawing in some kind of red pigment on the smooth surface of a rock on the upper Columbia Lake. It seems to represent a battle scene, and, though rude, denotes some conception of picture art. The Indians think that it was made prior to Indian times. Apparently it belongs to the same order of pictures as the drawings on the rocks of Lake Chelan and other places in the north-west, furnishing a worthy theme for the antiquarian.

The other object of historical interest is the remains of the temporary fort built by David Thompson of the North-west Fur Company in 1810. Thompson crossed the Rockies in that year in order to descend the Columbia and gain possession of its territory for his fur company. He was a brave, intelligent, and enterprising man with considerable knowledge of astronomy. But he waited one season too long. For, finding it late in the year 1810 when he had reached the sources of the Columbia, he decided to winter there and descend the River in the spring. He selected a beautiful spot capable of defence on all sides on Lake Windermere and there built a rude fort, the trench and mound of which still remain. In the spring of 1811 he went down the river (and this was the first party to traverse the entire course of the Columbia) full of hope that he might take possession for Great Britain and the North-westers, only to find that the Astor party of Americans had preceded them by three months in effecting what might be called permanent occupation.

This was one of the important links in the history of the control of the Northwest. Doubt has been raised as to the authenticity of this Windermere location, but there are certainly the remains of mound and trench, and the tradition has it that here was the place of the Thompson party of 1810, the first place located by white men on the upper Columbia.

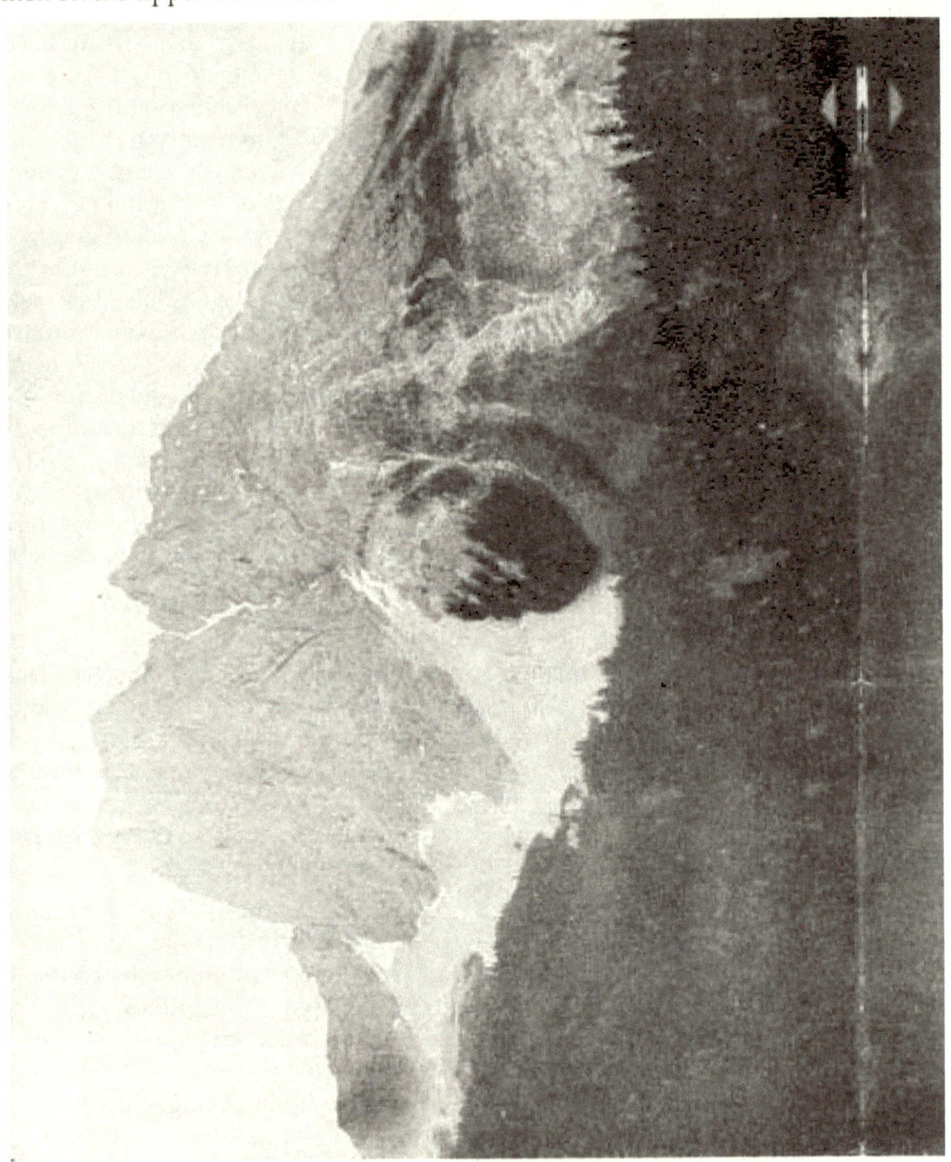

Mt. Burgess and Emerald Lake, One of the Sources of the Wapta River. B. C.

Photo. by C. F. Yates.

An interesting character lives on the shore of Lake Windermere in the person of Baptiste Morigeau. He is a man of sixty-six, the son of a French father and Indian mother. The father, Francis Morigeau, was born at Quebec in 1797, and came to the upper Columbia region as a free trapper in 1820. He trapped up and down the Columbia for many years, selling his catches to the Hudson's Bay Company, usually at Fort Colville. Baptiste was born at Windermere in 1842. Three years after that the father with his numerous family went to Colville. He had a number of horses and cattle, a large supply of valuable furs, ammunition, and traps. He located at Colville at just the right time. For, having taken up a large body of the rich land in that valley, he began raising hay and grain. His stock increased. He was surrounded with every species of rude plenty, and just at the most profitable time for him the gold discoveries began in 1854, followed the next year by the great Indian war. The fat cattle, the horses, the grain, hay, and vegetables of the Morigeaus were in great and immediate demand. Money came in to them by the handful. Baptiste states that they took in one hundred and fifty thousand dollars during the five years of Indian wars and settlement. Their lives were often in peril, but with good fortune, aided by their own connection with the natives, they escaped any serious harm.

On one occasion Indians were about to plunder them of their valuables and take possession of the barn where several of the family were thrashing grain with flails, when the oldest son, Aleck, suddenly turned his flail upon the marauders. So vigorously did he lay about him and so astonished were the Indians at the novel assault that they gave way and retreated.

Morigeau told us the interesting fact that there were practically no Indians living in the Windermere district until about a century ago. At that time some branches of the Shuswaps and of the Kootenais came in. Their relations were usually very amicable, but between the Shuswaps and the Okanogans was deadly and long-continued enmity. This was ended in a curious and interesting manner by the following event. The Shuswaps had captured the only daughter of the Okanogan chief. She was led with other captives into the Shuswap camp. The boasting warriors were gloating over the poor victim, and the squaws were discussing the greatest possible indignities and tortures for her, when an aged, white-haired chief got the attention of the crowd. He declared that his heart had been opened, and that he now saw that torture and death ought to end. He proposed that instead of shame and torture they should confer honour on the chieftain's child. He said: "I can hear the old chief and his squaw weeping all the night for their lost daughter." He then proposed that they adorn the captive with flowers, put her in a procession, with all the chiefs loaded with presents, and restore her to her father.

The girl meanwhile, who did not understand a word of the language, was awaiting torture or death. What was her astonishment to find herself decorated with honour, and sent with the gift-laden chiefs toward her father's camp. On the next day the mourning chief of the Okanogans and his wife, looking from their desolate lodge, saw a large procession approaching, and they said: "They are coming to demand a ransom."

Bonnington Falls in Kootenai River, near Nelson.

Photo by Allan Lean.

As the procession drew nearer, one of their men said that it looked like a woman adorned with flowers in the midst of the men with presents of robes and necklaces. Then they cried out: "It is our child, and she is restored to us." So they met the procession with rejoicing and heard the speech of the old Shuswap chief. And after that there was peace between the Shuswaps and the Okanogans.

Having returned from Lake Windermere to Golden by small boat,—one of the most charming of all water trips,—we are prepared to make a new start down the River.

The River from Golden holds a general north-westerly course to its highest northern point in latitude 52 degrees. There having received its northmost tributary, Canoe River, a furious mountain stream, it makes a grand wheel southward, forming what is known as the Big Bend. This section of the River was navigated by the bateaux of the trappers and the canoes of the Indians. There are, however, several bad rapids, of which Surprise Rapids, Kimbasket Rapids, and Death Rapids, are the worst. These cannot be passed by steamboats. The *voyageurs* seem to have run them sometimes, though they ordinarily made portages. A Golden steamboat captain assures us that none but fools ever ran Death Rapids,—and they were mostly drowned.

The Canadian Pacific Railroad follows the Columbia from Golden to Beavermouth, then turns up the Beaver to cross the Selkirk Mountains. The Beaver is a magnificent mountain stream, and from the railroad, high on the mountain side, the traveller can at many points look down hundreds of feet upon the river. Though the Selkirks are not quite so high as the main chain of the Rockies, they are even grander. The snowfall is materially greater in the Selkirks, and the glaciers are vast in extent. It is said that the snowfall at Glacier averages thirty-five feet during the winter, and that it lies from four to eight feet deep from October to April. There are thirty immense snowsheds on this section of the railroad.

Glacier is the great resort in the Selkirks. This splendid resort has attractions in some respects superior to those of Banff, Lake Louise, or Field. It is in the very heart of the Selkirks. The Great Glacier is only a mile and a half distant, a glacier which is said to cover an area of two hundred square miles; more than all the glaciers of Switzerland combined. From the watch tower at Glacier, this mass of ice, twisted and contorted, with all the colours of the rainbow playing upon it, is one of those visions of elemental force which only great mountains reveal. Like all the glaciers of the Northern Hemisphere, this is receding at a rapid rate. A record on the rock indicates the point to which the ice attained in July, 1887, and the ice is now over seven hundred feet distant from that point.

The Asulkan Glacier is a more beautiful sight, as viewed from Abbott rampart, than the Great Glacier. Every traveller should climb the trail to Abbott in order to get that sight. And with it he will view the twin peaks of Castor and Pollux yet farther south, while to the north the splendid peaks of Cheops, Hermit, and Cougar dominate the majestic wilderness.

Bridge Creek, a Tributary of Lake Chelan, Wash.

Photo. by F. N. Kneeland, Northampton, Mass.

But the most striking single sight is the granite monolith of Sir Donald. This is almost a counterpart of the Matterhorn of Switzerland, though not so high. It rises in one huge block to a height of 10,808 feet. It has been climbed, though this is one of the most daring and difficult of climbs. From the dizzy spire there is visible a perfect map of peaks, rivers, valleys, and lakes. It is said that a hundred and twenty glaciers can be seen.

Kootenai Lake, from Proctor, B. C.

Photo. by Allan Lean.

From Sir Donald and the Great Glacier issues the Illecillewaet River, well-named, for this means the "swift flowing." From its source in the Great Glacier to its entrance of the Columbia it descends thirty-five hundred feet in forty-five miles. It is swift. One of the most interesting places on this section of the road is the "Loops," a place where the track has to descend five hundred and twenty-two feet in seven miles. To accomplish this, it has been carried in a "double S" around the bases of Mts. Ross and Bonney. So close are the tracks that the two parts of the loop a mile in length are not more than eighty feet apart, one being almost perpendicularly above the other. Some miles farther down is the Albert Cañon on the Illecillewaet. On this point the distinction has been conferred of a complete pause of the train, while from it the passengers hasten to a platform to gaze down the perpendicular walls three hundred feet to the white torrent tearing its way through the rock.

Soon Revelstoke is reached, and we are again on the navigable waters of the Columbia. Every traveller, as he leaves the line of the Canadian Pacific Railroad, must pay his tribute of respect to the skill, energy, and intelligence with which this superb road is conducted. It has been said that English money supplied this road, Scotch energy built it, and Irish keenness and adaptability run it. Sir Thomas Shaughnessey, the manager, is certainly entitled to the respect and gratitude of thousands of tourists.

· With the railroad, all tourists will associate the Canadian Park managers. The Canadian Government is a singularly intelligent one. It has grasped the possibilities in these vast and varied scenic charms, and has used exceedingly good judgment in rendering them accessible to the travelling public. This entire mountain area bordering the railroad, to an extent of five thousand seven hundred and thirty-two square miles, has been set apart as a park, in charge of the Department of the Interior. Superb roads are constructed in available places, and improvements are continually in progress about the springs and falls and lakes and other points of interest. The Government, in fact, exercises entire control, but grants concessions to the railroad company in the matter of hotels and other conveniences.

As we bid good-bye to the Canadian Rockies, we may say that perhaps the world offers nowhere else such a sea of mountains, such knots and clusters and cordons of elevations, as in this strange and sublime region where the Columbia and its tributaries, the Kootenai, the Illecillewaet, the Wapta, the Beaver, the Canoe, seem to be playing hide-and-seek with the Thompson and the Fraser. There are not less than five distinct snowy ridges between the head waters of the Saskatchewan and the Pacific Ocean. The existence of this immense watershed of snowy mountains accounts for the vast volume of the Columbia. Although not half as long as the Mississippi, the Columbia equals it in volume.

Well joined, in truth, are the sublime River and the sublime mountains. One cannot fully understand the River unless he has seen its cradle and the cradle of its affluents beneath the shadows of the great peaks of British Columbia.

CHAPTER II

THE LAKES FROM THE ARROW LAKES TO CHELAN

The Lake Plateau—The Glacial Origin of the Lakes—Down the Arrow Lakes from Revelstoke—The Fine Steamers—Characteristics of the Scenery—By Rail from Robson to Nelson—Agricultural, Mineral, and Lumbering Resources around Nelson—Kootenai Lake and its Charms—On the River from Robson to Kettle Falls—Historic Features around Kettle Falls—On Lakes Cœur d'Alene, Pend Oreille, and Kaniksu in Northern Idaho—From Kettle Falls to Chelan—Appearance of Chelan River—First View of the Lake—Delights of a Boat Ride up the Lake—Comparison of Chelan with other Great Scenes—Storm on the Lake—Goat Mountain—Views from Railroad Creek—The Red Drawings—Rainbow Falls and Stehekin Cañon—The Wrecked Cabin and its Story—Railroad Creek and North Star Park—Cloudy Pass and Glacier Peak.

IN the progress of our journey down the River on the route of the old-time fur brigades, we have passed over what may be considered the first two stages of the stream. The first is the lagoon-like expanse of the section from Canal Flats to Golden, one hundred and fifty miles. The second is the more swift and turbulent part from Golden to Revelstoke, two hundred and fifty miles. At the latter place we enter upon a third stage of the River, the lake stage.

The region of the lakes constitutes one of the most unique and delightful of all parts of the River. Let the reader consult the map and he will find an area of probably one hundred thousand square miles in British Columbia, Washington, Idaho, and Montana filled with lakes. This lake region constitutes a plateau, crossed indeed by mountains and somewhat rough in surface, but of a uniform general elevation. It constitutes a sort of debatable region between the two great slopes, one from the Rocky summits to the lakes and the other from the lakes to tide-water. On those slopes the white waters of cataract and rapid are found; on the plateau, the deep, still lakes. A glance at the map reveals the fact that the larger of these lakes are long and narrow, and lie on north and south lines. A journey on them reveals the fact that they are deep and clear and cold. Join these facts with the additional one that they are surrounded by snowy mountains, and you have no difficulty in deciding their origin. They are glacial. At some time in the glacial ages, stupendous ploughshares of ice descending from Rockies, Selkirks,

Gold Range, Cascades, and Bitter Roots, gouged out profound cañons in the rents already wrought by earthquakes, and these became the lake beds.

Lower Arrow Lake, B. C.

Photo. by Allan Lean, Nelson.

Each one of the branches of the River in this plateau region has one or more of these expansions. On the Columbia itself are the Arrow Lakes. Kootenai Lake is an enlargement of the River of the same name. Okanogan Lake is likewise an expansion of its river. Christina Lake is the source of Kettle River. The Slocan River derives its icy torrents from Slocan Lake. Flathead, Kaniksu, and Pend Oreille lakes feed Clark's Fork, now more commonly known in its lower section as Pend Oreille River. Cœur d'Alene Lake supplies the Spokane River. Chelan pours its cold flood into the Columbia through a river of the same sweet sounding name. Wenatchee Lake gives life to the Wenatchee River.

We find at Revelstoke that the chief current of tourist travel follows the main line of the Canadian Pacific Railroad. Nevertheless, there is a rapidly increasing movement of travellers on the branch by steamboat over the Arrow Lakes and the Kootenai to what is known as the Crow's Nest line from Spokane to Calgary, Winnipeg, and other points east.

The Canadian Pacific line has excellent steamers, the *Rossland*, the *Kootenai*, the *Kaslo*, the *Kuskanook*, and others of similar grade. The journey on the *Rossland* or *Kootenai* down the Arrow Lakes from Arrowhead to Robson is one to dream of, one to recall in waking hours, and even, we almost suspect, in another life. The two lakes together constitute one hundred and thirty miles of steamboating, and every mile has its special charm. It was the peculiar joy of the *voyageurs*, after having toiled over the snowy and wind-swept Athabasca Pass and buffeted the foamy descent of Death Rapids, to reach the Arrow Lakes and lazily paddle down their tranquil deeps. In fact, pleasant as is our journey on the *Rossland*, we would rather reconstruct the bateaux of 1840 and in them make the whole long journey to the sea, a thousand miles away.

The traveller learns from the captain, if he can persuade that busy personage to indulge in conversation, that the Arrow Lakes derived their name from the fact that in early times great bundles of arrows could be seen stuck in the clay banks or in the crevices of the rocks at the head of the upper lake. The upper Arrow Lake has mountain banks rising thousands of feet to the zone of eternal snow. The shores are usually precipitous, though it is not uncommon to see smooth slopes furnishing timbered margins to enchanting little bays. At various places along the shores we see the beginnings of fruit and dairy ranches. It is only within four or five years that anything has been done here in the way of cultivation. The results thus far attained prove the wonderful adaptability of soil and climate to choice fruits. And the flowers,—Heaven bless them!—the sweetest and biggest and brightest of roses, pinks, sweet peas, larkspurs,—every kind that grows, are seen in profusion at almost every point where there has been any cultivation. By a little conversation with people at the landings we learn that the new-fledged ranches are very profitable. One tells us that he has made a net profit of two dollars and twenty-five cents per crate on his strawberries, or five hundred dollars an acre.

Perhaps the most attractive place on the Arrow Lakes is the point where the upper lake narrows into the stretch of fifteen miles of river joining the two lakes. The mountains on either hand, in great billows of forest green and blue, rise ever upward till they break against the eternal frost. The shores are clothed in dense forests, and on either hand bold promontories enclose sheltered bays, the very beau ideals of camping places.

Bridal Veil Falls on Columbia River.

Photo. by E. H. Moorehouse.

We find the lower Arrow Lake of a gentler type of scenery than the upper. The mountains no longer bear snow-peaks and glaciers on their crests, and there are no longer to be seen the stupendous rocky walls which in places enclose the upper lake. But as a compensation for the loss of this pre-eminent grandeur, the lower lake possesses a charm of colouring, both of water and shore, a richness of mountain outline and tints, and a certain serenity which may well make it an equal of its grander companion.

At the lower end of the Arrow Lakes the steamer stops and transfers her freight and passengers to the trains running from Robson to Nelson. This is necessitated by the fact that the Kootenai River, which enters the Columbia just below Robson, has a descent from Nelson of over two hundred feet. The railroad follows the Kootenai, which almost rivals the Columbia in magnitude. We pass the Bonnington Falls, the noblest waterfall on the entire system of Columbia's tributaries, with the exception of the Great Shoshone of the Snake.

Reaching Nelson, the metropolis of this entire lake country, we find a bustling, active, well-built little city of seven thousand people. The leading industries centring at Nelson are mining and lumbering. It has been discovered very recently, however, that the soil and air and climate are peculiarly adapted to choice berries and fruits. The shores of the river and lake at this point are rugged and rocky, at first thought ill adapted to horticulture. But it is well known that rough locations produce choicer fruit. Between the boulders or nestling against the hillsides, the peach and apple take on an added blush, absorb a more delicate nectar, exhale a more exquisite perfume. We are told that during the season of 1908 there were twenty thousand crates of berries, mainly strawberries, shipped from Nelson, at a price of two to three dollars per crate.

In every direction from Nelson is mineral wealth of untold quantity. Almost every mineral known, gold, silver, copper, zinc, lead, to say nothing of every kind of fine building stone, including marble, besides coal and iron, is found east, west, north, and south of Nelson. The town itself was founded by reason of the Silver King mine, which can be seen high up on the mountain side south of the place. The output of these mines has been immense. In spite of the comparatively hard times, the output of the three districts of the Kootenai, Rossland, and Boundary, was estimated at $21,025,500 in 1907. One interesting fact connected with the mining industry in the lake country is that at Nelson is located an electric zinc smelter, the only one of the kind in the world. Zinc is found in association with gold, silver, and copper, and, though valuable, is quite an impediment to the mining of the gold and silver. This unique smelter works by what is called the Snyder process, an electrical system, which, if it accomplishes all that is hoped for, will open every mine on the Kootenai.

From Nelson we find the way open by fine steamers to all parts of the Kootenai. This largest of all the lakes of the Columbia system, containing 141,120 acres of surface, bears a general resemblance to the Arrow Lakes, clear, deep, cold, with lofty mountains on either side and vast stretches of purple forests crowding to the very margin of the water. This lake consists of three arms, northern, southern, and western. The Kootenai River enters by the southern and leaves by the western.

Shoshone Falls, in Snake River, 212 Feet High.

Photo. by W. D. Lyman.

The northern part of the Kootenai region, especially around Kaslo, possesses vast mineral wealth. A railroad proceeds from Kaslo to Sandon in the heart of the mountains, and to Slocan Lake and thence to Nakusp on the upper Arrow Lake. The scenery of Slocan Lake is even more wild and rugged than that of the Kootenai. Both abound in fine trout. We saw a lake trout at Nelson of a weight of twenty-two pounds. Ducks and geese and swan are common on the water, limitless grouse and pheasants are found in the woods, while deer, elk, and bear are common in the wild maze of mountains and cañons;—a sportsman's paradise.

Tourists taking the route eastward go from Nelson on the elegant steamer *Kuskanook* to Kootenai Landing and there take up again the railway route by the Crow's Nest. Such as desire to go to Spokane can leave the line at Curzon and go southward to a connection with the Spokane International. There is also a rail connection more directly between Nelson and Spokane by the Spokane and Northern. This pursues more nearly the course of the Columbia River, of which the traveller obtains delightful glimpses at intervals. But for ourselves, we would rather go by rowboat from Robson down the River over the historical route of the old *voyageurs*. No rail route compares with the water.

The River is a superb water-way from Robson, British Columbia, to Kettle Falls, Washington, about ninety miles. In fact, the section of the River from Death Rapids above Revelstoke to Kettle Falls, including the Arrow Lakes, is the longest unbroken stretch of deep, still water on the entire River, being about three hundred miles.

Kettle Falls, too, is a historic spot. For here was Fort Colville of the Americans and also the old Hudson's Bay post. Here was the greatest centring of the fur-trade on the upper River. Here were the strongest of all the Catholic missions, and here were the most fertile fields and the earliest cultivated of any on the upper River. Here is the Colville Indian Reservation, and here for many years the wily and untamable old savage Moses herded his bands of "cuitans," watched the incoming whites with jealous eye, and, as opportunity offered, made way with such wandering prospectors or stockmen as he could find off their guard in rocky glen or forest depth. (And none ever knew what became of them.) Here Hallakallakeen (Eagle Wing) the great Nez Percé chief, commonly known as Joseph, who waged the Wallowa War of 1877 to its bitter conclusion, carried on the sad remnant of his days, and not far distant on the wild Nespilem, he held his summer camp. In all directions around Colville and Kettle Falls, up the Sans Poil and Kettle rivers, are opening mines and farms, one of the most promising sections of all the promising State of Washington.

Time forbids us to visit all the lakes in this wonderful lake section. But we must see the most important. While at Spokane, we should not fail to go, by trolley or train or auto or horseback, to the greatest of all Spokane resorts, Cœur d'Alene Lake. Of its beauties and delights, and of the "shadowy St. Joe River," and of the canoeing and fishing and hunting which may be found there galore, some of our pictures speak. And of them any one who has ever been there will also speak in no uncertain tone. It seems no whit short of the unpardonable sin to give no longer space to that wonderland of lakes, Cœur d'Alene, Pend Oreille, and Kaniksu, in Northern Idaho, each the centre of every conceivable scenic attraction. In their near vicinity, too, lie the great mines of the Cœur d'Alene district, the greatest silver lead mines in the world, whose fabulous wealth (forty million dollars a year) has built many a stone mansion at Spokane, or sent the prospectors of yesterday to the ends of the earth for the pleasure or display of to-day. But the limits of this chapter forbid description of these masterpieces. Though each lake has its individual character, there is a general similarity. All have the characteristics of their common glacial origin and mountainous surroundings.

Lake Pend Oreille, Idaho.

Photo by T. W. Tolman.

Lake Cœur d'Alene, Idaho.

Photo. by T. W. Tolman.

We may therefore make one visit and give descriptions of the one great inclusive scene or group of scenes which may be said to express the beauty, the sublimity, the wonder of the lakes of the Columbia River. And this one typical lake, the all-inclusive, is Chelan, "Beautiful Water."

The "Shadowy St. Joe," Idaho.
Photo. by T. W. Tolman.

True to our purpose of following the River from source to sea, we turn back now from Spokane in order to go from Kettle Falls to Chelan by boat. There are no regular steamboats running from Kettle Falls to Brewster at the mouth of the Okanogan, but from the last named point to Wenatchee the steamboat is the regular and indeed only means of public travel. Throughout the entire course of two hundred miles from Kettle Falls to Wenatchee the river is wild and swift. Yet steamers have traversed the entire distance, and Government engineers are now engaged in surveys looking to improvements such as will make steamboat traffic easy and profitable. We pass numberless points of interest, but "Chelan, Chelan," "Beautiful Water, Beautiful Water," is our goal.

We had thought that the Columbia was clear, but we did not then know what clear water really was. When we reach the mouth of Chelan River we know. We see a streak of blue cutting right across the impetuous downflow of the River. As we push our way into it we discover that it is so clear as to make little more obstruction to the view of rocks and fish below than does the air itself. This transparent torrent is the outlet of the lake. It is only four miles long and descends three hundred and eighty feet in that distance. It furnishes one hundred and twenty-five thousand horse-power at low water. The cañon, riven and tortured, through which it descends, is a fitting approach to the lake, unique Chelan. For having traversed the four miles, we find the lake outstretched before us.

At this first view the lake has that look of a serene obliviousness to the flight of passing centuries, that impress of eternity, that belongs to all great works of God or man. But majestic as is the view at the lower end of the lake, we are not content to remain there. "*Neskika Klatawa sahale*," cry we with a single voice, which being interpreted is, "Let us go up higher," the motto, by the way, of our Mazama (Mountain-Climbers') Club of the Pacific North-west. In skiffs, well-laden with provisions and ammunition, we set forth on our sixty-mile pull toward "where the spectral glaciers shone."

Delightful, delightful, almost ecstatic in truth, this rocking on the glassy swell; this bed of romantic spruce and pine boughs on the beach; this star-lit sky which is our only roof; this murmur of cascades falling from the bluffs; this trolling for five-pound trout; this disembarking on some rocky point and climbing a granite pinnacle from which a perfect maze of mountains, streams, and forests, lies extended below; this experience of the deadly attack of "buck-ague" which paralyses our arms as some goat or deer dashes by; and then the inexpressible delight with which we, "stepping down by zigzag paths and juts of pointed rock, came on the shining levels of the lake." We do not wish to hurry our oars. We must take time to look into the heavenly blue of the waters through the foam-streaks left by our advancing prows. We must suspend the oar-dip entirely at times while we gaze dizzied, with strained necks, up, up, thousands of feet, toward "Death and Morning on the Silverhorns." We must study shore and water as we pass slowly by, finding therein ample confirmation of the theory of glacial origin.

On the Cœur d' Alene River, Idaho.

Photo. by T. W. Tolman.

This is one of the deepest cañons on earth. Not such another furrow has Time wrought on the face of the Western Hemisphere, at least. At some points the granite walls rise almost vertically six thousand feet from the water's edge. Here, too, soundings of seventeen hundred feet have been necessary to touch bottom. Over a mile and a half of verticality! This surpasses in depth Yosemite, Yellowstone, Columbia, or even Colorado Cañon. As compared with those more familiar wonders, Chelan lacks the incomparable symmetry and completeness of Yosemite; it has not such a multitude of waterfalls and groups of "castled crags" as are seen within the basaltic gates of the Columbia; it does not display that variety of colouring, especially of the lighter and warmer hues, which astonishes the beholder of the Colorado or the Yellowstone, and it has no especially curious feature like the geysers of the last; but for immensity, for a certain chaotic sublimity, for the rich and sombre grandeur of the purple and garnet, dusky, and indigo-tinted shore views, Chelan surpasses any of the others, while in its water views,—such colourings and such blendings, light-green, ultramarine, lapis lazuli, violet, indigo, almost black,—such light and shade, "sea of glass mingled with fire," where every cloud in the changing sky and all the untold majesty of the hills find their perfect mirror, all hues and forms, a kaleidoscope of earth and heaven, beyond imagination to conceive or pen to describe or brush to portray,—in all this, Chelan is without a rival.

As we round a shaggy promontory, there the snow-peaks stand in battle array, azure, purple, amethystine, with lines and masses of glistening white, flushed on their topmost pinnacles with rosy light from the westering sun, solemn, solitary, very oracles of mountain revelation, so grand, so beautiful, so true, looking as though they had been there forever waiting for an interpreter,—before that scene we bow the head and make involuntary obeisance, the homage of the true in man to the true in nature, that is, the recognition of a common brotherhood in one divine origin.

Not of every scene on this lake of wonders can we speak. Yet every mile brought its special revelation. Sometimes we found the lake in storms. As we rowed in what seemed a summer calm, Winter from his throne eight thousand feet above sent forth his cloud-legions, which, like the "thunder birds" of Indian story, spread their wings and came down. The thunder clash went echoing in long reverberations "from peak to peak, the rattling crags among." "If a squall ever strikes you, put for the first crack in the bank that you see," had been the parting injunction of the lake sailors when we started on our cruise. We observed the warning and made the best possible time to a cranny in the ill-omened "Windy Cape." And there we lay till morning, when the tumult fell as suddenly as it rose, and lake and sky smiled as serenely at each other as ever.

The chief point on the lake, for photographing, hunting, fishing, and climbing, is Railroad Creek, fifty miles up the lake. Railroad Creek comes from the "Roof of the World," having its source in the very heart of a great group of glaciers. It descends probably six thousand feet in twenty-five miles. It is swift! The fury with which it hurls logs and even boulders down its cataract bed is fairly appalling. The very earth quivers beneath its flail-like strokes.

Gorge of Chelan River, the Outlet of Lake Chelan.

Photo. by T. W. Tolman, Spokane.

Nowhere, perhaps, can one see more work done by rivers than here. The entire course of one of these rivers can be traced from the lake. Rising in a snow bank six thousand feet above, its route marked by a streak of foam, sometimes falling in spray hundreds of feet, then hiding behind a cliff, to burst forth in snow-white "chute," augmented by similar streams from lateral cañons, it plunges into the lake with a perfect delirium of motion. So great is the erosion that were not the lake of enormous depth, it would soon be filled with the jetsam and flotsam of the hills.

The sunset effects looking up the lake from Railroad Creek are marvellous, though, alas, the cool black and white of the photograph cannot preserve the wealth of colouring, "the illumination of all gems," which for a few transcendent moments fills the mighty cañon "bank-full" with such radiance that one might think it the grand gathering place of all the rainbows of earth. The light greens and blues of the shallower water shade into deepest indigo toward the centre, reflecting the ever-changing hues of the cañon walls, a deep, rich, and sombre purple on the shaded side, while on the sun-lit side are poured forth upon the shaggy mountain slopes perfect inundations of orange, carmine, and saffron. From these floods of glory there falls into the lake a seeming rain of pearls and rubies, barred with stripes of gold and crimson. But the sun drops lower and the splendour fades, the conflagration of the sky is quenched, and it seems as though ten thousand ships, "all decked with funeral scarfs from stem to stern," were putting out from the glooming western shores, strewing darkness as they move,—and night is at hand.

Like all travellers to Lake Chelan, we must make a journey to the head of the lake, to the Stehekin River, and to Rainbow Falls. The view up the cañon of the Stehekin is the crowning glory of this panorama of sublimities. A forest of almost tropical luxuriance covers the morass through which the impetuous river makes its way. On either side tower the cañon walls, capped with snow. The background consists of glittering pinnacles of some of the Glacier Range. Majesty, might, elemental force, eternity,—such are the only words to express the emotions excited by this scene.

One curious thing to be seen at the mouth of the Stehekin, and at several other places on the lake is a series of rude drawings on the smooth, white surface of the granite bluff, the work of some prehistoric artist, unknown to the Indians, and of so ancient date that the lake is now twenty feet below their level. The drawings are of men, goats, tents, and trees, and are in strong red colours, of some very enduring nature. One is ashamed to record that alleged human beings in the form of white tourists have used these curious relics of bygone days as targets to shoot at from their boats, and have ruined some of the finest. Also that some vandal has desecrated the place by painting a glaring advertisement of his ferry underneath.

Although it may well seem to the tourist who has attained the head of Lake Chelan that nature has reached her acme of grandeur, and that it would tax his powers of belief to be informed that there is grander yet, we shall run the risk of saying just that, and bid him join us on side journeys up the mighty cañons of the Stehekin River and Railroad Creek. Lake Chelan being, as already indicated, in the very heart of the Cascade Mountains, and these mountains here attaining an average elevation of seven or eight thousand feet, with dozens of peaks of ten thousand or more, and the countless impetuous streams from those snowy heights having cut their way deep down toward the lake level, it follows as a matter of course that the entire Chelan region, for an area of probably ten thousand square miles, is perfectly gridironed with cañons. Many of them have never been explored or even entered. In them are myriads of lakes, waterfalls, parks, glaciers, and, in fact, every species of mountain attraction. There is no question that within this vast cordon of mountains there are more glaciers than in all the rest of the

United States combined, and, with the exception of the Sierras and the Canadian Rockies, there is certainly no other region on this continent that can for a moment enter into competition with it. Travellers have assured the author that the Alps in no respect except historical association, surpass, and some say, do not equal this crowning glory of our great North-west State.

Head of Lake Chelan—Looking up Stehekin Cañon.

Photo. by W. D. Lyman.

Amid the bewildering profusion of great cañons radiating from the lake, the two most accessible are those of the Stehekin River and Railroad Creek. The former enters the head of the lake, after a course of probably fifty miles from Skagit Pass. To ascend this cañon we must commit our lives and fortunes to cayuse ponies and a mountain trail, which, though good enough to the initiated, is a terror to the "tenderfoot."

Four miles up the Stehekin we reach Rainbow Falls, heralded by distant gusts and eddies of mist, which at first seem to be from woods on fire. But a dull roar, a harsh rumble, then a lighter splash,—and we see that what at first had seemed smoke eddying out of the cañon wall is the mist driven before the gusts created by the falling torrents. With a few more hurried steps we find ourselves before a fall three hundred and fifty feet high. Its clouds of spray swirl like a thunder-shower, drenching the rocks and trees far around. Picking our way amid the pelting mist to the top of a slippery hillock from which we can look right down into the very heart of the fall, we see, swinging against the mist, a perfect rainbow, a complete double circle, a blaze of lustre. The thrilling roar deepens as we hang over the slippery verge, and sounds like voices, trampling of armies, clatter of innumerable hoofs, rattling of artillery, all the grandeur and frenzy of conflict, seem to rise from that wild gorge. Now the mist eddies forth and blurs the vision, and then falls back, and that dazzling bow hangs there unmarred. The bridge of Iris or Heimdall, we say,—but no; it is no more a bridge, it is a perfect circle, the symbol of eternity. The symbol also of peace, for eternity is peace. That mist-hung bow becomes to us an emblem of the harmony of all jarring sounds and discordant forces. And so with that bow of peace swaying behind us, and the deep thunder fading in musical diminuendo, we pass on to the next wonder; and this is not far, for every mile brings its special revelation.

Time forbids that we pause for more than one added scene on the Stehekin, and this is the Horseshoe Basin, thirty miles up the river. This is in the upper cañon. Imagine yourself perched upon a granite pinnacle, looking possibly a little anxiously for bear in the thick copses at its bases, for this is said to be the greatest bear region in the country, but soon lifting your eyes to the heights on either side. Six thousand feet deep is that stupendous gorge. On the south side you see the "castled crags," glacier-crested, while on the north, Horseshoe Basin stands revealed. A long line of dark-red minarets, at whose foot stretches two miles of glistening and twisted ice, then below that a great terrace, vivid green with spring foliage, and over it falling a perfect symposium of waterfalls, if we may be allowed such an expression. Twenty-one falls and cataracts all in one view. They vary in descent from two hundred to two thousand feet. Joining at the foot of the terrace in one foaming torrent the waters of the Basin plunge in one fall of two hundred feet, thence pass under a snow tunnel and down a rocky chute swept clean by the flood to augment the already raging waters of the Stehekin. The Horseshoe Basin, though not grander, not so sublimely terrible, in fact, as some other scenes in the cañon, has that indescribable look of perfectness which belongs to the immortal works of nature and art. It has a symmetry of form and colour beyond any other in the entire region. The dark-red minarets which form the outer escarpment, ten thousand feet above sea-level, form a marvellous contrast and yet harmony with the green and blue and white of the glacier and the snow-field, and this in turn is margined with the deep-green and olive hues of the lower terrace, while joining and unifying all is the flashing and opalescent splendour of the cataracts.

Cascade Pass at Head of Stehekin River, Wash.

Photo. by T. W. Tolman, Spokane.

At the mouth of the Horseshoe Creek, lodged on a little rocky island, is a shattered cabin. We camp near this, and while we are engaged in preparing an appetising meal of fish and venison, a grizzled prospector appears coming down the trail. After the manner of the mountains, he makes himself at home and camps with us for the night. In the course of his conversation he narrates many stories of this wild region and of the prospecting and hunting adventures that have happened in it. Finally he tells us the story of the lost cabin, a story that certainly contains all the elements of a romance. It appears that some years ago two young fellows from the East, cousins, had come to the Stehekin to prospect. The old man who told us the story was then the only prospector in the cañon, and he soon made friends with the two adventurers. From broken pieces of conversation and finally some confidences on the part of one of the boys, he learned something of their story. They had been bosom friends all their lives, but had fallen in love with the same girl. The poor girl, not knowing which she did like best, told them that the only thing was for both to leave her for two years, and at the end of the time she would decide in favour of the one that had showed himself the braver and more successful man. Each kept his destination a perfect secret, but to their astonishment, within a month after, they found each other in Spokane. They concluded that it was the appointment of fate, and so went together to the wild country of Chelan, to seek a fortune.

After they had been there a short time they found a mutual distrust springing up, and finally, by the advice of the old man, they agreed to separate. George was to stay below. He was the more sullen and selfish of the two, and it was due to him that they had fallen out. Harry was of a frank and generous nature, and when it became evident that they must part he insisted that he should help build a cabin for George. And the cabin that they built was the very one that we now saw lodged against the rocks. Harry went up the cañon toward the Skagit Pass, and there in the lonely grandeur of the glaciers he plied his pick and shovel.

A few months later there came a mighty Chinook, the warm wind of the Cascades, which strips the peaks of snow within a day, transforms the creeks into raging torrents, and sends floods down every dry gulch. The night after the wind began to blow the old miner came to George's cabin, and in the intense darkness of the cloudy night they listened to the hurtling of the storm and the roar of the rapidly growing river. About midnight there came suddenly a succession of rifle shots near at hand, and in a few minutes a thunder and roar of water beyond anything that they had heard. Rushing out they saw that the water was already surrounding the cabin and they had to run in the darkness for their lives. Stumbling among the rocks they reached at last land high enough for safety, while the floods went tearing by. With the first light they looked out to see that the cabin had gone adrift, but sadder to tell, they soon found Harry, mangled, tortured, at the point of death, just strong enough to tell them that from his situation he had seen that a fearful flood was coming and he was trying to save George. But he had fallen in the darkness and crashed upon the rocks, and even in his suffering he had fired his rifle as a warning, hoping that it might be heard and save, and so it did. And the faithful fellow died content. "We tell the tale as it was told us." But the poor old wreck of a cabin took on something of a new significance as it leaned up against the rocks, while the restless river sobbed and frothed about it.

Doubtful Lake, Cascade Range, Washington, near Lake Chelan.

Photo. by T. W. Tolman, Spokane.

There is great strife among the Chelan people as to which is the grander section, the Stehekin or Railroad Creek. As a matter of fact, both are so superlatively magnificent that whichever place one is in, that he thinks the finer. But there is one feature of the case, and this is that the grandest part of Railroad Creek is seldom visited. Few have ever been to Glacier Lake, North Star Park, and Cloudy Pass, at the extreme head of the creek, and these are the central features of the scenery. They are about twenty-five miles from Lake Chelan, and the road and trail are mainly good, so that the journey to the head of the creek and return can be made very comfortably in four days.

Horseshoe Basin through a Rock Gap, Stehekin Cañon.
Photo. by T. W. Tolman.

˙ Neither words nor pictures are adequate to convey any true conception of Glacier Lake and its surroundings. Imagine a park of four or five thousand acres, set with grass and flowers, filled with ice-cold streams of water clear as crystal, and dotted here and there with trees of the most exquisite beauty. On every side except the one down which the creek descends, stupendous, glacier-crowned, and pinnacled peaks penetrate the blue-black sky at an elevation of ten or eleven thousand feet. At the south side of the park lies Glacier Lake, a mile long and half as wide, margined with vivid grass, brilliant flowers, and trees of the Alpine type, clear as crystal, unless darkened by some sudden scud from the heights. At the southern end of the lake is a bold bluff of five hundred feet, over which fall the waters of Railroad Creek, a white band across the darkness of the bluff. Above may be seen the source of this stream. It issues from a smaller lake, which lies in the very end of a vast glacier, a mass of ice two miles wide and about four miles long.

Passing west of Glacier Lake through the enchanted North Star Park, a veritable land of Beulah (at least when the sun is shining), we climb a thousand or twelve hundred feet higher, and find ourselves at one of those thrilling points in the mountains, a "divide." We are on the crest of the Cascade Mountains. To the east the water flows to Lake Chelan, thence to the Columbia, and thence to the Pacific by a journey of six hundred miles. To the west the water descends through the Sauk and the Skagit to Puget Sound, only a hundred and fifty miles away. This pass is almost always wrapped in clouds, and it is fittingly known as Cloudy Pass. The masses of warm vapour rising from the Pacific are hurled against the icy crowns of Glacier Peak, Mt. Nixon, Mt. Le Conte, North Star Peak, Bonanza Peak, and the rest of the wintry brotherhood, most not yet even named, and make of them a genuine *"patriam nimborum,"* in Virgil's phrase.

This is the breeding place of tempests. We had just reached the pass on one occasion, with a smiling sky below, and were just getting our cameras ready to catch the westward maze of peaks, when almost instantly there began to wheel and whirl above us great cloud-masses, seemingly from nowhere, formed right there, in fact, and before we had time to think, we were wrapped in a furious blizzard. With difficulty, benumbed, drenched, and exhausted, we managed to pick our way to camp, four miles below. This was in the early part of August. To be caught in a Chelan snowstorm is a serious matter at any time, and later in the year, may be all a man's life is worth.

But the greatest sight, the crowning feature, of all this panorama of sublimities is Glacier Peak seen from Cloudy Pass. This is pre-eminently the storm-king, the "Cloud-Compeller" (*Nephelegereta,* in the sounding word of Homer), and rarely can one catch an unobstructed view of its glistening cone. After much watching and waiting we caught the base and part of the double crown of the mighty mass. Glacier Peak is the "Great Unknown" among our Washington peaks. Every one has heard of Rainier, most people know of Adams, St. Helens, Baker, and Stewart, but Glacier Peak, alone in its solitary grandeur, not visible from the cities or routes of travel, is little known even to the people of the State. As its name denotes, it is the centre of a vast glacial system. To any tourist with a taste for adventure, Glacier Peak affords the finest field, while it offers an almost untouched mark for the scientist.

Lake Chelan.

Photo. by W. D. Lyman.

CHAPTER III

IN THE LAND OF WHEAT-FIELD, ORCHARD, AND GARDEN

Increasing Population and Cultivation as we go South—Chelan and Wenatchee Orchards—The Wheat-plains East of Wenatchee to Spokane—Spokane, the Metropolis of the Inland Empire—The Falls and their Power—Interesting Points in and around Spokane—The Palouse Farming Country—Snake River and its Orchards—Vast Irrigating Enterprises of the Upper Snake—Shoshone Falls—Walla Walla—Waiilatpu and Whitman Monument—Whitman College—Pendleton and its Wheat-fields and Historical Characters—Wallowa Lake—From Wenatchee to Priest Rapids—Origin of Name of Priest Rapids—Irrigating Enterprises below Priest Rapids—By Steamboat from Priest Rapids to Pasco—The Yakima Valley, its Fruits and Towns—Pasco and Kennewick and the Meeting of the Waters—Prospects of the Future for the Irrigable Country—From Pasco to Celilo—The Umatilla Palisades—Umatilla Rapids—Tumwater Falls—The Canal and Locks at Celilo—What Will be Accomplished by them for the Inland Empire—The Dalles—Its Historic Interest—Its Wool Business, its Horticultural and Agricultural Resources, its Scenery.

OUR journey on the River thus far has been mainly in those sections where scenery is the greatest product, and where the country, scantily inhabited, has almost as primitive an appearance as when the gay songs of the *voyageurs* raised the echoes against the rock-walls of the lakes, while paddles and bateau-prows started correspondent ripples on the clear surface.

But as we proceed southward into the State of Washington, we find more and more evidences of cultivation and inhabitancy. At the mouths of the streams and on the frequent "benches" and islands, orchards and gardens attest the enterprise and patience of the settlers. Around the lower end of Lake Chelan the big red apple, luscious peaches, plethoric pears, huge bunches of grapes, like the grapes of Eschol, make a picture of fruitfulness and delight. When we reach Wenatchee on the Columbia,—a river, a lake, and a town of the same name, meaning in the native tongue the "butterfly,"—we find ourselves in the uppermost of those belts of fruit land which have made the River so famous. As we stroll through these model orchards and vines and berry patches and gardens, and see the wonders wrought on the arid soil by the life-giving waters of the Wenatchee, we are almost ready to join the throng that are continually accepting the invitation to "be independent on ten acres of land and find health, wealth, and happiness in Wenatchee." In truth, these irrigated lands are marvels of productiveness. The valley of the Wenatchee is small, and not over twelve thousand acres are yet in productive bearing; but in 1907 not less than five hundred carloads of fruit and vegetables were shipped.

Like all the irrigated regions, Wenatchee is a place of pleasant homes, good schools and social advantages, and all the accompaniments of the finest type of genuine, whole-souled, ambitious Americanism. At Wenatchee we are on the main line of the Great Northern Railroad, and by it we can go west through the Cascade Mountains to Puget Sound, or east to Spokane. We must return again to Wenatchee in order to resume our journey down the River, but we will first turn eastward and make a tour of the great "Inland Empire" of Washington, Idaho, and Oregon.

A Harvest Outfit, Dayton, Wash.

Sunset Magazine.

One must necessarily visit Spokane on a journey through the great wheat country. Spokane, the metropolis and the pride of Eastern Washington, is a wonder to the Eastern tourist. Such a city, over one hundred thousand people, with costly brick and stone buildings, four, six, ten stories high, impressive public buildings, schools, churches, hotels, hundred-foot avenues well-paved, private dwellings of architectural excellence,—and hardly a soul there thirty years ago!

A grand spectacle the falls offered the eye in old Spokane, but now, alas, so cribbed and cabined is the noble stream by the march of industrial and electrical power that its wild energy is well-nigh gone except at the highest water. The total fall in the Spokane River is one hundred and forty-six feet, and the horse-power capacity at low water is forty thousand, at high water over half a million.

A Combined Harvester, near Walla Walla.

Photo. by W. D. Chapman.

Many points of interest must be hastily passed. The author feels great reluctance to omit a visit to the State College of Washington at Pullman, and the University of Idaho at Moscow. There are also historic spots, as one at Rosalia where a monument has recently been erected in commemoration of the Steptoe defeat in 1858, and the site of the first church in Eastern Washington on Walker's Prairie, where Eells and Walker started a mission for the Spokane Indians in 1838. There is also at the junction of the Spokane and Little Spokane, the site of Spokane House, a post of the Hudson's Bay Company, started in 1811. One might also well desire to visit the location of the old Spokane Bridge, where Colonel Wright crushed forever the pride and power of the Spokanes by killing eight hundred of their choicest horses.

On whatever side viewed, either past or present, or in the forecast of the future, Spokane is worthy of careful study. Its extensive railroad system and its network of electric lines reaching the many lakes, garden and fruit tracts, and rapidly developing suburbs, are concentrating the interests of a vast and wealthy region. But there are other cities to see and other boomers to hear and other bright futures to forecast, and so we turn our faces southward on the line of the O. R. & N. Railway, passing through vale after vale between the swelling prairies, with wheat,

wheat, wheat, oats, oats, oats, hay, hay, hay, cattle, horses, hogs, apple trees, and sugar beets, elegant farmhouses on the knolls and spacious barns in the hollows, — the great Palouse farming country, one of the most productive in the world. Whitman County has produced eight million bushels of wheat in a season, besides vast quantities of other products.

A hundred and forty miles from Spokane the great wheat plateau is broken by the profound abyss of Snake River. Dark, turbid, sullen, not so beautiful as the northern branches flowing out of the lakes, this largest of all the tributaries of the River goes on its swift and treacherous course to the union with the Columbia. Snake River is famous for its orchards. Almota, Penewawa, Alpowa, Kelly's Bar, Clarkston, Asotin, are the most prominent among many points where the cherries, peaches, nectarines, apricots, berries, grapes, go out by the carload and steamerload, earlier than anywhere else except on the banks of the Columbia itself, to all parts of the West and even at times to Chicago and New York. The region of these enormously productive fruit ranches is a narrow ribbon of fertile land at the bottom of a cañon fifteen hundred feet deep. Hot? Yes, hot! They say the mercury sometimes boils out of the top of the thermometer. But heat and water and good soil make the rich juice and bright cheeks of the peach and nectarine. Hundreds of miles up Snake River in the wide expanses of Southern Idaho the waters are being diverted for some of the largest irrigation enterprises on earth. There the Twin Falls canal, one hundred feet wide and deep enough for a steamboat, conveys the water to two hundred and eighty thousand acres of land. The Minidoka canal covers almost as much. That part of the Snake River Valley, three hundred miles long by fifty miles wide, will ere long count its inhabitants by the million.

Inland Empire System's Power Plant, near Spokane, 20,000 Horse-Power.

Photo. by T. W. Tolman.

Lower Spokane Falls.

Photo. by T. W. Tolman.

No one could consider that he had really seen Snake River unless he had visited the Great Shoshone Falls, or "Pahchulaka." This sublime manifestation of nature's power is about forty miles from the town of Shoshone on the Oregon Short Line. The total descent is nearly three hundred feet, of which eighty consists of cataracts and chutes broken by rocky islands, while the entire stream unites in the one final plunge of two hundred and twelve feet. It is ten hundred and fifty feet wide, and the walls of basaltic rock rise perpendicularly a thousand feet. Niagara is the only waterfall on the American continent that can be compared with Shoshone. Niagara is much wider but not so high. Its banks are tame, while those of Shoshone are wildly sublime.

The spectres of history rise up at every stage of a journey along Snake River. But we cannot pause. We pass on from the crossing of Snake River and soon find ourselves approaching Walla Walla. This is the most historic city of the Inland Empire and the oldest of the entire State of Washington, with the exception of Vancouver. The pleasant-sounding name signifies in the native tongue "Many Waters," though more literally, as the author has been told by an old Cayuse Indian, "Place where four creeks meet." The city of Walla Walla is thirty-two miles from the Columbia River in the midst of a broad and fertile valley, through which dozens of clear rivulets issuing from springs make their way through the birches and cottonwoods. The warm climate, rich soil, and abundant water, with multitudes of trees, give the "Garden City" an appearance of almost tropical luxuriance. On all sides for many miles stretch the wheat-fields, orchards, gardens, and alfalfa-fields. It is a land of plenty. It is commonly said that Walla Walla has more automobiles, more bicycles, more pianos, more flowers, and more pretty girls in proportion to population, than any other town in the North-west.

The special historic interest of Walla Walla is found in the fact that it was the location of the Whitman Mission and that the Whitman massacre took place at the Mission Station, Waiilatpu, six miles from the city. That spot is now marked with a marble crypt in which the bones of the martyrs rest, and a plain but imposing granite shaft stands upon the crest of the hill just above.

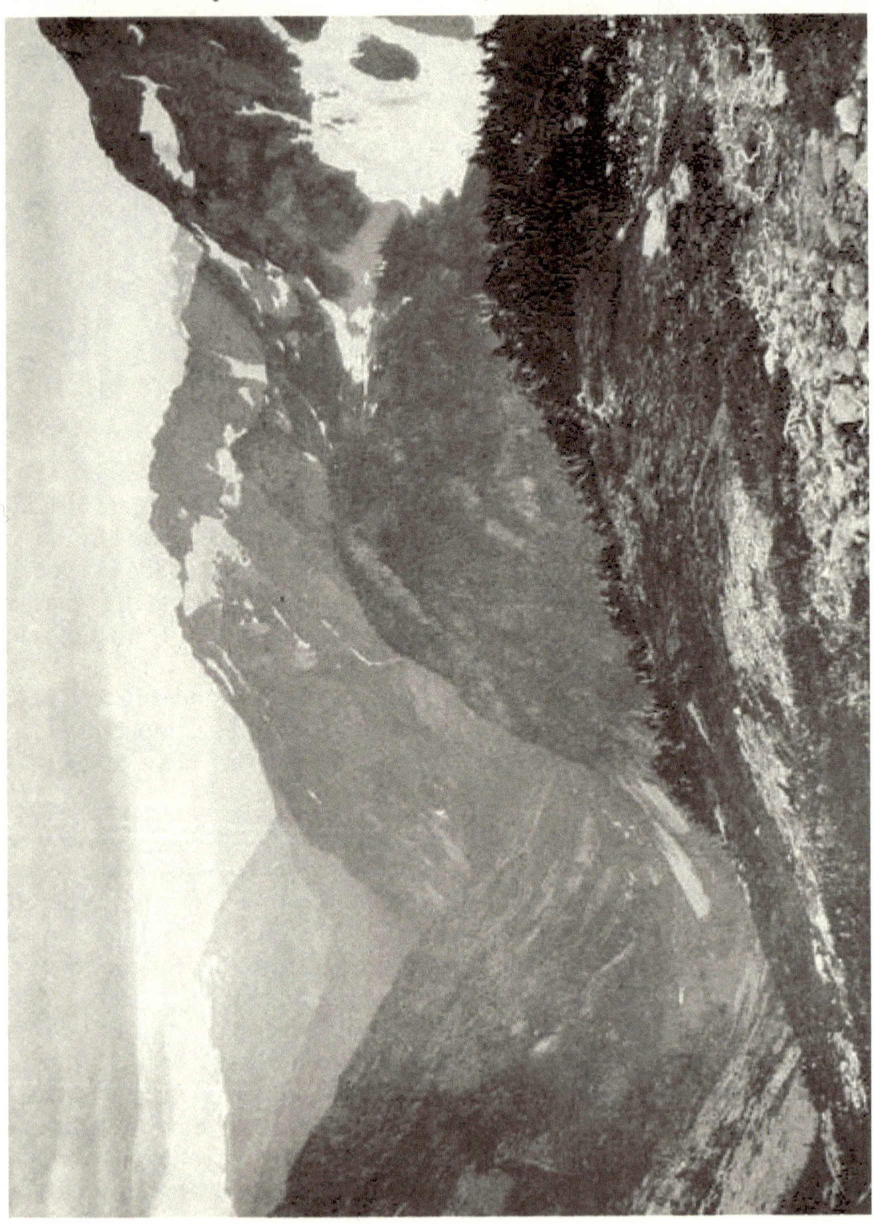

Cañon of the Stehekin, near Lake Chelan.

Photo. by T. W. Tolman.

Memorial Building, Whitman College, Walla Walla, Wash.

Photo. by W. D. Chapman.

A more living monument to the missionary is found in Whitman College. This institution, planned on the model of Amherst, Yale, and Williams, though co-educational, was founded by Rev. Cushing Eells in 1859 as an academy. It was not till 1883 that college work was undertaken. During that period the self-denying missionary and his family supported the infant institution by selling the products of their farm and devoting to it all except what was absolutely necessary for their own support. During years of slow, patient growth under very discouraging conditions, Whitman College has made friends East and West, and within the last few years it has become equipped with buildings and general facilities of high grade. An effort is now in progress, apparently sure of fulfilment, to raise two million dollars for buildings and general endowment. Walla Walla is becoming peculiarly known as the educational centre and the home city of the Inland Empire.

From Walla Walla we take a flying trip through the continued wheat belt on the Umatilla and its branches in Northern Oregon, a region similar to that around Walla Walla, rich and fruitful. Of this part of Oregon, Pendleton on the Umatilla is the metropolis. The Umatilla Indian Reservation, one of the most important in the history of this country, adjoins it. One of the most interesting persons in North-west history, now deceased, lived at Pendleton many years, Dr. William C. McKay, the son of Thomas McKay, and grandson of Alexander McKay, the last named being that one of the Astor company who lost his life on the *Tonquin*. Dr. William McKay was a three-quarter-blood Indian, but he was well educated and one of the most interesting men in our history. Another noted man, still living in the prime of life, is Major Lee Moorehouse, famous in earlier times as an Indian fighter and agent, and more recently as one of the most successful students and photographers of Indian life. Some of his pictures have gained national fame, and the publishers of this volume are indebted to his courtesy for their appearance here. Another interesting fact in connection with Pendleton is that here the Pendleton Indian robes and blankets are manufactured, and these have borne the name of their home place to all parts of the United States and even the world.

While in this part of Oregon we must take advantage of the opportunity to visit Lake Wallowa, with its tragic and pathetic memories of Indian war and early settlement and with its glorious scenery, almost equal to that of Chelan. Right over the lake, deep-set in precipitous mountain walls, towers the battlemented crest of Eagle Cap, which the people of Wallowa now declare to be the highest mountain in Oregon, 12,000 feet in elevation. Wallowa Lake is the veritable jewel of the Blue Mountains, a chain which, while not in general equal to the Cascades for height, grandeur, and variety, possesses in the Wallowa Basin a group of attractions not surpassed in any part of the North-west.

And now we must retrace our course after this long detour through the productive land bordering the tributaries of the River or we can in imagination fly on the wings of the south wind, which almost always blows across the Inland Empire, and find ourselves again at Wenatchee in order to resume our interrupted journey down the River. From Wenatchee to the foot of Priest Rapids, about sixty miles, there is no regular steamboat communication. We can, however, use the same means of transportation that we have hitherto used so liberally, imagination, and upon that airy and convenient ship we can descend the swift and tortuous stream. The fur brigades used to trust themselves to the skill of their paddles and boldly descend the rapids, seldom meeting with disaster. There are three principal rapids in this section of the River, Rock Island, Cabinet, and Priest. In the first the River is very narrow and split in sunder by ragged pinnacles of basaltic rock. At first observation it looks a reckless thing to push a boat out into the white water whirling through these fantastic points of rock. Yet a bateau or canoe skilfully handled will plunge like a race-horse down the foaming stretch, and emerge below bow down with little water aboard and inmates intact. Steamboats have both descended and ascended this rapid, though it is considered a somewhat dangerous performance. Cabinet Rapids are less picturesque and interesting than Rock Island, but they offer even more serious obstacles to navigation, the channel being narrow and the water shallow. The river has cut this part of its course through the great plateau, and its banks on either side are rocky walls a thousand feet high, with occasional sandy stretches, sad, barren, and monotonous. There is, in fact, not so much to catch the eye or enlist the interest of the tourist (if he were here) in this dismal expanse of rock and sand as there is either above or below. It is practically uninhabited. But as we proceed upon our way the banks fall away, wider expanses of land appear, and we discover an occasional band of cattle or a settler's hut on the generally bare, brown prairie. We are now approaching the longest rapid and the most serious impediment to navigation in the whole course of the River from Kettle Falls to Tumwater Falls. This is Priest Rapids. It is ten miles in length and represents a descent in the River of seventy feet. It would certainly be impossible of navigation by steamboats, were it not that the descent is distributed quite uniformly over the ten miles and the River in general is quite straight and with a fair depth of water throughout. The old *voyageurs* had little difficulty in racing down, and they seem to have usually ascended by *cordelling* their bateaux beside the rocks, and at some especially difficult places by lightening the load and carrying around. Steamers have both ascended and descended, but it is so slow and tedious (on one occasion requiring a steamer three days to ascend the ten miles) that it cannot be considered commercially navigable. It will doubtless become necessary to construct a canal and locks at this point to render the River continuously and profitably navigable.

Alexander Ross, in his *Adventures on the Columbia*, tells us how Priest Rapids came to be named. The first expedition of the Pacific Fur Company, of which Ross was a member, was making its way from Astoria up the River in 1811, and had reached the lower end of this fall. While reconnoitring and making preparations for proceeding, a large body of Indians gathered, watching operations with great interest. Among them was a fantastically dressed individual, with many feathers on his head, who was going through some kind of a performance which the explorers conceived to have a religious significance. Considering him a priest, they named the rapids thus.

Starting the Ploughs in the Wheat Land, Walla Walla, Wash.
Photo. by W. D. Chapman, Walla Walla.

The country around Priest Rapids is barren and unpromising in its natural state, but just below the foot of the rapids is one of the most interesting irrigation projects in the State. Along the west side of the River for twenty-five miles extends a belt of the most fertile land. An immense pumping plant run by electricity, which in turn is generated by the current, has been put in at the foot of the rapids. By this the water is conducted over the twenty thousand or more acres of land available, and it is the expectation that within a few years a dense population will line the river bank and repeat on a larger and finer scale the miracle of redemption by water already performed at various points on the River and its tributaries. Several town sites, of which the chief is Hanford, named from the president of the company, have already been laid out, and investments both in town property and orchard land are being rapidly made. The same process of irrigating is becoming inaugurated at many points from Hanford for a hundred and fifty miles down the River. It is plain to the observer that it is but a question of time when the shores of the River in this arid section will bloom and blossom like the rose, and repeat the history of Old Nile in massing of population and creation of cities and towns. It has been estimated that there are about a million acres of irrigable land contiguous to the River between Chelan and The Dalles. Since from five to twenty acres of irrigated land are ample to maintain a family, and since cities and villages are bound to grow on such tracts commensurate with their productive capacity, it seems probable that a million people will sometime live on this long belt of fertile soil redeemed by the River.

The beauty of irrigation on the Columbia is that it can be made to pump itself. For by taking advantage of such a fall as that of Priest Rapids (a half million horse-power at ordinary water), electric power can be generated by which limitless water can be raised sufficiently to cover any desired amount of land. Some have expressed the opinion that this process would exhaust the River, but this is hardly possible. For the great demands are in June and July when the River is at its flood. It has been estimated that at low water the Columbia at Celilo discharges 125,000 cubic feet per second, and at extreme high water, 1,600,000 cubic feet per second. Such a prodigious volume of water would be scarcely at all affected by any possible withdrawals.

The River from the foot of Priest Rapids is regularly navigated by several steamers connecting the new lands and towns with Pasco, the railroad centre seventy miles below. This section of the River is deep and tranquil, a superb watercourse. Below Hanford the River receives the Yakima River, which is the important agent in the irrigation of the great Yakima Valley. No one could say that he knew the Columbia River or the State of Washington without a visit to that valley, the largest in the State and the scene of the most extensive development in irrigated lands anywhere in the North-west. Three thousand carloads of fruit and vegetables were shipped from the Yakima in 1907. Buyers of Yakima fruits come from all parts of the East, from England, and even from France. Fortunes have been made in that fair land,—a fair land when supplied with water, but an arid waste without it. The United States Government has acquired control of most of the water system of the Yakima, and by means of storage basins in the mountain lakes where the

Yakima and its branches rise, will be able to supply water for over a million acres of land.

On the Historic Walla Walla River.

Photo. by W. D. Chapman.

The productive capacity of these fat lands when softened with an irrigating ditch and tickled with a hoe or cultivator is almost beyond belief. In 1907 an orchardist in what is known as Parker Bottom in the Yakima Valley raised on fifty-eight pear trees a crop of pears which was sold for over three thousand dollars. This statement is well attested, extraordinary as it sounds. It should be understood that such production does not represent an average yield. The trees were of large size and of the choicest variety, while conditions of production, price, and sale were of the best. Yet similar records may be found in Wenatchee, Hood River, Walla Walla, and others of the fine fruit-producing regions of the Columbia Valley. A man in the Touchet Valley near Dayton, who had been for twenty years a teacher at an average salary of a thousand a year, became discontented with his narrow conditions, and by making credit arrangements for a rich body of land has devoted himself for some years to the development of an apple orchard. He has a hundred acres of trees, young and of choice varieties, from which in the year 1907 he sold thirty-four thousand boxes of fruit for approximately fifty thousand dollars.

But while we have been flying in imagination over the spacious valley of the Yakima, our steamer has been speeding down the broad River, and we are now within sight of a vast prairie stretching east and south, bounded on the southern horizon by the azure wall, ridged with white, of the Blue Mountains. To the east, this great plain melts into the sky. In fact it extends to the Bitter Root Mountains, a distance of over two hundred miles. On the west bank of the River we see a narrower plain bounded by a steep treeless ridge. On either bank we see taking shape before us houses and trees, while extended over the River, like threads of gossamer in the distance, a bridge is outlined against the sky. We soon discover that we are near Pasco on the east bank and Kennewick on the west bank of the River. The bridge is that of the Northern Pacific and Spokane, Portland, and Seattle Railroads. A mile below the bridge the Snake River joins its greater brother.

This point is the very hub of the Inland Empire. Here the two great rivers unite. Here steamboating on a vast scale will take place in the near future. As soon as the locks are placed in the River at Celilo, a hundred and thirty miles below, steamers can move freely to the ocean. Here three transcontinental railroads pass, two down the River and one to Puget Sound. Another is in process of construction to Puget Sound. Here a body of the richest soil, on both sides of both rivers, embracing at least a hundred and fifty thousand acres, waits only for water to bloom and yield as Wenatchee and Yakima have already done. Here the long, hot summer insures the earliest production of any part of the North-west, and in early production the profit is found.

It is, in fact, obvious at a glance that here at the junction of the Columbia and Snake Rivers, at the crossings of the great railroads, and at the point of the greatest area of irrigable land in one body, with every advantage of soil, climate, and transportation, there is bound to be in the near future a large city. Already on the west side of the Columbia the beautiful little town of Kennewick, of three thousand inhabitants, where six years ago the jack-rabbits, coyotes, and sage-hens held sway, shows what can be done with water. For at that point the first irrigating canal was put through the waste, and the traveller can now see the results.

Blalock Fruit Ranch of a Thousand Acres at Walla Walla, Wash.

Photo. by W. D. Chapman.

Other irrigating enterprises are now in progress, and by the time the readers of this volume come to descend the River in the splendid steamboats which will sometime run through canals and locks the whole length from Revelstoke to the ocean, there will be one of the most splendid cities in the North-west at this meeting of the waters. Pasco is likely to be the location of the big city. From Pasco there are steamers running to Celilo, conveying wheat. The traveller who desires to know the River from its surface should take passage on such a steamer. We see the same characteristic features of the inauguration of irrigating enterprises from point to point, but mainly the shores are still uninhabited and barren, and the River, mainly untouched by sail or steamer, sweeps on its swift course, as lonely as when Lewis and Clark first turned their canoe prows westward.

As we pass the desolate sand heaps near the disconsolate little old town of Wallula, we can recall the old Hudson's Bay fort, the Indian wars, the struggle for possession, the missions, the incoming immigrants, all the tragedy and striving which marked the century just closed. Below Wallula the Umatilla highlands throw a barrier eight hundred feet high athwart the course of the stream, and the bold escarpments of rock, palisades grander than those of the Hudson, attest the energy with which the River fulfilled his mission of cleaving the intercepting barrier in two. Below these palisades, a vast plain extends many miles on the south to where the purple line of the Blue Mountains cuts the horizon. On the margin of this plain the little town of Irrigon (where is published a paper with the alliterative title of the *Irrigon Irrigationist of Irrigon, Oregon*), green and flowery in the wide aridity, shows us again what part water plays in reclamation of land. Of similar interest is Blalock Island, commemorating the name of Dr. N. G. Blalock of Walla Walla, whom the North-west honours as the father of great enterprises.

We pass several rapids on this section of the River, the chief of which are the Umatilla, John Day, and Hell-gate. These are somewhat serious impediments to navigation at low water. The Umatilla Rapid presents the curious feature of a reef extending almost directly across the River with the channel running parallel to it and at right angles to the course of the stream. Hence when the water is so low that the reef cannot be passed directly over, the steamer pilot must follow a channel running right across the current, a current which tends to throw him broadside onto the reef. The Government is at present engaged in blasting a channel directly through this reef. The country becomes more rugged as we descend, and at various points, if the sky be clear, we can see the great peaks of the Cascades to the west. Passing through the wild water of Hell-gate, where the steamer quivers as though great hands were reaching up from below and shaking her, we soon find ourselves at Celilo.

This is the beginning of the greatest series of obstructions on the River and the point where the Government is now constructing a canal, by means of which the entire upper course of the River will be brought into connection with the lower. In the distance of twelve miles the River falls eighty-one feet at low water and sixty feet at high water. The Tumwater Falls at the head of this series of obstructions has a descent of twenty feet at low water, but at high water the volume of the River is so great that it passes directly over the fall and a boat can shoot over the steep slope. Here was one of the most famous places in early history. On the north side was the Wishram village, noted in Irving's *Astoria*. This, too, was the greatest place for fishing on the upper River. Even now the Indians gather in autumn in great numbers and can be seen spearing the salmon. Several immense fish-wheels also can be seen upon the verge of the falls.

Witch's Head, near Old Wishram Village. The Indian Superstition is that these Eyes will Follow any Unfaithful Woman.

By Courtesy of Major Lee Moorehouse.

The most remarkable of all these obstructions is Five-Mile Rapids. This is the place to which in the first place the French *voyageurs* applied the name *Dalles,* meaning a trough through the flat plates of rock. It is sometimes called the "Big Chute."

Cabbage Rock, Four Miles North of The Dalles.

Photo. by Lee Moorehouse, Pendleton.

It is planned by the Government to overcome these obstructions by a canal and locks. The expense is estimated at four and a half million dollars. The resulting advantages will be vast. The greater part of the Inland Empire will be thrown open to steamer competition with the railroads. The freight tariff at the present time is heavier than in any other part of the United States. If the productive capacity of the region were not extraordinary, it could not have developed as it has with such a handicap. It is estimated that by the reduction of freight which will follow steamboat navigation, the Inland Empire will save not less than two million dollars annually. In the tremendous movement now sweeping over our country to improve waterways, the Columbia will bear its part and receive its improvement. It will be a great day for the storied and scenic River of the West when some magnificent excursion steamer descends the thousand miles from Revelstoke to the outer headlands. And with canals at Celilo, Priest Rapids, and Kettle Falls, with some improvements at minor points, at no immoderate expense, the thing can be done.

And now we reach the city of The Dalles. The traveller will find this a place hardly surpassed in historic interest by any other on the River. The old trading posts, the United States fort, the missions, the Indian wars, the early immigrations, the steamboat enterprises, all unite to give rare value to this picturesque "capital of the sheep country." For, aside from historic interest, The Dalles surpasses any other point in the United States as a wool shipping station. It is now becoming also the centre of a farming and orchard country. For it is now understood that the rolling hill land for many miles is adapted to wheat raising and to fruit of the finest quality. If our visitors to the River should happen to be in The Dalles in autumn they would find at the Wasco County Horticultural Fair one of the most attractive and appetising displays of fruit that the whole country affords.

The scenery about The Dalles, with the majestic River, the great white cones of Hood and Adams, and wide sweeps of rolling prairie and hollowed hills, is noble and inspiring. It may be considered the gateway of the open prairie to the east and the passage of the Cascade Mountains by the River to the west.

CHAPTER IV

WHERE RIVER AND MOUNTAIN MEET,
AND THE TRACES OF THE BRIDGE OF THE GODS

The Most Unique Point yet on the River—River, Mountains, and Tide—
The Only Place where the Cascade Range is Cleft—Distant View
of Mt. Hood and Gradual Appearance of Lesser Heights—Limits
of Region where River and Mountain Meet—Geological Character of this Region—Forces of Upheaval and Erosion and Volca-
no—We May Journey by Rail, by Steamboat, Horseback, Waggon,
or Afoot, but we Prefer a Rowboat—Paha Cliffs—On the Track
of Speelyei—Memaloose Island—Hood River and White Salmon
Valleys and their Fruit—Beginnings of the Great Heights—The
Sunken Forest—The Bridge of the Gods—Loowit, Wiyeast, and
Klickitat—Difference in Climate between the East-of-the-Mountains and the West—Sheridan's Old Blockhouse—Passing the
Locks—Petrified Trees—Fish-wheels—Castle Rock—Ascent of
Castle Rock—Story of Wehatpolitan—St. Peter's Dome—Oneo-
nta Gorge—Multnomah Falls—Cape Horn—Getting out of the
Mountains—Cape Eternity and Rooster Rock—This Section of
the Journey Ended—Comparison of the River with Other Great
Scenes.

IN the long journey down our River we have had a panoramic view of towering
mountains and broad plains, foaming cataracts and tranquil lakes, fruitful valleys and volcanic desolations, growing cities and lonely wastes. All illustrate that
infinite variety of the River which imparts its unrivalled charm.

But now we are approaching a point which is unique even in the midst of the
unique, varied in never-ending variety, sublime even in almost continuous sublimity, singular even upon our most singular River. This place is where the mountains and the River meet. By mountains we mean the great chain of the Cascades,
which under various names parallels the Pacific Coast all the way from Alaska
to Southern California. But not only do mountains and River meet here, but the
ocean sends his greetings, for at the lower end of the rapids which here mark the
gateway of the mountains, the first pulse-beat of the Pacific, the first throb of the
tide, is discernible, though it is a hundred and sixty miles farther to where the
River is lost in that greatest of the oceans. River, Mountains, Ocean,—a very symposium of sublimities.

Eagle Rock, just above Shoshone Falls in Snake River.
Photo. by W. D. Lyman.

There is, too, another especially interesting feature of this spot, and that is, it is the only place for twelve hundred miles where the Cascade-Sierra Range is cleft asunder. In fact it is the only place in the entire extent of the range where it is cut squarely across. This fact imparts not only scenic interest, but commercial value. It is the only water-level route from the seacoast to the Inland Empire.

The place where River and mountains meet had been heralded to us long before we reached it. For as we passed the plains of the Umatilla we got an intimation of the mountain majesty which we were approaching. Clear-limned against the south-western horizon, a glistening cone, cold-white in the earliest morning, rosy-red with the rising dawn, and warm with the yellow halo of noon, fixes our eyes and bids us realise that from the far vision of a hundred miles we can see and worship at the shrine of Oregon's noblest and most historic peak, Mt. Hood. As we speed on down the current we begin to see long lines of lesser peaks rising to the westward. The prairies of the Umatilla have been succeeded by picturesque bare hills, and these by ragged palisades of columnar basalt, with higher hills yet, crowned with gnarled oak-trees. Of the wheat-fields and orchards and sheep ranges centring at The Dalles, we have already spoken, and we have paused at Celilo and gazed on the historic "Timm," or the Tumwater Falls, and the "Big Chute," observing especially the Government canal and locks now started, from whose completion such vast commercial possibilities are plainly foreshadowed. Our present quest is therefore yet farther on, to the gateway of the mountains. This is found at the "Cascade Locks," fifty miles below Dalles City. The section of river which we have styled "Where River and Mountain Meet" may be considered as extending from the mouth of the Klickitat River, a few miles west of Dalles City, to Rooster Rock, about thirty miles east of Vancouver. The distance between these points is about fifty miles, and through this space we may see all the evidences of a titanic struggle between the master forces of fire and water and upheaval. As we descend the majestic stream with the majestic banks on either hand and mark the apparent ancient water-marks hundreds of feet above our heads, we recall the Indian myth of Wishpoosh in an earlier chapter. The opinion of geologists in regard to this extraordinary passageway of the River is that it represents ages of gradual elevation of the mountain chain and a cotemporary erosion by the River, so that as the heights became higher, the river bed became deeper. The one-time shore slowly mounted skyward, and as the new upheavals rose from the ocean deeps the lines of erosion were in turn wrought on them, and river shore succeeded river shore through long ages. With these fundamental forces of upheaval and erosion there were eras of local seismic and volcanic activity, more cataclysmic in nature, from which there came the magnificent pillars of columnar basalt and the first trenching of the profound chasms which subsequent lateral streams carved through the rising base of the great range.

Stehekin Cañon, 5000 Feet Deep.
Photo. by W. D. Lyman.

To view this great picture gallery of history and physiography, we may have the choice of nearly every method of travel, horseback, afoot, by team (though the waggon roads are not continuous), or by train, on either bank. The river himself offers his broad back for any kind of craft. Several swift and elegant steamers make daily trips between Portland and The Dalles, passing through the Government canal and lock at the Cascades. Launches, scows, sailing craft of almost every kind, are in constant movement, loaded with every sort of commodity. Of all the means of transit, however, we will, if you please, float down the stately stream in our well-tried skiff. Independent as the Coyote god Speelyei when he used to pass up and down the river, transforming presumptuous beasts or mortals into rock at will, we will drift with the current, partaking of the very life of the rich and multifarious nature about us. We can pause as we wish on jutting crag or fir-crowned promontory or at the foot of spouting cataract. We can camp for the night beneath some wide-spreading pine, and breathe the balsamic fragrance of the "continuous woods." We can trace the historic stages of bateaux or canoes or immigrant flatboats, and open and shut the camera at will amid the open volumes of our heroic age of discovery and settlement, or the yet vaster and grander epoch of Nature's creative day. No palace car or even floating palace of steamer for us when we can have two or three days of such unalloyed bliss in an open skiff moving at our own sweet will.

We shall find here a marked change in the movement of the river as compared with its prevailing character in the five hundred miles from the British line to The Dalles. The impetuous might above has become transformed into a slow and stately majesty. With the exception of the five miles at the Cascades round which the canal passes, the river below The Dalles is deep and calm, seldom less than a mile in width.

Of the almost numberless objects at which we level eye and camera, we can here describe but few.

A fitting introduction to this stage of our journey is found in Paha Cliffs at the mouth of the Klickitat, a perpendicular bastion of lava rock, not remarkable for height, but of such regularity and symmetry as to seem the work of men's hands. A short distance below the Paha Cliffs, also on the Washington side of the river, is a most singular semicircular wall of gigantic area, surrounding on the west what seems to be an immense sunken enclosure. The Indians have a story to the effect that once Speelyei, being on his way up the river before this wall existed, paused here to perform some unworthy deed (for Speelyei was a curious mixture of the noble and the base). Having done the deed, he began to fear that it would become known. So he hurriedly built a wall to keep in the report. But while he was engaged in building on the west, the report got out on the east. The wall that we now see is the remains of his building. Of a similar order of Indian fancy is the "Baby-on-the-Board" and the "Coyote Head" farther down the river, also on the north side. The Coyote Head is near White Salmon. It commemorates the transformation of a presumptuous Klickitat chief who wished to proclaim himself equal to Speelyei, so he crowned himself with a coyote skin and took his station on the great rock wall above the mouth of the White Salmon. And there he remains still, for Speelyei with a wave of the hand transformed the offending chieftain into rock.

Steamer "Dalles City," Descending the Cascades of the Columbia.

A few miles below the mouth of the Klickitat, there stands in mid-channel one of the most curious and interesting objects on the river, "Memaloose Island." This desolate islet of basalt was one of the most noted of the frequent "death" or burial places of the Indians. They were accustomed to build platforms and place the dead upon them. Apparently this island was used for its gruesome purpose for centuries. A large white marble monument facing the south attracts the attention of all travellers, and as we pass we see that it is sacred to the memory of Vic Trevett. He was a prominent pioneer of The Dalles, and in the course of his various experiences became a special friend of the Indians, who looked upon him with such love and reverence that when his end approached he gave directions that his permanent burial-place and monument should be on the place sacred to his aboriginal friends.

We have spoken of the region between the mouth of the Klickitat and Rooster Rock as the mountain section of the river. But as we move on down the stream we discover that there are numerous nooks and glens adjoining it which are the choicest locations for fruit and garden ranches. At a point just about midway from The Dalles to the Cascades there is a remarkable break in the otherwise unbroken and constantly rising mountain walls. This break constitutes one of the most charming residence regions on the Columbia shores, and at the same time the avenue of approach to the most magnificent of mountains. There are here two great valleys. One of these is that of Hood River, better called by its musical Indian name Waukoma, "The Place of Cottonwoods." It proceeds directly from the foot of Mt. Hood, twenty-five miles distant to the south. The valley on the north bears a similar relation to Mt. Adams, forty miles distant, and is drained by the White Salmon River. From favourable points on the River, or from the heights which border it, we obtain views of the two peaks which create an unappeasable longing to tread their crags and snow-fields. Though truly mountain valleys, these two valleys are of spacious extent. They are moreover so richly provided with sun and water and all the ingredients of soil necessary to produce the choicest fruit that they have become the very paradise of the orchardist. The Hood River apples grace the tables of royalty in the old world and delight the palates of epicures in both hemispheres, while to the eyes and the nostrils of any one of delicate sensibilities their colour and fragrance impart a still more æsthetic charm.

As we pass on down the river from those two vales of beauty and plenty, we begin to see the first of those lofty crags on either hand, the basaltic pinnacles, turretted, spired, castellated, which make the distinguishing feature of Columbia River scenery for these fifty miles. Mitchell's Point, Shell Mountain, Wind Mountain, Bald Mountain, and Mt. Defiance are the first group. The lowest of the group attains an elevation of nearly two thousand feet, almost perpendicular, while at the summit of the crags rise a thousand feet higher yet long grassy slopes alternating with splendid forests.

As we near the Cascades we note another curious phenomenon. This is the sunken forest on either side. At low water these old tree trunks become very observable, and their general appearance suggests at once that they are the remains of a former forest submerged by a permanent rise in the river. This explanation is confirmed by the fact that from The Dalles to the Cascades the river is very deep and sluggish. When we reach the Cascades a third fact is revealed and that is that at the chief cataract the river bank is continually sliding into the river. Trees are thrown down by this slow sliding process, railroad tracks require frequent adjustment, and on clear, still nights there is sometimes heard a grinding sound, while a tremor from the subterranean regions seems to indicate that the upper stratum is sliding over the lower toward the river. In fact, the mighty force of the stream is all the time eating into the bank and gradually drawing it down.

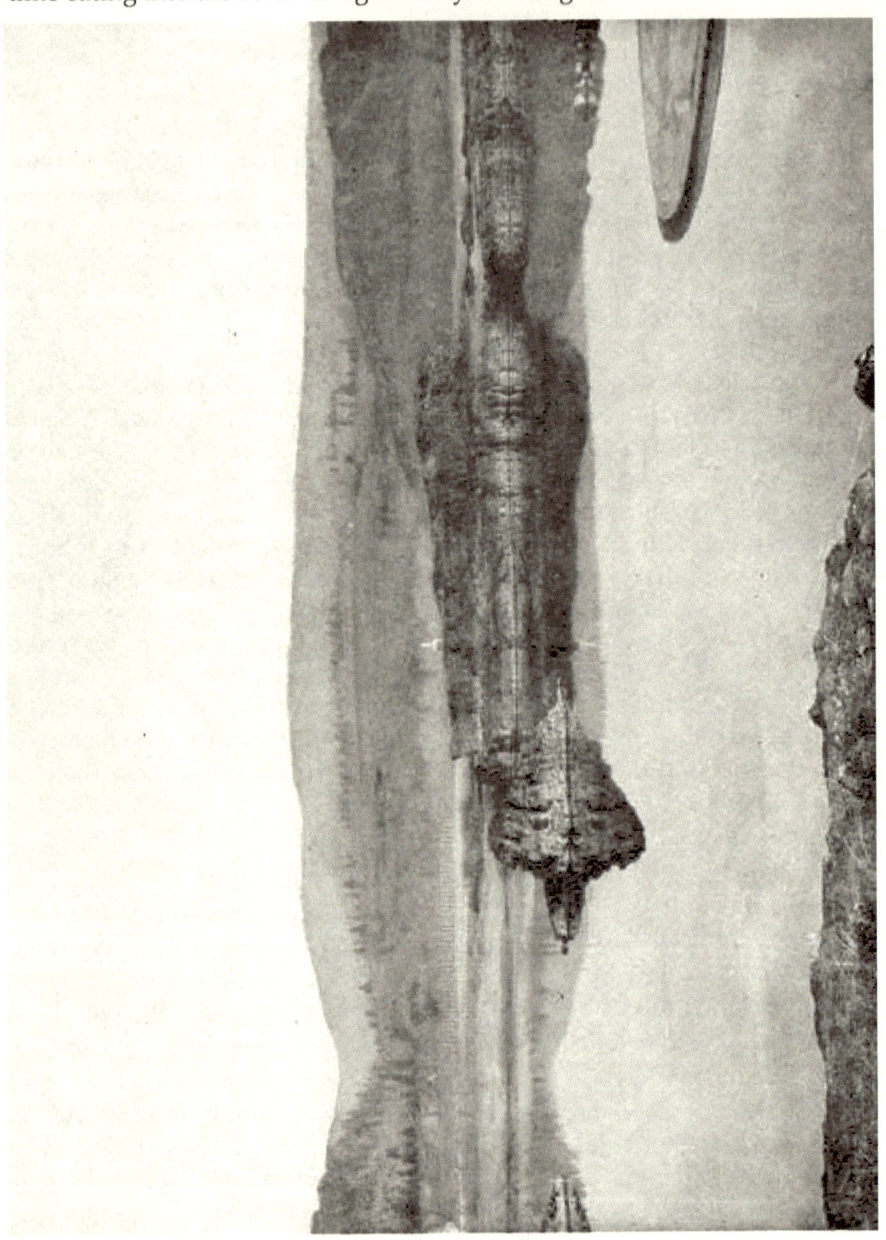

Memaloose Island, Columbia River.

Photo. by E. H. Moorehouse.

From those and other indications the conclusion has been drawn that some prodigious avalanche of rock at a not long distant time dammed the river at this point, creating the present Cascades and raising the water above so as to submerge the forest, whose remains now attract the attention of the observer at the low stage of water.

To confirm this theory we have the Indian story of the "tomanowas bridge," the quaintest and most interesting of the long list of native myths.

The region around the old site of the "Bridge of the Gods" may be considered as the dividing line between the Inland Empire and the Coast Region. Above, it is dry, sunny, breezy, and electrical, the land of wheat-field and sheep ranges, cowboys and horses and mining camps. Below, it is cool, cloudy, still, and soft, the region of the clover and the dairy, the salmon cannery, the logging camp, and boats of every sort. Above, the rocks look dry and hard, and glitter in the sun. Below, the rocks are draped in moss, and from every cañon and ledge there seems to issue a foaming torrent. It is, in truth, the meeting place of mountain and River.

On all sides around the Cascades there are objects of natural and historic interest. Stupendous crags, often streaked with snow, lose themselves in the scud of the ocean which is almost constantly flying eastward to be absorbed in the more fervid sunshine of up-river. Perhaps the most impressive of these vast heights is Table Mountain, on the north side of the River, near the locks, said to have been one of the supports of the "Bridge of the Gods." Its colours of saffron and crimson add to the splendour and grandeur of its appearance. Just below the locks on the north side stood the old blockhouse built by a young lieutenant in 1856 as a defence against the Klickitat Indians. The blockhouse is now in ruins, but the name of its builder has been fairly well preserved, for it is—Phil Sheridan.

The total extent of the cataract at the Cascades is five miles and the descent is about forty-five feet, of which half is at the upper end at the point passed by the locks. We enter the locks in the wake of one of the steamers, and in a few minutes find our craft emerging from the lower end of the massive structure into the white water which bears us swiftly down the remaining part of the Cascades. It looks dangerous to commit an open boat to that sweeping current, but as a matter of fact the course of the river is straight and deep, though swift, and it is entirely feasible for any one of reasonable skill to manage a small boat in the passageway to the tranquil expanses below.

As we speed swiftly down the river, we note the little station of Bonneville, named for the historic fur-trader whom the fascinating pages of Irving have brought down to this era. A short distance below Bonneville our eyes catch sight of a white sign-board bearing the words, "Petrified Tree." Sure enough, there is the tree, and a marvellously fine specimen of silicification it is, too. When the railroad was built along the river bank at this point, the graders ran into a perfect forest of petrified wood. The logs and limbs were piled up by the cord near Bonneville, but the larger part has been taken in various directions for cabinets and ornaments.

But a short time is needed to fly down the Cascades, and at their lower end we reach what may be called the Lower River. For here a slight rise and fall of tide betokens the presence of the ocean. No more rapids on the River, but a tranquil, majestic flood, broadening like a sea toward its final destination, a hundred and sixty miles away.

Horseshoe Basin, near Lake Chelan, Wash.

Photo. by T. W. Tolman, Spokane.

If we were to describe in detail all the marvels of beauty and grandeur and physical interest which engage our attention at every stage of the journey, our volume would end with this chapter, for there would be no room for anything more. One class of objects of curious interest to almost all travellers, though of no special charm to scientist or nature lover, is the fish-wheels at the Cascades. These are very ingenious contrivances set in the midst of a swift place in the stream and made to revolve by the current. As they revolve, the huge vans dipping the water scoop up almost incredible numbers of the salmon which have made the Columbia famous the world over. A weir is built to turn the fish from the outside course into the channel of the wheel, with the result that numbers are taken almost beyond belief, sometimes as high as eight tons a day by a single wheel. Another picturesque sight, both at the Celilo Falls and the Cascades, is the Indian fishermen perched upon the rocks and with spear and dip-net seeking to fill their larder with the noble salmon.

But now to contemplate the works of God and Nature rather than those of man. We must, as already seen, by the necessities of space, ask our readers to share with us only the masterpieces of this gallery of wonders. Probably all visitors to the River would agree that the following scenes most nearly express the spirit and character of the sublime whole: Castle Rock, St. Peter's Dome, Oneonta Gorge, Multnomah Falls, Cape Horn, and Rooster Rock. To these individual scenes we should add, as the very crown of all, the view at the lower Cascades both up and down the great gorge. With the majestic heights, scarred with the tempests and the earthquakes of the ages, swathed in drifting clouds and oftentimes tipped with snow, and the shimmering of the River, and the answering grandeur of sky and forest, — this grouping of the whole is more inspiring than any one scene.

The first special object to fix our attention below the Cascades is Castle Rock. It is an isolated cliff of basalt, nine hundred feet high, covering about seventeen acres, its summit thinly clothed with stunted trees. It stands right on the verge of the River, nearly perpendicular on all sides, marvellous for symmetry from every point of view. At first sight one gets no conception of its magnitude, for it is dwarfed by the stupendous pinnacles, three thousand feet high, which compose the walls of the cañon. It is said that some Eastern lady, seeing it from a steamer's deck, exclaimed, "See that fine rock! I wish I had it in my back yard at home." Being informed that she would have to find a pretty spacious back yard to accommodate an ornament covering seventeen acres, she was too much astonished to believe it. But to any one viewing it deliberately and from every point of view, and especially landing, as we in our happy method of travel can do, and going about its base, it becomes evident that Castle Rock might be called a mountain in almost any other place. It was for a long time regarded as an impossible thing to reach the summit. For some years there was a standing offer of one thousand dollars for any one who would place the Stars and Stripes on the summit. But no one took the dare. At last in 1901, when the rivalry between two steamboat lines was keen, Frank Smith of the Regulator Line, with George Purser and Charles Church, accomplished the seemingly impossible, and, by ropes and staples and fingers and teeth and toenails, scaled the almost perpendicular walls, and unfurled the Regulator banner to the breeze where no flag ever flew before, nor human foot ever trod. It was probably the most risky climb ever taken in the North-west. A little later, by the aid of the experience of this party, several others attained the summit. Among these were George Maxwell, who set the Oregon Railway and Navigation flag as high as that of the Regulator had gone, and two photographers, W. C. Staatz and George M. Weister. With them went a young lady, Lilian White, who, though she did not reach the summit, went higher than any of her sex have gone. Later Mr. Whitney, manager of the great McGowan Cannery, went up and placed the Stars and Stripes upon the top.

Castle Rock, Columbia River.

(Copyright by Kiser Photograph Co., 1902.)

The Lyman Glacier and Glacier Lake in North Star Park Near Lake Chelan.

Photo. by W. D. Lyman.

We said that no earlier human steps had trodden that beetling height and that Miss White had gone higher than any of her sex. But if we accept the romantic Indian tale of Wehatpolitan, our statement needs correction. For this story is to the following effect. Wehatpolitan was the beautiful child of the principal chieftain in these parts. She loved and was loved by a young chief of a neighbouring tribe. But when she was sought by her lover in marriage, the stern father denied the request and killed the messenger. But the lovers were secretly married and met clandestinely at various times. In course of time the father, thinking the infatuation of the forbidden lovers to be at an end, gave Wehatpolitan to a chief whom he had favoured. The latter kept constant watch of the girl, and one night he saw her stealing steathily away, and tracking her he found the secret of her midnight wanderings. As soon as the new lover had imparted to the father these tidings, the latter with deep duplicity sent word to the other chieftain that if he would come to the lodge, all would be forgiven and he and Wehatpolitan would be duly wed. Rejoicing at the happy outcome to all their troubles, the faithful lover hastened to his own, but no sooner had he arrived than he was seized upon and slain by the revengeful parent. Not long after this the heartbroken girl gave birth to a child, but her father at once decreed that the child must share its father's fate. Hearing this pitiless word, Wehatpolitan caught up her child and disappeared. All that day they searched in vain, and on the next day, the Indians heard wailings from the top of Castle Rock, from which they soon discovered that the poor girl with her child had gone to that apparently inaccessible height. The old chief, repenting of his harsh course, called aloud to his daughter to come down and he would forgive her. But fearing new treachery she paid no heed, and the wailings continued. Overcome with grief the remorseful chief offered all kinds of rewards for any one who would climb the rock and save Wehatpolitan and her child. But though many tried, none could succeed. On the third day the wailings ceased. Then the half-crazed father himself essayed to climb. He seemed to succeed, for at least he disappeared among the crevices of the rock high up toward the summit. But he never returned. The Indians thought that he reached the top and that finding the lifeless bodies of his daughter and her child he had probably given up all hope of getting down and had lain down and died with them. But even yet heart-breaking wailings come down from time to time, especially when the Chinook blows soft and damp up the river, and these wailings have been thought by Indians to be the voice of the spirit of the unhappy Wehatpolitan, because it could never descend to the happy hunting grounds of the tribe.

Another native idea is to the effect that Castle Rock (which ought to be called Wehatpolitan's gravestone) is hollow and is filled with the bodies of former generations now turned to stone. As a matter of fact, the party of 1901 found evidence of a great cave, but so far there has been found no practical ingress. So the interior is still an unexplored mystery. Immense quantities of spear-heads and arrow-heads are found along the river at this point, and these are apparently of an earlier age than most of those found in this country.

Loosing from the enchanted shore of Wehatpolitan's monument, we see for several miles on the Oregon side a cordon of perpendicular cliffs, red and purple in hue, streaked with spray, and touched here and there with the deep green of firs which have rooted themselves with claw-like roots into the crevices. Most symmetrical and beautiful, though not the highest of this line of elevations, is St. Peter's Dome. Its summit is over two thousand feet above the river. While in height it is surpassed by certain crags of Chelan or Yosemite, as well as its brothers on the river, it has no rival in beauty there, or elsewhere, so far as the author has seen, among the wonders of the American continent. Every hour of the day, every change of sky or season, reveals some new and unexpected beauty or sublimity in this superb cliff.

Hunters on Lake Chelan, with their Spoils.

Photo. by W. D. Lyman.

We are almost sated with sublimities by the time we pass on down below St. Peter's Dome, but one of the most unique scenes of all is close at hand. This is Oneonta Gorge. A swift stream issuing from the cliffs on the south side of the River attracts our attention, and we moor our boat to the roots of a tall cottonwood and make our way inward. The wall is cleft asunder, its sides almost meeting above. At places the smooth sides of the Gorge leave no space except for the passage of the pellucid stream, and we have to wade hip deep to make our way. Showers of spray descend from the towering roof above, and in places we are well-nigh in darkness. Then there is a widening and through the broken wall the lances of sunshine pierce the gloom with rainbow tints. Marvellous Oneonta with the sweet-sounding name! It, too, has its wealth of native myth, of which our narrowing limits forbid us to speak.

A Morning's Catch on the Touchet, near Dayton, Wash.

Sunset Magazine.

And now leaving Oneonta, we can see that we have passed the maximum of the mountains, and are already looking into a broadening valley, with the yet more lordly volume of the river widening toward the sunset. While our eyes are thus drawn toward the river, the diminishing walls of the cañon, and the fair entrance to what may be called the genuine West-of-the-Mountains, we perceive on the Oregon shore a series of waterfalls, higher and grander than has even been the wont, and in the midst of them, far-famed Multnomah. A spacious sweep of circling mountains, a perpendicular wall, indented with a deep recess, and crowned upon its topmost bastions with a row of frightened looking trees, and partially visible through intercepting cottonwoods at the River's margin a moving whiteness,—such is the first vision of this matchless waterfall. A short space farther carries us past the screen of cottonwoods, and the whole majestic scene lies before us. Like St. Peter's Dome or Castle Rock or Niagara or Yosemite or Chelan or Mt. "Takhoma," this scene of Multnomah Falls with its surroundings wears that aspect of eternity, that look of final perfectness, which marks the great works of nature and of art. The cliff almost overhangs, so that except when deflected by the wind against a projecting ledge the water leaps sheer through the air its eight hundred feet of fall. It is mainly spray when it reaches the deep pool within the recess of the mountain, and from that recess the regathered waters pour in a final plunge, from which the stream takes its way through the cottonwoods to the River.

We disembark and climb to the pool which receives the great fall. We find it sunless and almost black in hue from the intensity of the shadows. The maidenhair fern which grows at the edge of the pool is nearly white in its cool dark abode. The water falls into the pool with a weird, uncanny "chug," rather than a splash, so great is the sheer fall and so largely does the water consist of spray alternating with "chunks"—if we may so express it—of water. The pool is large enough to hold a steamboat and of considerable depth. A pretty rustic bridge spans the gorge through which the stream passes on its way from the pool, and below the bridge is the final fall of seventy-five feet. On account of its proximity to Portland and the frequent steamboat excursions, Multnomah has become quite a resort. While the creek is only of moderate size in summer, and the fall is notable rather for beauty than energy, yet when swollen by the rains and melting snows of winter and spring it takes on the dimensions of a river. Then the fall hurling its great volume over the eight hundred feet of open space assumes an appalling sublimity.

Oneonta Gorge—Looking In.

Photo. by E. H. Moorehouse.

And now with the sounds of the fall ringing in our ears and our eyes turned back for a final reluctant gaze, we make our way across the River and a short distance down to the next wonder on the Washington side. This is Cape Horn. It is a long palisade of basalt, not high compared to most of the river walls, being only about two hundred feet high, but it is the most complete example of continuous basaltic formation on the River. The beauty and symmetry of the formation, the deeps of the River reflecting the escarpment of rock, the wide-opening vista of hazy islands and extending plains down-stream;—all these together compose a scene unique in itself and, though so different, placing Cape Horn in the same gallery of royal pictures which we have been gathering.

A few miles below Cape Horn it becomes apparent that we are about to issue from the mountain pass. The heights have fallen away. Deep valleys appear and many habitations attest the cultivable character of the region. But as if to show that she has not exhausted her resources, wonder-working Nature has set one more masterpiece in the long line, and this is Rooster Rock, with a mighty rampart of rock adjoining and closing the southern horizon. Together they mark the western limit of the mountains. That rampart, which was once well named Cape Eternity, though the name does not seem to have been preserved, is a sheer massive precipice of a thousand feet. Though not nearly so high as some of the cliffs above, it is not surpassed by any for the appearance of solid and massive power. Rooster Rock is distinguished by a singular and exquisite beauty, rather than magnitude or grandeur. It is only three hundred and fifty feet high, but in form and colour and alternation of rock and trees it is the most beautiful object on the River.

With a farewell to Cape Eternity and Rooster Rock we are out of the mountains, and this stage of our long journey is at an end. If we were to compare the section of the River which we have described in this chapter with other great scenes in our country, we would say that this section of the Columbia from Paha Cliffs to Rooster Rock possesses a greater variety than any other. Chelan has loftier cliffs, clearer and deeper water, and a certain chaotic and elemental energy beyond comparison. The Yellowstone has a greater richness of colouring and larger waterfalls, together with the unique features of the geysers. Yosemite has loftier waterfalls and has cliffs that in some respects are even more imposing. Puget Sound has finer distant scenes, with lagoons and channels and archipelagoes. Each of these grand exhibitions of nature's works is equal or even superior to the Columbia Gorge in some special feature. But the River has every feature. It has cliffs and mountains and waterfalls and cataracts, valleys and forests, broad marine views near and distant, colour and form, shore and sky, earth and air and water, a commingling of all elements of beauty, grandeur, and physical interest. Add to this, that, up or down, the broad waters of the River are accessible to every form of floating craft, and that Portland, one of the most beautiful and progressive cities of the West, destined to become one of the great cities of the world, sits at the very gates of admission to this symposium of grandeurs and wonders, and we have such an aggregation of charms that we may well suppose that all the other great scenic regions would bow before our great River and acknowledge him as the king of all.

Cape Horn, Columbia River—Looking Up.

Photo. by E. H. Moorehouse, Portland.

CHAPTER V

A SIDE TRIP TO SOME OF THE GREAT SNOW-PEAKS

Attractions of our Mountain Peaks—Relations to the Rivers—Locations of the Greatest and their Positions with Regard to the Cities and the Routes of Travel—The Mountain Clubs—The Peaks, Especially Belonging to the River: Hood, Adams, and St. Helens—A Journey to Hood—Beauty of the Approach through Hood River Valley—Lost Lake—Cloud-Cap Inn and Elliot Glacier—Extreme Steepness of the Ascent—Magnificence of the View—Mt. Adams—The Hunting and Fishing—The Glaciers—The Vegetation about the Snow-Line—The Night Storm—Morning and the Ascent—Views Around, Up, Down—Ascent by the Mazama Club in 1902 and the Transformation Scene—General Similarity of Ascent of our Peaks—Zones of a Snow-Peak.

"Nesika Klatawa Sahale"

MOST countries have rivers of beauty and grandeur; many have lakes of scenic charm; many have hills and mountain chains; but there is only one country in the United States that has all of these features, and, in addition, a number of isolated giant peaks, clad in permanent ice and snow. That country is the Pacific North-west. Throughout Oregon and Washington and extending partly through California is a series of volcanic peaks which gather within themselves every feature of natural beauty, sublimity, and wonder.

The fifteen most conspicuous of these peaks, beginning with Baker or Kulshan on the north, and ending with Pitt on the south, are spaced at nearly regular intervals of from thirty to fifty miles, except for the one group of the Three Sisters, which, though distinct peaks, are separated only by narrow valleys. Most of these great peaks are somewhat remote from the cities or the great routes of public travel, and hence are not easily accessible to ordinary tourists. None of them, except Hood and Rainier or Tacoma, possesses hotel accommodations. The natives are more accustomed to "roughing it," and braving the wilderness than most Eastern people are, and hence many parties go annually from the chief cities of Oregon and Washington to the great peaks. Some of them, as Glacier Peak and Shuksan, are so environed with mountain ramparts and almost impassable cañons as to be practically unknown. The most approachable and the most visited are Hood,

Rainier, and Adams.

Looking up the Columbia River from the Cliff above Multnomah Falls, Ore.

Copyright, Kiser Photograph Co., 1902.

The greatest influence in organising visits to these mountains, and in cultivating an appreciation of them among the people of the region, as well as in inform-
ing the world regarding them, has existed in the mountain clubs. The chief of these

are the Mazama (Wild Goat) Club of Portland and the Mountaineers of Seattle. Membership is not confined to those two cities, though mainly located there. The Mazama Club may be called the historic mountain climber's club, and it has done incalculable good in fostering a love of mountains and in arranging expeditions to them.

The three peaks which may be considered as especially belonging to the Columbia River are Hood, Adams, and St. Helens. As the traveller on the River views the unsullied spires and domes of these great temples of nature, he longs to worship in their more immediate presence. As a logical consequence of this sentiment, after having floated down the Columbia from The Dalles to Rooster Rock, we feel that life would be at least partly in vain if we should fail to plant feet on the topmost snows of at least two of these great heights.

We will first visit Hood. Though not the highest, this is the boldest and most picturesque of all. Moreover by reason of its location, seen conspicuously as it is from Portland and the Willamette Valley, and because of its nearness to the old immigrant road into Oregon, Hood was the first noticed, and the most often described, painted, and berhymed of any of the wintry brotherhood. As the Puget Sound region became settled, and great cities began to grow up there, Mt. Rainier ("Takhoma") began to be a rival in popular estimation. When measurements showed that Rainier was three thousand feet higher, and Adams over one thousand feet higher than the idolised Hood, a wail of grief arose from the Oregonians, and for a time they could hardly be reconciled. But as they became adjusted to the situation, they planted themselves upon the proposition that, though Hood was not the highest, it was the most beautiful, and that its surroundings were superior to those of any other. For this proposition there is much to be said, though, in truth, we must accept the dictum of Dogberry that "comparisons are odorous"

The usual approach to Mt. Hood by the Hood River route is indeed of striking attractiveness. This picturesque orchard valley is like an avenue of flowers leading to a marble temple. One of the finest points in the vicinity of Hood River, seldom visited because it is off the road and buried in forests, is Lost Lake. Perhaps the grandest view of Mt. Hood is from this lake. The bold pinnacle, rising out of the broad fields of snow, they in turn most wondrously encircled in forests of rich hue, is mirrored in the clear water with a perfectness that scarcely can be matched among the many lakes of its kind in all the land. In these days of swift transit, Hood River keeps up with the procession, for there is a regular automobile line from the town to Cloud-Cap Inn at the snow-line of the great peak, twenty-four miles distant. The distance, though it represents a rise of seven thousand feet, is traversed all too quickly to fully enjoy the valley, filled with its orchards, and rising in regular gradation from the heat of the lower end to the bracing cold of the upper air. In Cloud-Cap Inn the traveller may find the daintiest, most unique specimen of a mountain resort in our mountains. The Inn is owned by a wealthy Portland man, and is maintained rather as an attraction to visitors than with the expectation of making money.

Spokane Falls and City, 1886.

Photo. by T. W. Tolman, Spokane.

Spokane Falls and City, 1908.

Photo. by T. W. Tolman, Spokane.

From the Inn one can climb in a few minutes to Photographer's Point, from which he can look right down on the Elliot Glacier, not a large, but an exceedingly fine specimen of that most interesting of all features of a great peak.

Hood, though so steep, can be ascended from several points. It was for a long time supposed to be unscalable from the north side. But William Langille, one of the most daring and successful mountain climbers of Oregon, soon found his way up the sharp ascent, and, once marked out, that route has been followed by the great majority of climbers. Though very steep, there has never been an accident on this route except in one case, when a stranger undertook the climb alone and never returned. He probably lost his footing and fell into a crevasse. With the usual precautions of ropes and ice hatchets and caulks, a party can make their way over the steep slope, and its very steepness makes the ascent quicker and less exhaustive than to overcome the longer and more gradual ascents of Adams or "Takhoma." While it takes but about four or five hours for an average party to go from snow-line to summit of Hood, either of the other mountains named demands from seven to ten hours.

And having reached the summit, what a view! If the day be entirely clear—a rare occurrence—you will behold a domain for an empire. On the south, the long line of the Cascades, with the occasional great heights, Jefferson, Three Sisters, Thielson, Diamond, Scott, and, if it be very clear, even Pitt. To the north, the giant bulk of Adams, the airy symmetry of St. Helens, and the lordly majesty of Rainier, rule sky and earth, while in mazy undulations the great range, alternately purple and white, stretches on and on until it blends into the clouds.

Seemingly almost at the feet of the observer, a dark green sinuosity amid the timbered hills, now strangely flattened, as we stand so high above them, marks the course of the River on its march oceanward. If the day be very clear, a whitish blur far westward shows where the "Rose City" on the Willamette reigns over her fair domains, while a dim stretch of varied hues denotes the Willamette Valley. Some climbers have even asserted that late in the afternoon of extremely clear days the glint of the western sun can be seen upon the Pacific, a hundred and fifty miles distant. Toward the east lie the vast plains of the Inland Empire, marked at their farther limit by the soft curves and lazy swells of the range of the Blue Mountains.

While it is an ungracious and even a fruitless undertaking to compare such objects as the great mountains or the views from the respective summits, it may be said that Hood has one conspicuous feature of the view, and that is that it is nearest the centre of the great mountain peaks, as well as systems, and also best commands the outlook over the great valley systems and river systems of this part of the Columbia Basin. And therefore, though the view is not equal in breadth to that from the summit of Adams or Rainier, it is unsurpassed for variety and interest. It may be said to cover more history than the view from any other peak. Across the southern flank lies the old Barlow Road, over which came the greater part of the immigration in the days of the ox-team conquest of Oregon in the forties and fifties. Thirty miles east is The Dalles with its old fur-trader's station, its old United States fort, its mission station, its Indian wars, its early settlement, the most historic place in Eastern Oregon. From the old town, during all the years from the opening of the century, there descended the River the trappers, missionaries, immigrants, miners, soldiers, hunters, home-seekers, of a later day, adventurers and promoters of every species, to say nothing of the generations of Indians who lived and died along the banks.

To the west of our icy eyrie, Portland and Vancouver, with the rich valleys around them, represent the earliest explorations and developments of the fur-traders, as well as the earliest days of the era of permanent settlement. There in the westward haze is the little town of Champoeg where the Provisional Government of Oregon was established. In fact, in whatsoever direction we may look, we see illustrations of the heroic age of Old Oregon, the drama of native races, rival powers of Europe and America, the march of empire, a section of humanity and the world in the making.

When our visit to Hood is ended we must cross the River and traverse another paradise, the White Salmon Valley, leading to Mt. Adams, the old Indian Klickitat. Adams is in such a position that its true elevation and magnitude cannot be understood from Portland or The Dalles or most of the routes of travel. Therefore until comparatively recent times it was generally supposed that Adams was an insignificant mountain in comparison with Hood, which looms up with such imposing grandeur from every point along the chief highways of commerce. It was discovered by the Mazama Club in 1896 that Adams carried his regal crown at a height of twelve thousand four hundred and seventy feet above the level of the sea, while the previously established height of Hood was only eleven thousand two hundred and twenty-five. Since then Adams has been held in much greater respect by mountain lovers, and many journeys have been made to and on it.

Around Mt. Adams is a region of caves. As one rides through the open glades he may often hear the ground rumble beneath his horse's hoofs. Mouths of Avernus yawn on every side. Some caverns have sunken in, leaving serpentine ravines. One cave has been traced three miles without finding the end. Some of these caves are partially filled with ice. There is one in particular, fifteen miles south-west of the mountain, which is known as Ice Cave. This is very small, not over four hundred feet long, but it is a marvel of unique beauty. Its external appearance is that of a huge well, at whose edge are bunches of nodding flowers, and from whose dark depths issue sudden chilly gusts. Descending by means of a knotty young tree which previous visitors have let down, we find ourselves on a floor of ice. The glare of pitch-pine torches reveals a weird and beautiful scene. A perfect forest of icicles of both the stalactite and stalagmite forms fills the cave. They are from ten to fifteen feet in length and from one to three in diameter. From some points of view they look like silvered organ-pipes.

These caves have been formed in some cases by chambers of steam or bubbles in the yet pasty rock which hardened enough to maintain their form upon the condensation of the vapour. Others were doubtless produced by a tongue of lava as it collected slag and hardened rock upon its moving edge, rising up and curling over like a breaker on the sand. Only the "cave of flint" instead of turning into a "retreating cloud" had enough solid matter to sustain the arch and so became permanent. Others were no doubt formed by pyroducts. A tongue of flowing lava hardens on the surface. The interior remains fluid. It may continue running until the tongue is all emptied, leaving a cavern. Such a cavern, whose upper end reaches the cold air of the mountains, might be like a chimney, down which freezing air would descend, turning into ice the water that trickled into the cave, even at the lower end.

In the Heart of the Cascade Mountains, above Lake Chelan, Wash.

Photo. by T. W. Tolman, Spokane.

For sport, the region about Mt. Adams is unsurpassed. The elk, three kinds of deer, the magnificent mule deer, the black-tail, and the graceful little white-tail, two species of bear, the cinnamon and black, the daring and ubiquitous mountain goat, quail, grouse, pheasants, ducks, and cranes, are among the attractions to the hunter. Of late years great bands of sheep have driven the game somewhat from the south and east sides. In the grassy glades that encircle the snowy pile of Adams no vexatious undergrowth impedes the gallop of our fleet cayuse pony or obscures our vision. On the background of fragrant greenery the "dun deer's hide" is thrown with statuesque distinctness, and among the low trees the whirring grouse is easily discerned. Nor is the disciple of Nimrod alone considered. After our hunt we may move to Trout Lake, and here the very ghost of the lamented Walton might come as to a paradise. Trout Lake is a shallow pool half a mile in length, encircled with pleasant groves and grassy glades, marred now, however, by the encroachment of ranches. Into it there come at intervals from the ice-cold mountain inlet perfect shoals of the most gamey and delicious trout. On rafts, or the two or three rude skiffs that have been placed there, one may find all piscatorial joys and may abundantly supply his larder free of cost. A few ranches here and there furnish accommodations for those who are too delicate to rest on the bosom of Mother Earth. But no extended trip can be taken without committing oneself to the wilderness delights of sleeping with star-dials for roof and flickering camp-fire for hearth. And what healthy human being would exchange those for the feverish, pampered life of the modern house? Let us have the barbarism, and with it the bounding pulses and exuberant life of the wilderness.

But now, with stomachs and knapsacks filled, and with that pervasive sense of contentment which characterises the successful hunter and angler, we must get up our cayuse ponies from their pastures on the rich grass of the open woods, saddle up, and then off for the mountain, whose giant form now overtops the very clouds. About two miles from Trout Lake the trail crosses the White Salmon, and we find ourselves at the foot of the mountain. For eight miles we follow a trail through open woods, park-like, with huge pines at irregular intervals, and vivid grass and flowers between, a fair scene, the native home of every kind of game.

As we journey on delightedly through these glades, rising, terrace after terrace, we can read the history of the mountain in the rock beneath our feet and the expanding plains and hills below. All within the ancient amphitheatre is volcanic. There are four main summits, a central dome, vast, symmetrical, majestic, pure-white against the blue-black sky of its unsullied height. The three other peaks are broken crags of basalt, leaning as for support against the mighty mass at the centre. Around the snow-line of the mountain many minor cones have been blown up. These have the most gaudy and brilliant colouring, mainly yellow and vermilion. One on the south-east is especially noticeable. From a deep cañon it rises two thousand feet as steep as broken scoriæ can lie. The main part is bright red, surmounted by a circular cliff of black rock. Probably the old funnel of the crater became filled with black rock, which, cooling, formed a solid core. The older material around it having crumbled away, it remains a solid shaft.

But fire has not wrought all the wonders of the mighty peak. Ice has been most active. The mountain was once completely girdled with glaciers. Rocks are scratched and grooved five miles below the present snow-line. The ridges are strewn with planed rocks and glacial shavings and coarse sand. Some of the monticules on the flanks of the mountain have been partially cut away. Many have been entirely obliterated. But the ice has now greatly receded. Instead of a complete enswathement of ice there are some six or seven distinct glaciers, separated by sharp ridges, while the region formerly the chief home of the ice is now a series of Alpine meadows. Like most of the snow peaks, Mt. Adams is rudely terraced, and the terraces are separated into compartments by ridges, forming scores and hundreds of glades and meads. In some of these are circular ponds, from a few square rods to several acres in area. These lakes are found by the hundred around the mountain and in the region north of it. They are one of the charms and wonders of the country. About most of them tall grass crowds to the very edge of the water. Scattered trees diversify the scene. Throughout these glades flow innumerable streams, descending from level to level in picturesque cascades, and composed of water so cold and sparkling that the very memory of it cools the after thirst. Sometimes the tough turf grows clear over, making a verdant tunnel through which "the tinkling waters slip." Here and there streams spout full-grown from frowning precipices.

But we are not content to stand below and gaze "upward to that height." We must needs ascend. In climbing a snow peak a great deal depends on making camp at a good height and getting a very early start. By a little searching one may find good camping places at an elevation of seven thousand or even eight thousand feet altitude. This leaves only four thousand or five thousand feet to climb on the great day, and by starting at about four o'clock a party may have sixteen hours of daylight. This is enough, if there be no accidents, to enable any sound man of average muscle, — or woman either, if she be properly dressed for it, — to gain the mighty dome of Adams.

At the time of our last ascent we camped high on a great ridge on the south side of the mountain, having for shelter a thick copse of dwarf firs. So fiercely had the winds of centuries swept this exposed point that the trees did not stand erect, but lay horizontal from west to east.

With pulses bounding from the exhilarating air, and our whole systems glowing with the exercise and the wild game of the preceding week, we stretch ourselves out for sleep, while the stars blaze from infinite heights, and our uneasy camp-fire strives fitfully with the icy air which at nightfall always slides down the mountain side.

Sweet sleep till midnight, and then we found ourselves awake all at once with a unanimity which at first we scarcely understood, but which a moment's observation made clear enough. A regular mountain gale had suddenly broken upon us. It had waked us up by nearly blowing us out of bed. Our camp-fire was aroused to newness of life by the gale, and the huge fire-brands flew down the mountain side, igniting pitchy thickets, until a fitful glare illuminated the lonely and savage grandeur of the scene. The whole sky seemed in motion. Then a cloud struck us. Night, glittering as she was a moment before with her tiaras of stars, was suddenly transformed into a dull, whitish blur. The vapour formed at once into thick drops on the trees and was precipitated in turn on us. Occasional sleet and snowflakes struck us with almost the sting of flying sand when we ventured to peep out. Covering ourselves up, heads and all, we crowded against each other and grimly went to sleep.

Birch-Tree Channel; Upper Columbia, Near Golden, B. C.

Photo. by C. F. Yates, Golden.

A Typical Mountain Meadow, Stehekin Valley, Wash.

Photo. by T. W. Tolman, Spokane.

We woke again, chattering with cold, to find it perfectly calm. The morning star was blazing over the spot where day was about to break. The sky was absolutely clear, not a mote on its whole concavity. The wind had swept and burnished it. The mountain towered above us cold and sharp as a crystal. There was a still, solemn majesty about it in the keen air and early light which struck us with a thrill of fear. The light just before daybreak is far more exact than the scarlet splendour of morning or the blinding blaze of noon. The world below us was a level sea of clouds. We seemed to be on an island of snow and rock, or on a small planetoid winging its own way in space. Yet beyond the puncturing top of a few of the Simcoe peaks a wavering line that just touched the glowing eastern sky, told of clear weather a hundred leagues up the basin of the Columbia. Out of the ocean of cloud, the great peaks of Hood and St. Helens rose, cold and white, like icebergs on an Arctic sea.

Coffee, ham, and hardtack, and then out on the ice and snow, just as the first warm flush of morning is gilding the mighty mass above us. The snow, hardened by the freezing morning, affords excellent footing, and in the sharp, bracing air we feel capable of any effort. We gain the summit of a bright red knob, one of the secondary volcanoes that girdle the mountain. At its peak are purple stones piled up like an altar, as indeed it is, though the incense from it is not of human kindling. The sun is not fairly up, but from below the horizon it splits the hemisphere of the sky into a hundred segments by its auroral flashes. And now we begin to climb a volcanic ridge, rising like a huge stairway, with blocks of stone as large as a piano. This is a tongue of lava, very recent, insomuch that it shows no glacial markings, and yet enough soil has accumulated upon it to support vegetation. It can be seen, a dull red river, three hundred yards wide, extending far down the mountain side. How well the old Greek poet described the process that must have taken place here: "Ætna, pillar of heaven, nurse of snow, with fountains of fire; a river of fire, bearing down rocks with a crashing sound to the deep sea."

The ridge becomes very steep, at an angle of probably thirty-five or forty degrees, and we climb on all fours from one rock to another. At last we draw ourselves up a huge wedge of phonolite and find ourselves at the summit of the first peak. Six hundred yards beyond, muffled in white silence, rises the great dome. It is probably five hundred feet higher than the first peak. To reach it we climb a bare, steep ridge of shaly, frost-shattered rock, in which we sink ankle deep, a difficult and even painful task with the laboured breathing of twelve thousand feet altitude.

But patience conquers, and at about noon, seven hours and a half from the time of starting, we stand on the very tip of the mountain. Ten minutes panting in the cold wind and then we are ready to look around. Within the circle of our vision is an area for an empire. Northward is a wilderness of mountains. High above all, Mt. Rainier lifts his white crown unbroken to the only majesty above him, the sky. The western horizon, more hazy than the eastern, is punctuated by the smooth dome and steely glitter of Mt. St. Helens. Far southward, across a wilderness of broken heights, rises the sharp pinnacle of Mt. Hood, and far beyond that, its younger brother, Jefferson. Still beyond, are the Alpine peaks of the Three Sisters, nearly two hundred miles distant. Our vision sweeps a circle whose diameter is probably five hundred miles. Far westward the white haze betokens the presence of the sea. A deep blue line north-eastward, far beyond the smooth dome of St. Helens, stands for Puget Sound. Numerous lakes gleam in woody solitudes.

High School, Walla Walla, Wash.

Photo. by W. D. Chapman, Walla Walla.

Having looked around, let us now look down. On the eastern side the mountain breaks off in a monstrous chasm of probably four thousand feet, most of it perpendicular. We crawl as we draw near it. Lying down in turn, secured by ropes held behind, fearful as much of the mystic attraction of the abyss as of the slippery snow, we peep over the awful verge. Take your turn, gentle reader, if you would know what it seems to gaze down almost a mile of nearly perpendicular distance. Points of rock jut out from the pile and eye us darkly. That icy floor nearly a mile below us is the Klickitat glacier. From beneath it a milk-white stream issues and crawls off amid the rocky desolation. At the very edge of the great precipice stands a cone of ice a hundred feet high. Green, blue, yellow, red, and golden, the colours play with the circling sunbeams on its slippery surface, until one is ready to believe that here is where rainbows are made. We roll some rocks from a wind-swept point, and then shudder to see them go. They are lost to the eye as their noise to the ear, long before they cease to roll. Silence reigns. There is no echo. The thin air makes the voice sound weak. Our loudest shouts are brief bubbles of noise in the infinite space. A pistol shot is only a puff of powder. Even the rocks we set off are swallowed up and we get no response but the first reluctant clank as they grind the lip of the precipice. Nor do we care much for boisterous sounds. We are impelled rather to silence and worship.

But now once more to earth and camp! For pure exhilaration, commend me to descending a snow peak. For a good part of Mt. Adams one may descend in huge jumps through the loose scoriæ and volcanic ashes. Some of the way one may slide on the crusty snow, a perfect whiz of descent. How the thin wind cuts past us, and how our frames glow with the dizzy speed! Such a manner of descent is not altogether safe. As we are going in one place with flying jumps on the softening snow, a chasm suddenly appears before us. It looks ten feet wide, and how deep, no one could guess. To stop is out of the question. We make a wild bound and clear it, catching a momentary glance into the bluish-green crack as we fly across. We make the descent in an incredibly short time, only a little more than an hour, whereas it took us over seven hours to ascend. And then the rest and mighty feasts of camp, and the abundant and mountainous yarns, and the roaring camp-fire, whose shadows flicker on the solemn snow-fields, until the stars claim the heavens, and, while the wailing cry of the cougars rises from a jungle far below us, we sleep and perform again in dreams the day's exploits.

Of all scenes in connection with Mt. Adams, the most remarkable in all the experience of those who witnessed it, and one of those rare combinations which the sublimest aspects of nature afford, was at the time of the outing of the Mazama Club in 1902. The party had reached the summit in a dense fog, cold, bitter, forbidding, and nothing whatever to be seen. All was a dull, whitish blur. In the bitter chill the enthusiasm of some of the climbers evaporated and they turned away down the snowy waste. Others remained in the hope of a vanishing of the cloud-cap. And suddenly their hopes were realised. A marvellous transformation scene was unveiled like the lifting of a vast curtain. The cloud-cap was split asunder. The great red and black pinnacles of the summit sprung forth from the mist like the first lines in a developing photographic plate. Then the glistening tiaras and thrones of ice and snow caught the gleams of the unveiled sun, and lo, there we stood in mid-heaven, seemingly upon an island in space, with no earth about us, just the sun and the sky above and a great swaying ocean of fog below. But now suddenly that ocean of fog was rent and split. The ardent sun burned and banished it away. Mountain peak after peak caught the glory. Range after range seemed to rise and stand in battle array. The transformation was complete. A moment before we were swathed in the densest cloud-cap, blinded with the fog. Now we were standing on a mount of transfiguration, with a new world below us. Every vestige of smoke or fog was gone. We could see the shimmer of the ocean to the west, the glistening bands of Puget Sound and the Columbia. Far eastward the plains of the Inland Empire lay palpitating in the July sun. The whole long line of the great snow-peaks of the Cascades were there revealed, the farthest a mere speck, yet distinctly discernible, two hundred miles distant. One unaccustomed to the mountains would not believe it possible that such an area could be caught within the vision from a single point.

It may be understood that the description of one of our great snow-peaks is, in general terms, a description of all. With every one there are the same azure skies, the same snow-caps, the same crevassed and glistening rivers of ice, the same long ridges with their intervening grassy and flowery meads, purling streams, and reflecting lakes. With the name of each there rises before Mazama or Mountaineer the remembrance of the camp of clouds or stars upon the edge of snow-bank, the sound of the bugle at two o'clock in the morning of the great climb, the hastily swallowed breakfast of coffee and ham, while climbers stand shivering around the flickering morning fire, the approaching day with its banners of crimson behind the heights, the daubing of faces with grease-paint and the putting on of goggles, amid shouts of laughter from each at the grotesque and picturesque ugliness of all the others, then the hastily grasped alpenstocks, the forming in line, and at about four o'clock, while the first rays of the sun are gilding the summit, the word of command and the beginning of the march.

Each great peak has its zones, so significant that each seems a world in itself. There is first the zone of summer with its fir and cedar forests at the base of the peak, from a thousand feet to twenty-five hundred above sea-level. In the case of most of our great peaks this zone consists of long gentle slopes and dense forests, with much undergrowth, though on the eastern sides there are frequently wide-open spaces of grassy prairie. Then comes the zone of pine forest and summer strawberry, with its fragrant air and long glades of grass and open aisles of columned trees, "God's first temples," pellucid streams babbling over pebbles and white sands, and occasionally falling in cascades over ledges of volcanic rock. This zone rises in terraces which attest the ancient lava flow, at an increasing grade over the first, though at most points one might still drive a carriage through the open pine forests. Then comes the third zone, a zone of parks. The large pine trees now give way to the belts of subalpine fir and mountain pine and larch, exquisite for beauty, enclosing the parks and grouped here and there in clumps like those in some old baronial estate of feudal times. This is the zone of rhododendron, shushula, phlox, and painted brush. Through the open glades the ptarmigan and deer wander, formerly unafraid of man, but now, alas, under the ban of civilisation. The upward slope has now increased to twenty or twenty-five degrees, and to a party of climbers a frequent rest and the quaffing of the ice-cold stream that dashes through the woods afford a happy feature of the ascent. At the upper edge of this zone, at an elevation of probably seven thousand feet, beside some dashing stream or some clear pool, fed from the snows above, is the place for the camp. And such a camp! Oh, the beauty of such an unspoiled spot!

Lake Chelan.

Photo. by F. N. Kneeland.

On the Banks of the Columbia River, near Hood River.

Photo. by E. H. Moorehouse.

It is from such a camp at the upper edge of the paradise zone that a party sets forth at the four o'clock hour to attain the highest. So the march on the great day of a final climb carries us at once into a fourth zone. This is the zone of avalanche and glacier, the zone of elemental fury and warfare, a zone of ever-steepening ascent, thirty degrees, a zone of almost winter cold at night, but with such a dazzling brightness and fervour in the day as turns the snow-banks to slush and sends the fountains tearing and cutting across the glaciers and triturating the moraines. Vegetation has now almost ceased, though the heather still drapes the ledges on the eastern or southern exposures, and occasionally one of the tenacious mountain pines upholds the banner of spring in some sheltered nook. This wind-swept and storm-lashed zone is also the zone of the wild goats and mountain sheep. On the precipitous ridges and along the narrow ledges at the margin of glaciers they can be seen bounding away at the approach of the party, sure-footed and swift at points where the nerve of the best human climber might fail. This zone carries the climbers to ten or eleven thousand feet of elevation on the highest peaks. And here is the place for the Mountaineers and Mazamas to take the half-hour rest on their arduous march. A sweet rest it is. We pick out some sheltered place on the eastern slope, and stretch ourselves at full length on the warm rocks, while the icy wind from the summit goes hurtling above us. And how good the chocolate and the malted milk and the prunes and raisins of the scanty lunch taste, while we rest and feel the might of elemental nature again fill our veins and lungs and hearts.

But then comes a fifth zone, the last, the zone of the Arctic. This is the zone of the snow-cap. The glaciers are now below. All life has ceased. The grade has ever steepened, till now it is forty degrees or more. The snow is hummocked and granulated. Here is where part of the climbers begin to stop. Legs and lungs fail. Camp looks exceedingly good down there at the verge of the forests. They feel as though they had lost nothing on the summit worth going up for. A nausea, mountain sickness, attacks some. Nosebleed attacks others. Things look serious. Icy mists sometimes begin to swirl around the presumptous climbers. Frost gathers on hair and mustache and eyebrows. The unaccustomed or the less ambitious or weaker lose heart and bid the rest go on, for they will turn toward a more summer-like clime. Generally about half an ordinary party drop out at this beginning of the Arctic zone. But the rest shout "Excelsior," take a firmer grasp of alpenstock, stamp feet more vehemently into the snow, and with dogged perseverance move step by step up the final height. Inch by inch, usually in the teeth of a biting gale, leaning forward, and panting heavily, they force the upward way. And victory at last! There comes a time when we are on the topmost pinnacle, and there is nothing above us but the storms and sun. And then what elation! Nothing seems quite to equal the pure delight of such a triumph of lungs and legs and heart and will.

Rooster Rock, Columbia River—Looking Up.

Photo. by E. H. Moorehouse, Portland.

CHAPTER VI

THE LOWER RIVER AND THE OCEAN TIDES

Remarkable Change in Climate and Topography—Farms and Villages—First View of Mt. Hood on West Side—Vancouver and its Historic Interest—The North Bank Railroad—View at the Mouth of the Willamette—Sauvie's or Wapatoo Island—Beauty of the Willamette and its Tributaries—Simpson's Poem—Approach to Portland—Site of Portland—Transportation Facilities—Portland's Commerce—Homes and Public Buildings—Art in Portland—The Historical Society Museum—The *Oregonian* and its Editor—Once more on the River—The Fishing and Lumbering Villages—Scenery of the Lower River—Astoria and the Outlook to the Ocean—Industries of Astoria—The Fisheries—The Fleet of Fishing Boats on the Bar—The Ocean Beaches and the Tourist Travel—Through the Outer Headlands to the Pacific.

HAVING returned from our side trip to the mountain peaks of Hood and Adams and having resumed our station on the bank of the River just below Rooster Rock, we see that we are now in a new world. We are at sea-level. Dense forests clothe the shores, except for the places where the axe of the settler or the saws of the lumberman have made inroads. Moss drapes the rocks. Ferns and vines take possession wherever the trees have been removed. Even in summer a feeling of humidity usually pervades the air. A certain softness and roundness seems to characterise both the vegetable and animal world. The smell of the sea is in the atmosphere, even though the sea is yet distant. No longer do our eyes wander over boundless expanses of rolling prairie, crowned to the highest knolls with wheat-fields, as on the other side of the mountains. The mountains fall away, and low bottoms, sometimes oozy with the inflowing river or the creeks from the forests, stretch away in the lazy, hazy distance. The River no longer flows tumultuously and with that militant energy which is so characteristic of the long stretches from Kettle Falls to The Dalles. It has a calm and stately majesty, the repose of accomplished warfare and victory. It has hewn its way down to the level of the ocean and no longer needs to fret and storm. It has conquered a peace.

Below Rooster Rock, the shores are flats with low hills in the background, and the River expands to a width of from one to two miles. If we still imagine ourselves in a small boat, we find the most delightful of sensations in gliding past the grassy islands and shores thick with fir or cottonwood. Or if we choose to take our way to one of the elegant steamers, *Spencer* or *Bailey Gatzert*, we shall still partake of the same life and feel the same sense of repose and contentment which belong by natural right to this portion of the River.

Band of Elk on W. P. Reser's Ranch, Walla Walla, Wash.

Photo. by W. D. Chapman.

Soon after leaving Rooster Rock, we begin to pass frequent pleasant farms on either bank. On the Washington side we see two pretty villages, Washougal and La Camas. The first has the historical distinction of being at or nearly at the highest spot reached by the English explorer Broughton in 1792, and named by him Point Vancouver. La Camas is the location of the most extensive paper mills in the North-west.

If, while we are in this section of the River and our eyes are bent eagerly forward to catch the ever-changing shore and river lines, we happen to glance backward, our gaze is fastened as with a magnet, and for a moment utterance fails. For what do we see? Glistening white, ethereal, Mt. Hood rises before us, a vision which, of the many mountain visions that we have seen, seems the most beautiful. Mt. Hood indeed is the background of many a noble scene upon the River, but there is none quite equal in amplitude, in variety, to this,—River, forest, shore, foreground of timbered hills, Cascade Gorge, distant white and purple chain of Cascade Mountains, and the volcanic cone overtopping and overawing all. This view of Mt. Hood from the vicinity of La Camas has perhaps been oftener the subject of painting than any other.

A few miles below La Camas we reach the most historic and perhaps the most beautiful spot upon the Columbia, Vancouver. As the capital for twenty years of the Hudson's Bay Company's Fur Empire, associated with the name of Dr. John McLoughlin, the centre of almost every event of importance in the early history, connected with both American and British occupation, and later as the location of the United States military post and preserving the names of Grant, Sheridan, McClellan, Hooker, and others of our famous generals, Vancouver has indeed a rich historic setting. But aside from such associations with the past, every tourist must note the location of Vancouver as one of rare beauty. In fact, the spot is almost ideal for a great city. The splendid River, a mile and a half in width, offers limitless facilities for shipping, while, beginning at the water's edge, a gradually rising slope of land extends in a superb swell several miles to the north. Every feature of scenery that could delight the eye—Mt. Hood with the Cascades to the east, the Willamette Valley to the south, the Portland and Scappoose hills to the west, the River blending all—seems to have been lavished on Vancouver. It has been a surprise to many that the great city had not grown here rather than at Portland, which, though on an equally fine location, is on the tributary and much smaller Willamette. The chief reasons of this were the nearer proximity of Portland to the rich farming country of the Tualatin and the presence in the Columbia a mile below Vancouver of a sand-bar which embarrassed shipping. This is now removed.

At Vancouver the newly-built "North Bank" Railroad (Spokane, Portland, and Seattle) has constructed across the Columbia a bridge a mile and three quarters in length, said to be the largest and costliest of its kind in the world. This same railroad has also bridged the Willamette a few miles west of Vancouver, thus effecting an entrance to Portland. This railroad is one of the most interesting and remarkable undertakings of the age. It is said that its cost from Spokane to Portland exceeded forty million dollars. Vancouver expects much from this road, even anticipating that much of the shipping hitherto centring in Portland will be diverted to the larger river. However that may prove, it is plain that Vancouver has the promise as well as the memory of great things.

Oregon City in 1845.
From an Old Print.

Fort Vancouver in 1845.

Six miles west of Vancouver is one of those imposing scenes in which our River so abounds. This is the junction of the Willamette with the Columbia. This spot was noted by Broughton in 1792 as one of exceptional beauty, and to it he attached the name Belle Vue Point. It is indeed a combination of both historical and scenic interest. The Willamette steals shyly and coquettishly through green islands to fall into the strong arms of the stately Columbia. The western arm of the Willamette, commonly called the "Slough," joins the Columbia eighteen miles below at the picturesque little town of St. Helens. Between the Columbia and the Slough lies Sauvie's Island, named from a Hudson's Bay man, and famous throughout Hudson's Bay times as well as Indian times. The island was the seat of power of the Multnomah tribe. The scene of the book known as the *Bridge of the Gods* by Frederick Balch is mainly upon this island, and in that book will be found some glowing descriptions of this beauty spot. To the Indians it was known as Wapatoo Island. In the ponds grew the plant called the wapatoo, an onion-like root, very nutritious and palatable, and, with salmon, constituting the chief food of the natives. Not only so, but the Multnomah Indians used the wapatoo as a commercial stock, carrying on regular trade with both the coast and the up-river tribes.

According to the early explorers there were great annual fairs on Wapatoo Island, when Indians from ocean beach, from valley, from mountains, and from River, both up and down, would gather to exchange products, to gamble, race horses and boats, and have a general period of hilarity and good fellowship.

The gathering of the wapatoos developed upon the patient "klootchmen" (women) of the tribe. They would go out in canoes to the shallow water where the roots grew and then, stripping naked, would hang over the side of the boat and dislodge the wapatoos with their toes from the soft mud. Soon the surface would be covered with the floating roots. The squaws would gather these into the canoes. Then they would move to another place for another load. Sometimes they would spend almost the whole day in the water. The wapatoo still grows in the ponds and lagoons of the island. These ponds formerly abounded in ducks and geese and cranes and swans. Even yet there is fine hunting. During the damp soft days of the Oregon winter, the Nimrods of Portland betake themselves thither in great numbers.

From the steamer, as we enter the mouth of the Willamette, or from the greater elevation of the lighthouse, one may command one of the lordliest views that even this land of lordly views affords. Five snow-peaks, Hood, Rainier-Tacoma, St. Helens, Adams, and Jefferson, rise snow white from the purple forests of the Cascade Range. Up the Columbia the great gorge through which we have passed stands open to view, while down-river the sinuous and hazy lines of low-lying shore betoken the nearer proximity of the ocean. Up the Willamette, enchanting islands, with low watery shores, occupy the foreground, while a short distance back from the western bank, a chain of picturesque hills, heavily timbered, encloses the vista. On the east side a low bench with bluffy promontories, crowned with the beautiful smooth-barked madrona tree, rises from the green meadows.

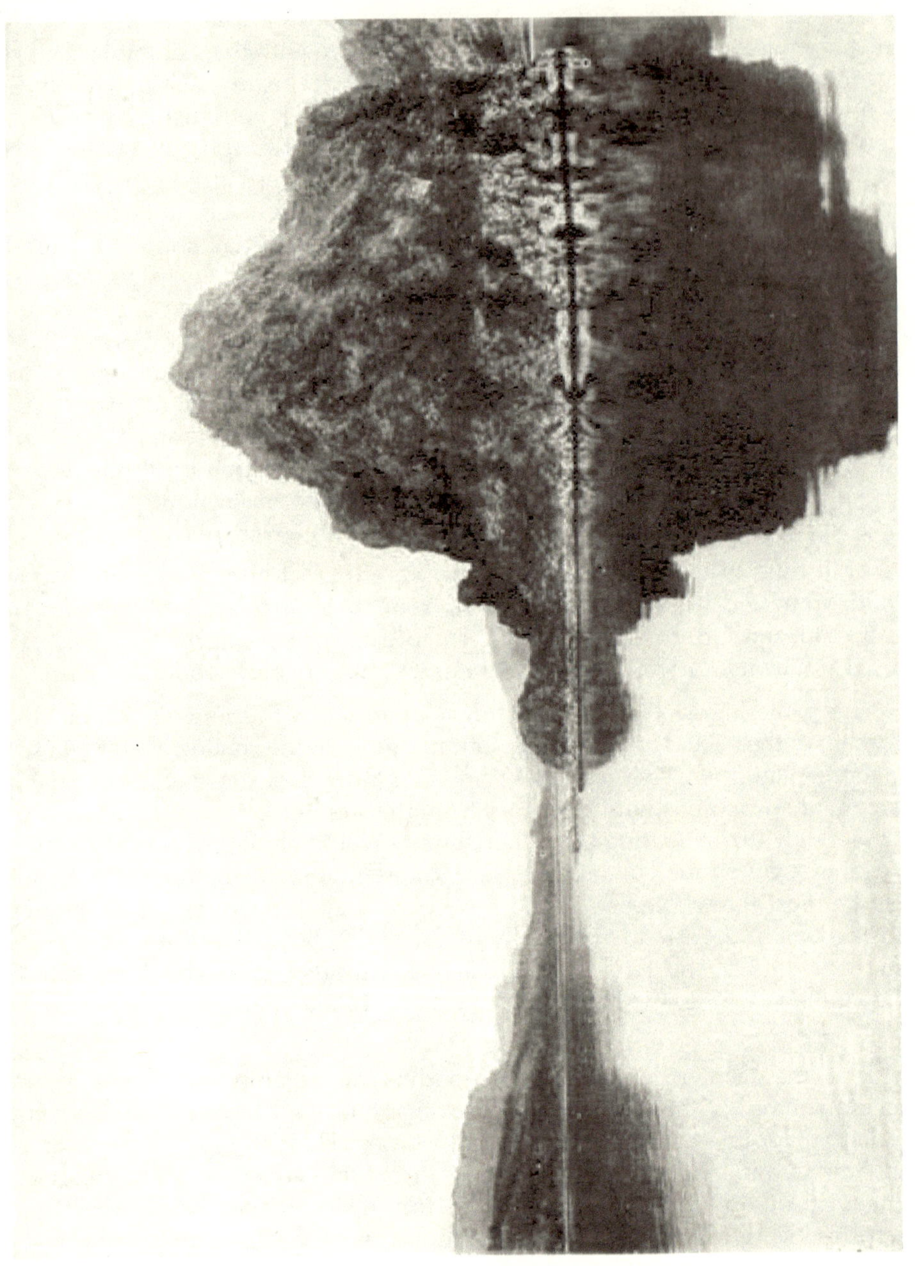

Lone Rock, Columbia River, about Fifty Miles East of Portland.

Photo. by E. H. Moorehouse, Portland.

If we could, from so fair an entrance, ascend the Willamette to its source in the Cascade Mountains two hundred miles away, and if we could turn into the Tualatin, the Yamhill, the Clackamas, the Molalla, the La Creole, the Santiam, the

Calapooia, affluents worthy of union with the Willamette, and if we could tarry among the vales and meadows and oak-crowned hills and distant Coast and Cascade ranges of mountains, all across that superb valley, fifty miles wide by a hundred and fifty long, as beautiful as Greece or Italy,—we would then all agree that the Willamette deserves a volume by itself and that it is almost a crime to introduce it so briefly here. Every old Oregonian, in thinking of the Willamette, at once associates it with the apostrophe to it by S. L. Simpson, the gifted and unfortunate poet of Oregon, whose genius deserved a wider recognition than it ever received. The first stanza of his poem is this:

> From the Cascades' frozen gorges,
> Leaping like a child at play,
> Winding, widening through the valley,
> Bright Willamette glides away.
> Onward ever, lovely River,
> Softly calling to the sea,
> Time that scars us, maims and mars us,
> Leaves no track or trench on thee.

And now that we have fairly entered the Willamette, it becomes speedily evident that we are in the near vicinity of a large and prosperous city. Steamboats, an occasional steamship, sailing ships, sometimes huge four-masted steel ships towed by coughing tugs, long booms of logs in tow of some spluttering stern-wheeler, scows of every description, gasoline launches, rowboats,—a motley fleet, they seem to be making they way with all possible haste upon the stream.

We are indeed approaching Portland, the metropolis of the Columbia, the "Rose City," in many respects the most interesting and attractive of Western cities. The approach to Portland is one hard to match for stately beauty. The city occupies both sides of the Willamette, the main business part on the west side, but the larger residence part on the east.

The first settler on the original site of Portland was a man named Overton. Lownsdale, Chapman, and Lovejoy bought him out. Then Captain John H. Couch in 1845 located a donation land claim on what is now the northern part of the west side city. At that time the site was somewhat cut up with gulches and clothed in the densest of dense forests, with perfect jungles of every species of undergrowth. But duller eyes than those of the gallant mariners, Couch, Flanders, Ainsworth, Pettygrove, and Lovejoy, could have seen beneath the tangled thickets the making of a city, though it may well be questioned whether even they, in their wildest flights of fancy, ever pictured the scene of to-day, where the city of these sixty years' building now sits, a queen upon her circling throne of hills. The location of Portland is almost ideal. The hills to the west rise to a height of about eight hundred feet, but many fine homes are located there, and car lines cross the hills in many directions. Above the fogs and smoke these high-line homes have every possible charm. On the east side of the Willamette the land is a level bench with limitless room for expansion. There are a few picturesque elevations on the east side, as Mt. Tabor and Mt. Scott, and these have been used for homes with the taste which characterises the entire city.

Willamette Falls, Oregon City, Ore.

Photo. by E. H. Moorehouse.

Portland is the centre of every species of transportation facility. It has one of the most extensive and well-equipped electric railway systems in the United

States. In addition to the urban lines, there are interurban lines in every direction, to Vancouver, Troutdale, Oregon City, Milwaukee, Hillsboro, and Salem, the last named the capital of the State and fifty miles distant. We find also that four transcontinental railroads have a terminus in Portland, the Southern Pacific, the Northern Pacific, the Union Pacific, and the Great Northern. Steamship lines run to Alaska, Puget Sound, San Francisco and other California ports, to all the coastwise ports of Oregon, to the Hawaiian Islands and the Orient, and to Mexico and South America. Sailing ships convey the products of the North-west to all the ports of the world.

As a result of these facilities for commerce we find such figures as the following: During the year 1907 there entered and cleared at Portland twelve hundred and twenty ocean-going vessels, registering more than 1,700,000 tons, net, and with a carrying capacity of 3,500,000 tons. In the cargoes of this total, were 175,000,000 feet of lumber and 18,000,000 bushels of wheat, flour included. Portland has in fact reached the front rank as a wheat and flour shipping port, being in the class with Galveston and New York, some of the time having led both of them. In December, 1907, Portland's record of wheat shipments, exclusive of flour, was 3,000,000 bushels. The Bureau of Statistics of the Department of Commerce and Labor gave the value of all breadstuffs shipped from Portland for the eleven months ending November 30, 1907, at $10,536,234. During the same period the shipments of the same commodities from San Francisco totalled $4,143,592, while from the three Puget Sound ports of Seattle, Tacoma, and Everett, the aggregate was $13,989,178. During November, 1908, there were shipped 903,000 bushels of wheat, 180,145 barrels of flour, 209,246 bushels of barley, and 9,752,552 feet of lumber. During the year 1908 the value of wheat and flour reached a total of $18,340,405, while the lumber exports aggregated 162,089,998 feet.

Perhaps the most gratifying feature of the shipping trade to Portland people has been the increase in the size of ships entering the River. In 1872 the average wheat cargo exported was 33,615 bushels, while now it is four times as much. The record cargo was that of the British bark *Andorinha*, in the fall of 1908, 189,282 bushels. The channel from Portland to the Columbia Bar and that across the Bar have so much improved that no lightering was necessary during the year 1908, and ships of twenty-five and twenty-six feet draft have gone from Portland to the ocean without difficulty. In connection with this fact we are told that in June, 1907, the International Sailing-ship Owners' Union abolished the differential of thirty cents per ton which had stood for some years against Portland. These conditions, together with the completion of the North Bank Railroad, by which a greatly added traffic from the Inland Empire will be turned to Portland, seem to indicate that Portland is on the direct road to a greater commercial leadership than she has yet known. The lumber industry centring in Portland is as remarkable as that of grain. Oregon's available forests, according to Government estimates, reach a total of three hundred billion feet, board measure. It is estimated that during the years 1906-8 the lumber cut in Oregon reached about two billion feet each year, of which about one fifth was sawed in Portland. It is asserted, in fact, that Portland is the largest lumber producing city in the world. Lumbermen believe that it is only a question of a few years when Portland will cut a billion feet of lumber a year. While grain and lumber are the great articles of export from Portland, there are vast totals of fruit, hay, live-stock, dairy and poultry products, fish, and manufactured articles of many kinds.

Among the Big Spruce Trees, near Astoria, Oregon.

Photo. by Woodfield, Astoria.

Portland in 1908. Mt. St. Helens, Sixty-five Miles Distant.

But to the thoughtful traveller it is of more interest to see the use made of wealth than the wealth itself. Portland now contains about two hundred thousand people, said to have more per capita wealth than any other city, with two exceptions, in the United States. What are these people doing with their accumulations? For answer the traveller visits the schools, the public buildings, the churches, the stores, the places of amusement, the homes, and he finds every evidence of taste, good judgment, refinement, and artistic skill. The Portland Hotel, the *Oregonian* building, the Marquam Grand Theatre, the Marquam building, the Chamber of Commerce building, the Corbett block, the Wells-Fargo building, the First Congregational, Presbyterian, Catholic, and Baptist churches and Jewish Synagogue, the Union Depot, the City Hall, the City Library,—these and many other structures challenge the admiration of travellers from even the best-built cities of the East. During the year 1907, building permits were issued to an amount exceeding nine million dollars, of which nearly half was expended for dwelling houses. Portland is indeed a city of homes, and workingmen own their own houses to an unusual degree.

As the visitor traverses Portland's streets, he sees amply demonstrated the propriety of the cognomen, the "Rose City." Almost every yard boasts its roses, and on almost every porch the scarlet rambler or some other climber casts its rich colouring. Soil and climate are said to produce an ideal combination for the finest grades of roses, as well as of many other species of flowers. The Portland Fair of 1905 was the means of beautifying a section of the city near Macley Park. While most of the structures were of a temporary nature, the unique and interesting Forestry building has been left, and this is a rare attraction to the Eastern visitor. The two tasteful and significant groups of statuary, *The Coming of the White Men* and *Sacajawea*, still grace the spot where they were dedicated. Portland contains many other attractive works of art at available points. Among these is the Skidmore Fountain, on one of the most crowded thoroughfares of the city, a real gem of art.

No visitor to Portland should fail to visit the City Hall and the valuable and interesting historical collection of the Oregon Historical Society. Mr. George H. Himes, the Secretary of the Society, has devoted years to the gathering of this museum of pioneer relics. Some of them are priceless. Here is the first printing press in Oregon, used for some years by Rev. H. M. Spalding at the Nez Percé Mission. Here is Mrs. Whitman's writing desk. Here is Captain Robert Gray's sea-chest. The ages of discovery, of the fur-traders, of the missionaries, of the pioneers, are all lived over again in the inspection of these relics.

Probably most people who have followed the course of public thought and action in the West, if asked what agency and what man would first come into their minds at the mention of the name of Portland, would answer at once,—"The *Oregonian* and its editor, Harvey Scott." This great journal and its great editor, associated together most of the time for over forty years, have indeed constituted one of the most potent forces in framing the thoughts and the institutions of the Columbia River people. It is frequently said that Harvey Scott and Henry Watterson are the only great American editors yet remaining of the old type, the type of a personal intellectual force and a public teacher. The present type of editor is rather an advertising manager than a political and social leader, a business man rather than a generator of ideas.

Portland Harbour, Oregon.

Photo. by E. H. Moorehouse, Portland.

There are many additional features of interest in and around Portland. Whether viewed artistically, commercially, financially, socially, or historically, this fair

metropolis of the Columbia River Empire is in a class by herself. Only by personal acquaintance can the student of the West satisfy himself as to Portland.

But once more we must address ourselves to the River. One may go to Astoria by rail down the southern bank, or he may, if he prefer, as we certainly do, go by water. He can go by almost every species of boat known to man, from an ocean steamship to one of the lateen-sailed fishing boats which abound on the lower River.

When we have retraced our course to the mouth of the Willamette and have again committed ourselves to the oceanward flow of the Columbia, we find a continuance of the same low, oozy, and verdant banks, the same timbered hills on either side in the middle distance, and the same dominant snow-peaks and unbroken Cascade Range in the farthest background. We pass many little towns, whose leading occupations are manifestly lumbering and fishing. We try to live over again the sensations which we think must have been felt by Lewis and Clark or Broughton, as they, first of civilised men, lifted the veil from this solitude.

In this section of the River there are no stupendous pinnacles as in the Gorge of the Cascades. Yet the scenery is infinitely varied, and although less bold, it is, in its way, equally attractive with the loftier scene. One unique spot attracts the eye, and almost recalls the beauty of Rooster Rock. This is Mt. Coffin, on the Washington side, near the mouth of the Cowlitz River. This was one of the "Memaloose" or sepulture places of the Indians. There in early times their dead, in great numbers, were deposited upon platforms after the usual Indian fashion.

After passing the ingress of the Cowlitz, we find the River widening to yet grander proportions. Islands become numerous. Among these islands not a few desperate affrays and even tragedies have occurred among warring fishermen, union against non-union. Lurking among these islands, too, are numerous unlicensed vendors of spirits. In the uncertainty as to which of the States may have jurisdiction at places, these illicit traffickers move from island to island and cove to cove and one overhanging forest to another, evading officers of both States and of Federal Government alike. Sometime a novelist will be inspired with the poetry and humour and tragedy and pathos of this fisher life on the lower River, with its mingling of the life of law-breaker and desperado, and this section of our River will blossom into literature and find a place with the moonshiners of the South and the cowboys of the Rockies. All the material is ready. The River waits only for its Owen Wister or Hamlin Garland or Jack London to introduce it to the world of readers.

But the River moves and we must move with it. Many signs indicate to us that we are approaching the ocean. If we are moving in a small boat, we may pause to camp under some one of the thick-topped spruce trees whose stiff spicules pierce our unwary hands like pins. If we should spend a night we would find the water heaving and falling two, four, or five feet, with the ocean tides. Broader and broader grows the River. Numerous salmon canneries and seining stations appear. Passing a fishing village on the north bank called Brookfield, we notice a very curious rock, Pillar Rock, in the River a quarter of a mile from shore. It rises forty feet directly out of the water. We are told by one versed in Indian lore that this is the transformed body of a chief who tried to imitate the god Speelyei by wading across the River. For his presumption he was turned into a rock.

Soon after passing Pillar Rock we see the curious spectacle of a house on piles apparently right in the middle of the River. More curious still, we see horses seemingly engaged in drawing a load through the very water itself. The mystery is soon solved. The house is built on a sand-bar. It is a seining station. The horses are pulling a seine from its moorings at the point of the sand-bar to the point where its load may be discharged. Lumber, salmon, and water, — this is the world in which we now live and move and have our being.

Fish River Road, in Upper Columbia Region, B. C.

Photo. by Trueman, Victoria.

We next enter a broad expanse of the River, nine miles wide, on the north side of which is a deep cove. There is the historic spot in which Robert Gray on May 3, 1792, paused at his highest point to fill his water casks and to float the Stars and

Stripes over Oregon, claimed for the United States of America. As we look westward, the headlands seem to part in front of us, and between them sky and water join. The greatest ocean is before us, though still twenty miles away. The River has reached the end of his fourteen-hundred-mile journey. Soon we pass, on the Oregon side, the bold promontory of Tongue Point, and Astoria, the second largest city on the navigable waters of the Columbia, is before us.

To the history of this oldest American town west of the Rocky Mountains we have already referred many times. Interesting in so many features of the past, Astoria is full of problems and suggestions, commercial and otherwise, for the present and the future. The city has grown slowly, always wondering why Portland should have so outstripped her. She certainly has such a location that it seems a crime not to utilise it for a great city. The River is here five miles wide. Upon its ample flood all the navies of the world might ride at anchor, sheltered from the sea by the long low sand-ridge of Point Adams. The site of the city, though somewhat rugged and broken, is entirely capable of reduction to a convenient grade, and is singularly noble and commanding. From the plateau three hundred feet high upon which the splendid waterworks are located, is a view of imposing grandeur;—River in front, dense forest to rear, with the blue saddle and pinnacled horn of Saddle Mountain,—Swallalochost in Indian speech, with its thunder-bird of native myth,—and the ocean to the west. We find Astoria to be a well-built city of about fifteen thousand permanent inhabitants, with perhaps five or six thousand more during the height of the fishing season. Almost every resource of industry offers itself in this favoured region about the mouth of the River. Though the country is densely timbered in its native state, the soil is such that when cleared it is of the finest for dairy and vegetable purposes. The mildness of the climate keeps the clover and grass green and the flowers in bloom the long year through.

As might be expected the chief industries as yet developed are lumbering and fishing. There are magnificent forests of fir, spruce, cedar, and hemlock, in all directions, while in and around Astoria there are six immense establishments for transforming the timber into merchantable lumber. This lumber aggregates something like a hundred and twenty million feet annually, and it goes to all the ports of the world. There is occasionally floated to the bar and thence to San Francisco, a log-boom chained in substantial fashion and containing several million feet of logs. Such a great boom is one of the most curious sights of the River-mouth. But transcending all else in importance at Astoria is the business of canning and drying salmon. What silver is to the Cœur d'Alene, what wheat is to Walla Walla, what apples are to Hood River, that salmon are to Astoria. The people think, act, and reason in terms of salmon. And well they may. He who has not seen Chinook salmon from the Columbia River has not seen fish. Nay, he cannot even be said to have really lived in the larger sense of the term. Take a genuine Chinook salmon of fifty or sixty pounds, caught in June, fat, rich, glistening,—but words are a mockery. Nothing but the actual experience will convey the impression. The salmon output on the River has for some years run from two hundred and fifty thousand to five hundred thousand cases per year, twenty-four cans to the case. The amount dried and smoked represents something like an equal amount. This is for the River from Astoria to The Dalles. The great bulk of this, however, is put up at Astoria or in its immediate vicinity. It is estimated that from thirty million to forty million salmon are caught yearly on the Oregon side of the lower River. This represents a value of four or five million dollars, about half of this going to the fishermen and half to the cannerymen. Some ten thousand men are engaged in fishing about the mouth of the River. These men are largely Finns, Russians, Norsemen, Italians, Sicilians, and Greeks. They have various co-operative associations and are independent of the cannerymen, to whom they furnish the fish at some stipulated price, usually five cents a pound.

Multnomah Falls, 840 Feet High,
on South Side of Columbia River about Sixty Miles above Portland.

Photo. by E. H. Moorehouse, Portland.

There are many tragedies at the mouth of the River. The best fishing is just off the Bar and the best time to draw the nets is at the turn of the tide. In a fishing boat in the chill of the early morning, the fishermen will frequently become benumbed and drowsy, and will neglect the critical moment. When the tide fairly turns on the Bar it runs out like a mill race, and woe to the boat that waits too long. It goes out to sea, reappearing perhaps, bottom-up, in the course of the day, with owners and cargo gone. Some experienced men have asserted that not less than a hundred fishermen are lost every summer. Many boats are now fitted with gasoline power, and loss of life is lessened thereby.

To the visitor at the River's mouth the fairest sight of all in connection with the fishing industry is the incoming fleet of boats in the early morning, or the outgoing fleet of evening. On a June night it scarcely grows really dark at all, and as the faint glow of the north turns at two or three o'clock into the morning flush, the lateen sails can be seen like a flock of gulls on the rim of the ocean. When the full radiance of the dawn, with its bars of carmine and saffron, has "turned to yellow gold the salt-green streams," the fleet is within the outer headlands. Hundreds, sometimes thousands of them, a regular cloud of them, converge from all parts of the offing to the wharves of lower Astoria.

With all its benefits the fishing industry brings almost infinite trouble. The two States of Oregon and Washington never agree on laws governing the periods of lawful fishing. Sometimes Federal authorities bear a part in the imbroglio. Gill-net men, seiners, fish-trap men, union men, non-union men, local, State, and Federal officials, all combine in one great general mix-up. In the midst of the confusion the countless salmon pursue their course up the River and its tributaries in summer, back to the ocean again in autumn. The Federal Government maintains fish hatcheries on a number of streams, and from them young salmon to the number of millions are turned out each year to replenish the diminishing supply.

A great and constantly growing tide of tourists from all parts of the Willamette Valley and the upper Columbia region go to Astoria during the summer. The fine steamers, *T. J. Potter, Hassalo, Charles D. Spencer,* and others of less size, convey these thousands of tourists to Astoria, while the railroad from Portland brings yet other thousands. From Astoria, the North Beach is reached by steamer to Ilwaco, and thence by rail to all points of the fishhook of land which extends from the northern headland of the River to the mouth of Willapa Harbour. During the season this beach is almost a continuous city from Cape Hancock to Leadbetter Point, twenty miles distant. Clatsop Beach on the south side of the River is reached by rail from Astoria. Every charm that an ocean resort can possess has been lavished on these two beaches on either side of the River. The bathing, boating, climbing, fishing, hunting, clamming, crabbing,—they are all there. To the population of that part of the River country east of the Cascades, the transition from the dust and heat of the summer to the cool and rest and freshness of the beach, with its breath from six thousand miles of unbroken sea, is almost like a change of scenes in a play. Both these beaches, especially Clatsop Beach, are the location of a rich store of Indian legend and romance. "Cheatcos" and "Skookums" haunt the forests, and the spirits of Tallapus and Nekahni and Quootshoi have been enthroned on every peak and cape.

*   *   *   *   *

Chinook Salmon, Weight 80 Pounds.

Photo. by Woodfield, Astoria.

All rivers must reach the sea, and all journeys must end. And so both our River and our journey find their end in the ocean. From Astoria we can see the outer headlands and the ocean space between. As we survey this merging of the Great River with the greater deep, our eyes turn in fancy to that clear, bright lake, fourteen hundred miles away in the snowy peaks of British Columbia, from which the River flows. And in imagination we view again the vistas of lagoons and islands, cliffs and glaciers, lakes and cañons, plains and forests, through which the Columbia takes its course, while once more the changing scenes of the historical drama associated with that splendid waterway are enacted before our eyes.

Lake Adela, near Head of Columbia River, B. C.

Photo. by C. F. Yates.

But now all these scenes and vistas must be left behind, and we must pass between the capes. The long sandspit of Point Adams lies on the south, and the bold rock-promontory of Cape Hancock on the north, seven miles apart, each crowned with a lighthouse. Between them we secure a view of the great jetty in course of construction by the Federal Government. This is one of the most important improvements in connection with the River. When this work, together with the canal and locks at Celilo, is completed, the River may be regarded as really navigable on a large scale. The work on the jetty was inaugurated soon after the jetty-building by Captain Eads at the mouth of the Mississippi River had drawn the favourable attention of people and Government to this method of deepening river mouths. The jetty consists of a double line of piling, filled with rock and mattresses of woven willows. This constitutes a solid core against which the current of the River on one side piles the silt, while on the other the ocean waves pound the sand into a permanent barrier-reef. The philosophy of it is so to narrow the entrance that the accelerated current of the River will scour out the channel to an increased depth. Piles have been set in place by an ingenious system of pneumatic pipes by which compressed air bores a hole in the sand. Into this hole the pile is dropped, and the sea-waves in a moment fill in and tamp the sand around it. Thus the ocean is made to fence itself out. Upon the jetty a railroad has been built, and a train, loaded with rock and willows, runs out on this every eleven minutes for dumping material into the space between the piles. Very gratifying results have already been secured. There is now a depth of twenty-six feet on the Bar at low water. The crest of the Bar has been cut much deeper at several narrow points, and this indicates the progress that may be expected. It is hoped that the completed jetty will maintain a permanent channel of forty feet at low water. In stormy weather the work on the jetty is difficult and dangerous. The impact of the Pacific waves when lashed by a sixty-mile "sou'-wester" is something terrific. Large sections of piling have been torn out, and much loss has resulted. But patience and money triumph over all obstacles, and the work goes steadily on. Some conception of the magnitude of the commerce to be accommodated by this great work may be formed from the fact that in the year 1907 the freight handled on the lower River by both river and ocean vessels amounted to 4,251,681 tons, valued at $76,583,804. This is but a fraction of what will come with the full development of the Columbia Valley and with the needed improvements to navigation. The Federal Government maintains life-saving stations on both sides of the River. Many a tale of daring could these heroes of the beach tell, should we stop to question them.

We are at the point of the jetty. The buoys rise and fall behind us. The horrible blare of the fog-horn sounds across the thunder of the surf, as we cross the imaginary line from headland to headland. Sea-captains tell us that ten miles from the River's mouth—so powerfully does the mighty current cleave the sea—they can dip up fresh water. But now, to west and north and south, the deep blue, though crossed by the pale green of the River water, assures us that we are fairly upon the Bar. The River of the West is all behind us. If it be very clear, we can just discern upon the horizon's verge, cameo-like and glistening white, Mt. Hood, monarch of the Oregon Cascades, for ever standing guard over the disappearing River.

Bridal Veil Bluff, Columbia River, Oregon

Photo. by E. H. Moorehouse, Portland.

As the shore line grows vague, it would not be difficult for the imagination to conjure up the navigators of the Old World who sailed these seas, then unknown seas of mystery and romance. Looming up through the ocean mists we may see strange ships and stranger crews emerge,—junks with Oriental castaways swept hither by storms and ocean currents; caravels with the dauntless sailors of the sixteenth century; buccaneers and pirates, a motley flotilla. Then the stout crafts of Drake, Behring, Heceta, Cook, Malaspina, Valdez, Bodega, Vancouver, La Pérouse; ships of discovery, of trade, of war, of adventure, of science; flags of Spain, of Russia, of Portugal, of France, of England;—on they throng from the hazy Pacific rim toward the Oregon shore. And soon we seem to see, circling around them, canoes with their red-skinned paddlers from the River's mouth. But ships and flags, explorers and natives, fade like a dissolving view. In their place appears a gallant bark, with banner streaming free. What ship? What banner? The *Columbia Rediviva*, and the Stars and Stripes—the flag that still waves over the land of the Oregon.

*   *   *   *   *

And now our vessel rises and falls upon the long swell of the Pacific. Our journey on the Columbia River is ended, and we are upon the open sea.

Band of Kootenai Indians, B. C.

Photo. by Allan Lean, Nelson.

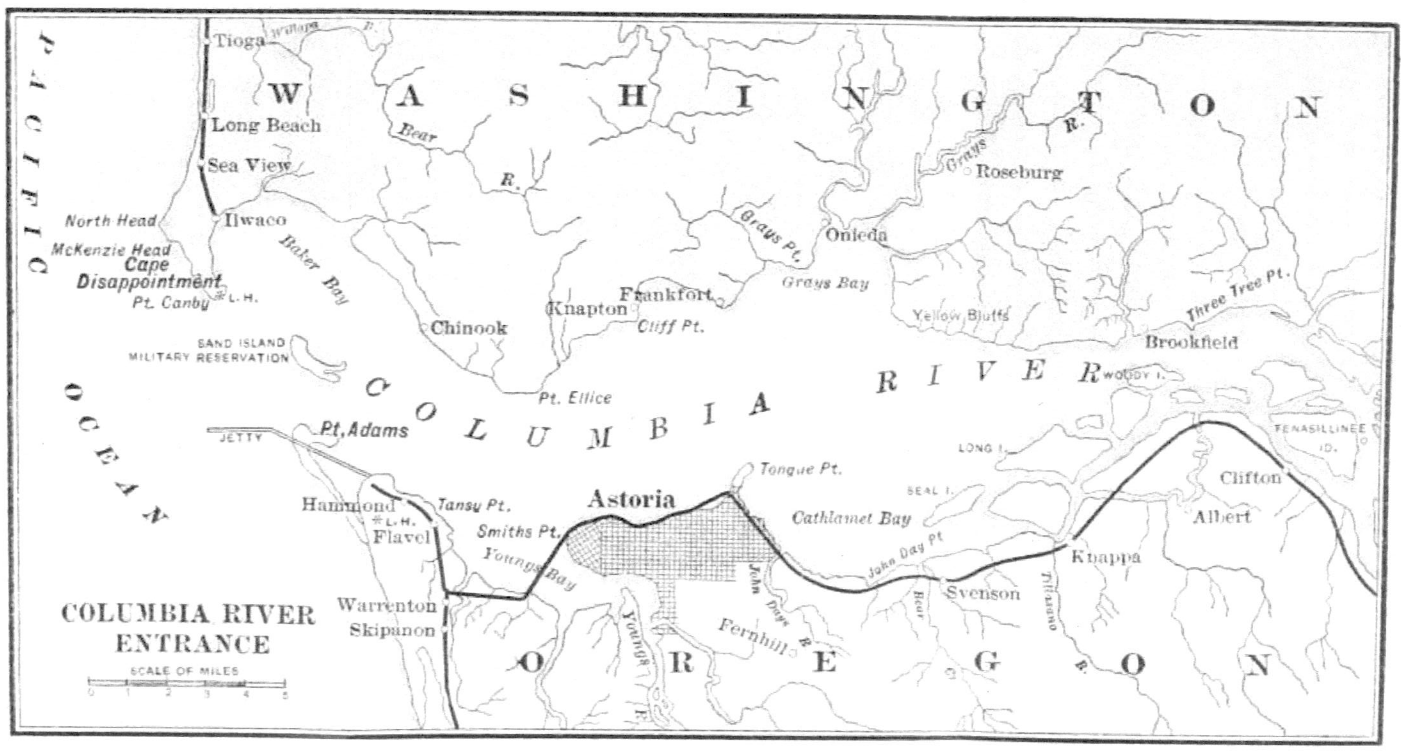

Map–Columbia River Entrance.

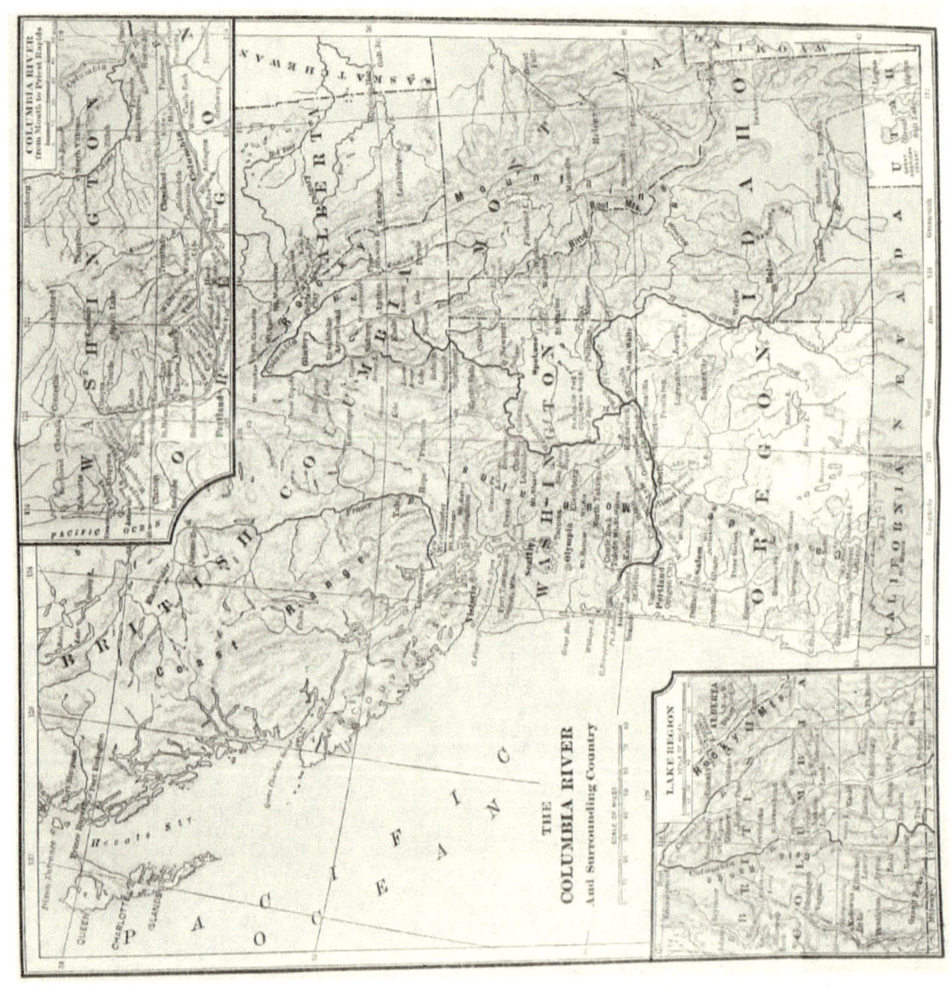

Map–The Columbia River and Surrounding Country.

INDEX

Lector House believes that a society develops through a two-fold approach of continuous learning and adaptation, which is derived from the study of classic literary works spread across the historic timeline of literature records. Therefore, we aim at reviving, repairing and redeveloping all those inaccessible or damaged but historically as well as culturally important literature across subjects so that the future generations may have an opportunity to study and learn from past works to embark upon a journey of creating a better future.

This book is a result of an effort made by Lector House towards making a contribution to the preservation and repair of original ancient works which might hold historical significance to the approach of continuous learning across subjects.

HAPPY READING & LEARNING!

LECTOR HOUSE LLP

E-MAIL: lectorpublishing@gmail.com

9 789356 142886